IMAGES
of America

BATAVIA REVISITED

On the Cover: Taken in the early 1920s, this photograph shows Main Street looking west from a point a little east of the Jackson Street intersection. The trucks are tankers carrying Socony gasoline to the grand opening of a supply depot on Jackson Street. The latter was most likely the facility operated by William W. Buxton at the corner of Jackson and Ellicott Streets. (Courtesy of the Genesee County History Department.)

IMAGES
of America

BATAVIA REVISITED

Larry D. Barnes

ARCADIA
PUBLISHING

ISBN 978-0-7385-7404-2

Published by Arcadia Publishing
Charleston, South Carolina

Printed in the United States of America

Library of Congress Control Number: 2010931930

For all general information, please contact Arcadia Publishing:
Telephone 843-853-2070
Fax 843-853-0044
E-mail sales@arcadiapublishing.com
For customer service and orders:
Toll-Free 1-888-313-2665

Visit us on the Internet at www.arcadiapublishing.com

To Jerianne, my wife, who has provided both emotional support and guidance in the form of constructive criticism

Contents

Acknowledgments		6
Introduction		7
1.	The Evolving Community	11
2.	Moving the Railroad Tracks	41
3.	Building the Oak Street Bridge	49
4.	Urban Renewal and Batavia	57
5.	Landmark Preservation	87
6.	Monuments and Other Public Art	105
7.	Prominent Batavians of the Past	117

Acknowledgments

As with all projects of this sort, there have been many people behind the scenes who have made significant contributions for which I am very grateful. Judy Stiles of the Genesee County History Department, Genesee County historian Susan Conklin, and Kathleen Facer of the Richmond Memorial Library have been especially helpful in gathering both pictures and information. I want to thank Arthur Brisbane, Elizabeth Rowsick, and Michael Smith for generously sharing images from their personal collections. I also want to thank Wendy Kail of the Tudor Place Foundation and Susan Nurse of the Memorial Art Gallery of the University of Rochester for assistance in obtaining images from their respective institutions. Finally I would be remiss if I did not express appreciation for the assistance of Rebekah Collinsworth Mower at Arcadia Publishing. She has always been immediately available whenever I needed her expert guidance.

The majority of the images used in this book are from the archives of the Genesee County History Department (GCHD). Other sources, not already acknowledged above, include the Batavia city historian archives (BCH), Richmond Memorial Library (RML), Landmark Society of Genesee County (LSGC), and the personal collection of the author.

INTRODUCTION

Batavia, located in western New York about halfway between Rochester and Buffalo, was laid out in 1801 by Joseph Ellicott, surveyor and resident land agent for the Holland Land Company. Ellicott literally created the community out of a wilderness. There were no houses or stores. There were only the trails of the Native Americans who passed through the area. Woodsmen had to chop down trees to make way for the thoroughfares.

The land on which Batavia came to stand had earlier been claimed by both Massachusetts and New York. In fact, all of what is now western New York was a part of the conflicting claims. These claims were based on the wording of charters that had been granted to the states prior to the American Revolution when Massachusetts and New York were British colonies. The matter was resolved in a 1786 treaty that established a boundary known as the Preemption Line. It ran south from Lake Ontario to the Pennsylvania border, passing near present day Geneva. The treaty awarded the land west of this boundary to Massachusetts, but the right of governance to New York. Once this arrangement went into effect, Massachusetts began selling the land to investors.

A large portion of this Massachusetts territory eventually came into the hands of Robert Morris, the financier who had helped fund the American Revolution. Morris, in turn, contracted to sell the westernmost 3.5 million acres to a group of Dutch investors who had formed the Holland Land Company. The Dutch, however, were concerned by the fact that the Seneca Indians had never been a party to its sale. Consequently the Dutch insisted that this matter be addressed before closing their deal with Morris.

In 1797, Seneca Indian claims to the land in western New York were relinquished in a treaty negotiated at Big Tree, a location close to present-day Geneseo. After many days of difficult negotiation between them and representatives of Robert Morris, the Seneca negotiators traded their land for $100,000, keeping a few limited areas as reservations. Thus were born the reservations that still exist today. In short order, the land then passed into the hands of the Holland Land Company. It thereafter was known as the Purchase.

The Dutch intended to have the Purchase surveyed, followed by relatively quick sale of large sections to developers. Joseph Ellicott, who had established his competence in other major undertakings, was hired to survey the 3.5 million acres now belonging to the Holland Land Company. Ellicott carried out his task in a remarkably short period of time. Parcels were ready to sell in 1800.

Having observed Joseph Ellicott's skills as a surveyor, his Dutch employers next offered him the job as resident land agent. Ellicott accepted and soon went to work selling the land. He established a land office in the newly founded community now known as Batavia. However, hopes of quickly selling large areas to developers proved too optimistic, as sales tended to be to individuals wanting land for their personal use. The Holland Land Company was still trying to sell all its holdings when it closed out operations in 1836.

Joseph Ellicott remained resident land agent until 1821, when he was dismissed by his Dutch employers who had become increasingly dissatisfied with his performance. Five years later,

Ellicott took his own life. Despite its tragic end, Ellicott's presence in western New York played a major and positive role in its development. It is no accident that we find squares, streets, avenues, a township, and a village named after him. His body rests in the Batavia Cemetery on Harvester Avenue.

The official seal of the City of Batavia includes a male figure wearing knickerbockers, the clothing worn by early Dutch settlers in what is now eastern New York State. He is portrayed standing in front of the Holland Land Office. The author, however, has never been able to understand the rationale for the seal. The Dutch investors who made up the Holland Land Company never set foot in the United States and probably didn't wear knickerbockers. Their U.S. representative who maintained his office in Philadelphia, Paolo Busti, was of Italian descent and would not have dressed in this manner. Furthermore there has never been a significant Dutch presence among the immigrants living in Batavia. Perhaps Batavia will use its 2015 centennial, celebrating 100 years as a city, as an occasion to consider another design for its seal.

During a brief period of time that coincided with the founding of Batavia, New York, the whole nation of the Netherlands was called "The Republic of Batavia." Students of history know that there is a city in the former Dutch East Indies that was once named Batavia. It was an outpost of Dutch traders. There was also the Dutch sailing ship *Batavia* that became infamous as the result of a murderous mutiny on its native voyage to the East. In all these instances, the name seems to stem from an area of the Netherlands once inhabited by a tribe known as the Batavii. Some historians believe the name "Batavii" may translate roughly as "superior men."

When it came time to give a name to our community, Joseph Ellicott reportedly favored calling it Bustiville in honor of Paolo Busti, the Holland Land Company's general agent in Philadelphia. Busti objected, and the name Batavia was eventually chosen to honor the homeland of the Dutch investors who made up the Holland Land Company. With tongue in cheek, but only partially so, the author suggests that a new city seal be struck that reads, "Batavia: Home of Superior Men and Women."

At one time, the population of Batavia exceeded that of Buffalo; however, over time, Buffalo's more favorable geographic position helped it to become a far larger city. Nevertheless, Batavia has its own natural advantages. It missed the boom days brought to places like Lockport, Albion, and Brockport by the Erie Canal, but it has gained from being on U.S. Route 5, which runs from Albany to Buffalo, the New York State Thruway, and the mainline of the former New York Central Railroad. It is able to benefit from the shopping, cultural, and employment opportunities offered by Buffalo and Rochester. Both are within easy commuting distance. At the same time, its location in a prosperous agricultural region has permitted it to maintain the advantages of a small city and rural surroundings.

Like many communities in the northeast, Batavia has experienced economic challenges common to what has been called the Rust Belt. There was a period when there was apparently considerable wealth that manifested itself in the impressive homes that lined East and West Main Streets. Several large manufacturing concerns employed many hundreds of workers. In retrospect, the beginning of the 20th century appears to have been Batavia's golden age. Since that time, most of the larger manufacturing operations have either gone out of business or moved away. Gone, for example, are Massey-Harris; Batavia and New York Wood Working; Wiard Plow; Eaton, Yale, and Towne; Doehler Die Casting; E. N. Rowell; and Sylvania Television. The private mansions occupied by single families and their many servants have disappeared as well.

There has been a change in housing with one-family occupancy decreasing in frequency. One of the laments heard repeatedly concerns the purchase of older homes by absentee landlords who then divide the structures into multiple apartments. Over time, it appears that the owners are sometimes more interested in maximizing their income than in maintaining the property. This situation has periodically produced calls for stepped-up code enforcement or other measures to address the problem. Thus far, such efforts seem to have had limited impact and the deterioration of some neighborhoods has become a political issue.

Batavia has also joined the many communities that have seen retail business leave the downtown areas and move into shopping centers outside the city limits. Pictures of downtown Batavia streets in the early to the mid-20th century show sidewalks crowded with shoppers. Those shoppers now get in their cars and drive to the surrounding town of Batavia or beyond to Buffalo and Rochester. This changing retail picture has also been characterized by locally-owned stores, such as Carr's Department Store and Salway's Hardware Store, being replaced by the big box stores of national chains.

A compounding factor in these economic challenges is the lack of foresight earlier leaders had when they drew the city's boundaries so close to the center of the community. The situation is additionally complicated by their failure to anticipate the problems produced in giving a village (and later a city) the same name as the surrounding township. An elaboration on the impact of these two matters follows below.

The city of Batavia is surrounded by the town of Batavia. As the city grew, housing, retail businesses, and industry expanded into the town. Today, unless one is alert to roadside signs, it is not at all evident as to when one has crossed the boundary separating the two. In fact, the author has encountered residents of the town of Batavia who thought they lived in the city of Batavia. When someone says that he or she lives in Batavia, it is necessary to ask, "Do you mean the town or the city?" Still, the matter would be just one of confusion were it not for the two other considerations of the differing tax bases and the duplication of governing bodies.

As noted above, local retail activity, once centered in the city of Batavia, is now concentrated in the town. Stores such as Home Depot, Lowes, K-Mart, WalMart, Target, and OfficeMax are all in the town. Similarly, manufacturing and distribution operations attracted to the area in recent years have also tended to choose locations in the town. On the other hand, much of the tax exempt properties such as nonprofit organizations, low income housing, housing for the elderly, the Veterans Administration Hospital, and the United Memorial Medical Center are located in the city. The resulting differences in the tax base have produced a situation where residents of the town currently have a zero property tax rate while residents of the city pay approximately $10 per thousand of assessment.

The two Batavias also result in extensive duplication in government and associated services. There are two separate governing bodies serving a relatively small population, a professional manager and council in the city and a supervisor and town board in the town. There are two independent planning boards. The same is true of the zoning boards. The city and town each has its own department of public works. There are two court systems. Separate fire departments result in seeing town fire trucks speeding through the city to reach a fire in the town while nearer city trucks stand idle. Town plows pass over city streets, their blades raised, en route to town roads. None of this would be happening if Joseph Ellicott and others who shaped the boundaries had anticipated today's state of affairs.

The existence of two Batavias has even affected how this book has been written. At one level, it would make sense to have it cover both the town and the city, since they are linked together in both a physical and a historical sense, but the town has its own historian who might choose to produce her own publication. So the author, as the city historian, has chosen to limit this book to the city.

Over the years, there have been several occasions on which merger of the town and city into one entity has been discussed; however, none of these discussions have gotten very far. Residents of the town express a desire to keep their own elected leaders and avoid the possibility of being swallowed up by the more populous city electorate. Town residents also fear losing their lower property tax rate. Resistance has come from city residents who, among other things, might lose the personal representation they now have in the city's six relatively small wards. Comfort with the familiar way of doing business and anxiety over an unknown future has worked to keep things unchanged. Some suspect resistance also comes from those who stand to lose political power, as it's unlikely that a merged government would continue having 14 elected leaders governing only 20,000 residents.

Despite the failure of previous proposals to merge the town and city, the idea is once more on the table at the time of publication. This time, pressure from New York state combined with financial incentives offered by the state have again led to formal exploration of a merger. Both the town and the city governments have agreed to form a joint committee to prepare a concrete proposal that will eventually be put to voters for acceptance or rejection.

This book focuses on several aspects of Batavia's history including its long-term, gradual evolution and the abrupt and major impact that came from realigning railroad tracks, building the Oak Street Bridge, and urban renewal. Landmark preservation, the history of public art, and some prominent citizens of the past will also be addressed. The reader should not expect it to be an exhaustive treatment of these subjects, for one cannot address that in 128 pages. The reader should also keep in mind that this publication mainly serves to provide visual images from the past and necessarily omits a great deal of detail that would be found in a narrative. Nonetheless, the author believes it should provide both enjoyment and enlightenment to the typical reader.

Historical information used in the captions and elsewhere has been taken from a number of sources, but especially from the publication *History of the City of Batavia*, written by former city historian Ruth M. McEvoy. Other sources include the Landmark Society publication *The Architectural Heritage of Genesee County, N.Y.*, past issues of the *Daily News*, the vertical files of the Richmond Memorial Library and Genesee County History Department, the Genesee County Clerk's Office, and records in the Batavia city historian archival collection.

A few words need to be written in regards to accuracy of the information. An effort has been made to achieve accuracy, of course, but it is likely that mistakes have crept into the material. Historical records in Batavia, like other communities, contain numerous errors that are often discovered only by cross-checking different sources, alert reading, and a little luck. The two examples below illustrate the problem.

One example of error has been in the reporting of E. N. Rowell's 1883 murder of his wife's lover. It was a sensational case in which the local industrialist was acquitted by a jury sympathetic to the emotions of a cuckolded husband. Newspaper accounts of the murder place the location of the crime at either 123 or 125 Bank Street, depending on the article one reads. It was only when the author reviewed property deeds from the 1800s that he was able to establish the correct address at 123 Bank Street.

Another error, more significant because it has been repeated again and again by a succession of writers, is the owner and occupant of the former Brisbane Mansion at 10 West Main Street. It has been repeatedly stated that the structure was built and occupied by James Brisbane, first postmaster of Batavia, when it was in fact built by his son, George Brisbane, two years after the death of James. The problem seems to stem from there being a second James Brisbane, George's son, who inherited the mansion when his parents died and then sold it to the city. Writers have apparently failed to recognize that there were two James Brisbanes who lived two generations apart and the historical accounts have thus become impossibly confused.

One

The Evolving Community

The face of Batavia has undergone major change over the years, sometimes suddenly, but most often gradually. This chapter focuses on the changes that have been part of a long-term, ongoing, and gradual shift in the appearance of the community. More abrupt and major shifts, such as that created by relocating railroad tracks, a new bridge, and urban renewal, will be covered in separate chapters.

Among the ongoing, relatively gradual changes, fires have played an important role. Some involved individual structures such as those that destroyed Ellicott Hall, the Emmanuel Baptist Church, and St. James Hotel. Other fires, particularly early in the community's history, wiped out several buildings all at once. The desire to prevent or better fight such fires was a major factor that led to incorporation as a village in 1823. It also led to passage of a village ordinance requiring that new downtown structures be built of brick or stone rather than wood.

The desire to use land for a new purpose has frequently led to change. For example, the Dailey Mansion was razed to provide a site for the current St. Joseph's Church. The Richmond Mansion was torn down to serve as a site for a proposed new library that voters later rejected in favor of an addition to the old library. The Cary Mansion was torn down by St. Jerome Hospital for expansion of its nursing school. Christ Scientist Church was leveled in order to construct retirement housing.

Population growth spurred the development of new housing. Between 1860 and 2000, Batavia grew from 2,560 to 16,258 residents. Housing designed specifically to accommodate low-income families and/or the elderly also emerged.

The landscape was changed when new industries such as Johnston-Harvester, the Wiard Plow Company, and the Batavia and New York Wood Working Company came into being. It changed again when they went out of business or moved on.

Many people find the most interesting changes have involved the movement of buildings to new locations. There are at least 42 homes in the city that were once located on a different building lot.

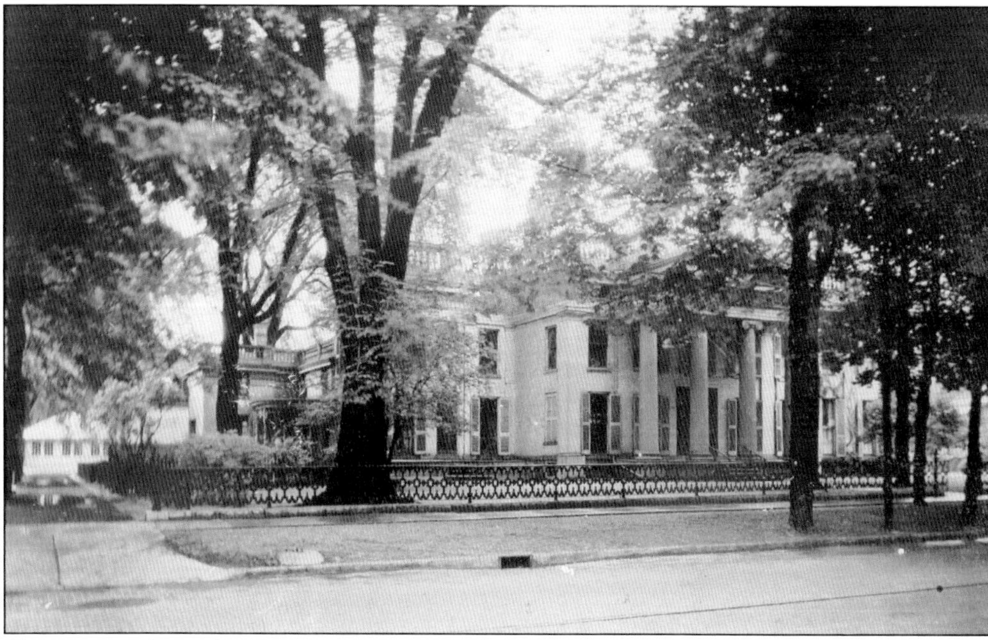

This mansion, located on East Main Street, was the home of Dean and Mary Richmond. The original building was built in the 1830s by William Davis. When the Richmonds purchased it in the 1850s, they greatly expanded the structure into what became Batavia's finest residence. As seen in the image below, a greenhouse and formal garden were located to the rear. (Courtesy of GCHD.)

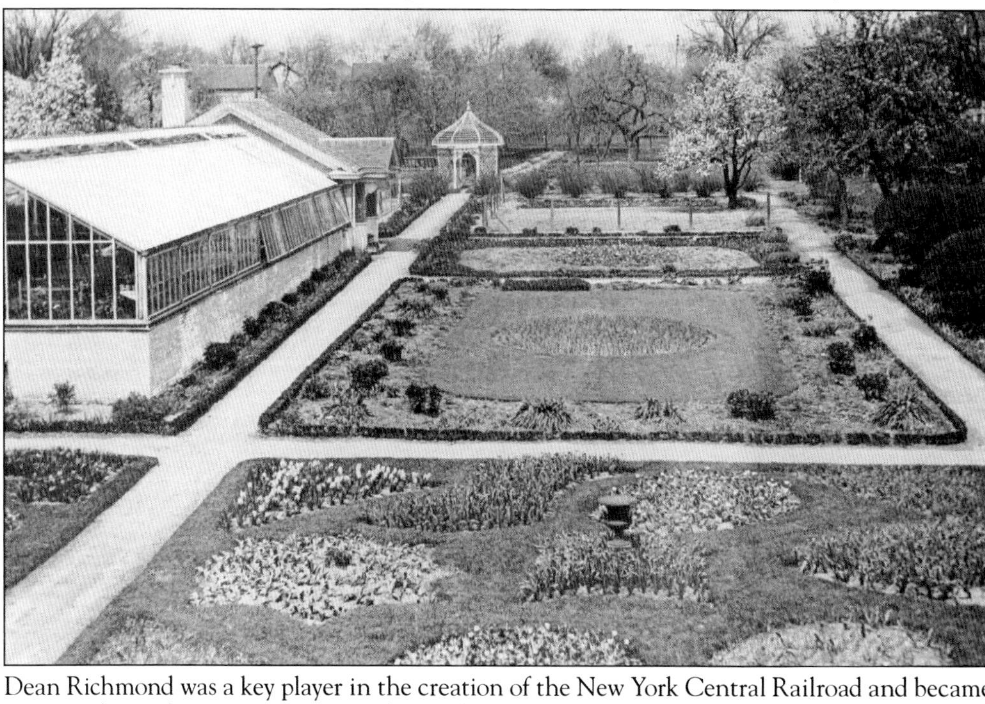

Dean Richmond was a key player in the creation of the New York Central Railroad and became its second president. Mary Richmond gave the Richmond Memorial Library to the community as a memorial to one of the Richmond sons. The mansion was torn down in 1970, and the site became the parking lot east of St. Joseph's church. (Courtesy of GCHD.)

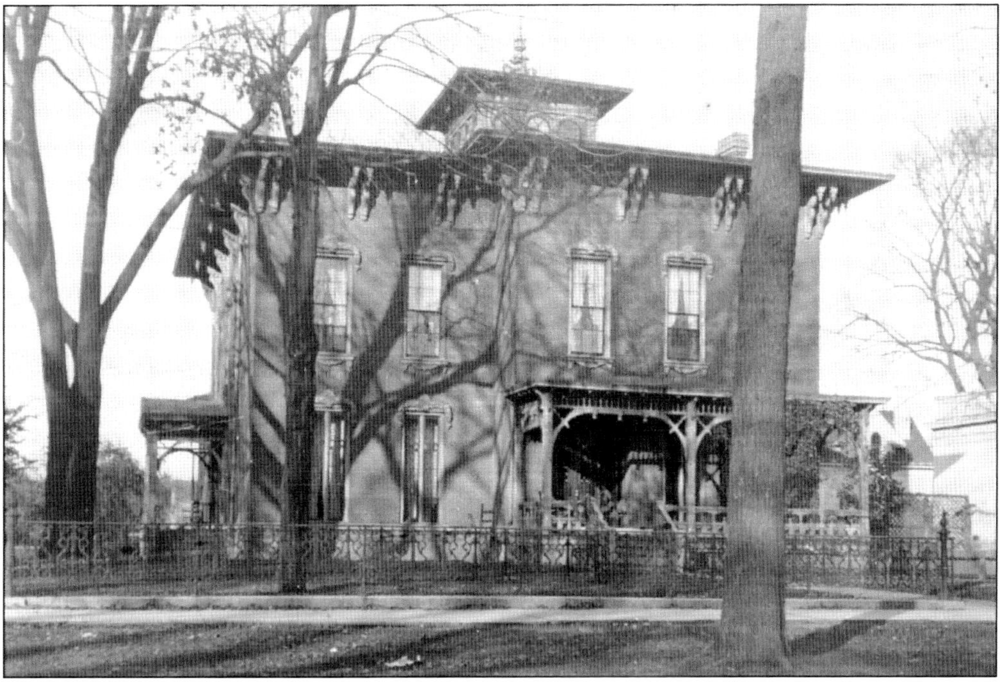

The Dailey house was located immediately west of the Richmond Mansion. Its last owner was Monica Dailey who, despite being a talented and promising vocalist, turned into a recluse. She willed the house to St. Joseph's parish. It was torn down in 1965 to make way for the current St. Joseph's Church building. (Courtesy of GCHD.)

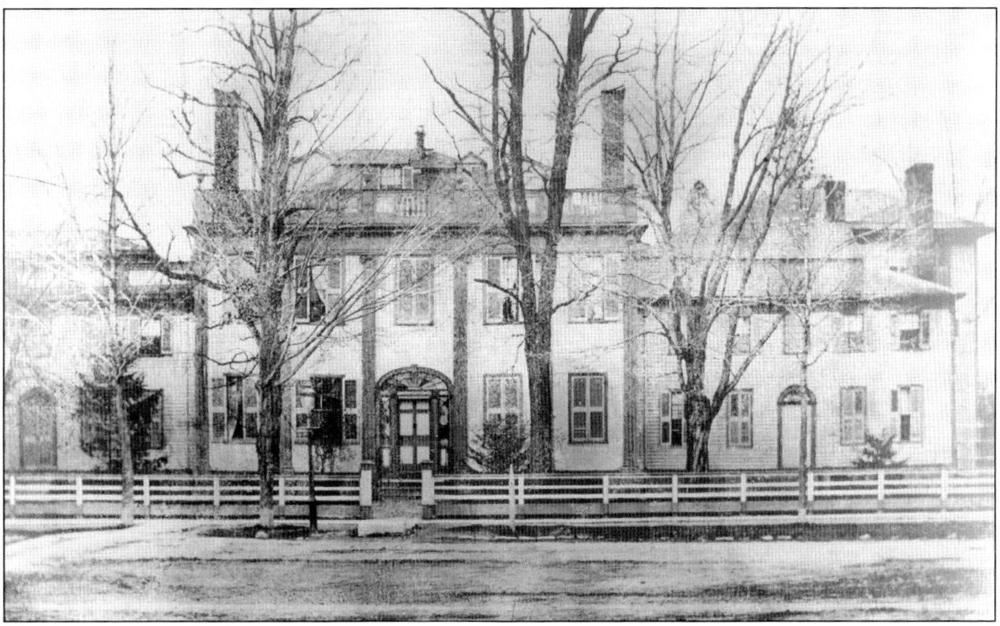

This mansion, located where Dellinger Avenue now intersects West Main Street, was built by Joseph Ellicott. Beginning in 1802, it was constructed in stages over a period of several years. The earliest section housed a temporary land office. Before being razed in the 1880s, it was occupied by a finishing school for young ladies. (Courtesy of GCHD.)

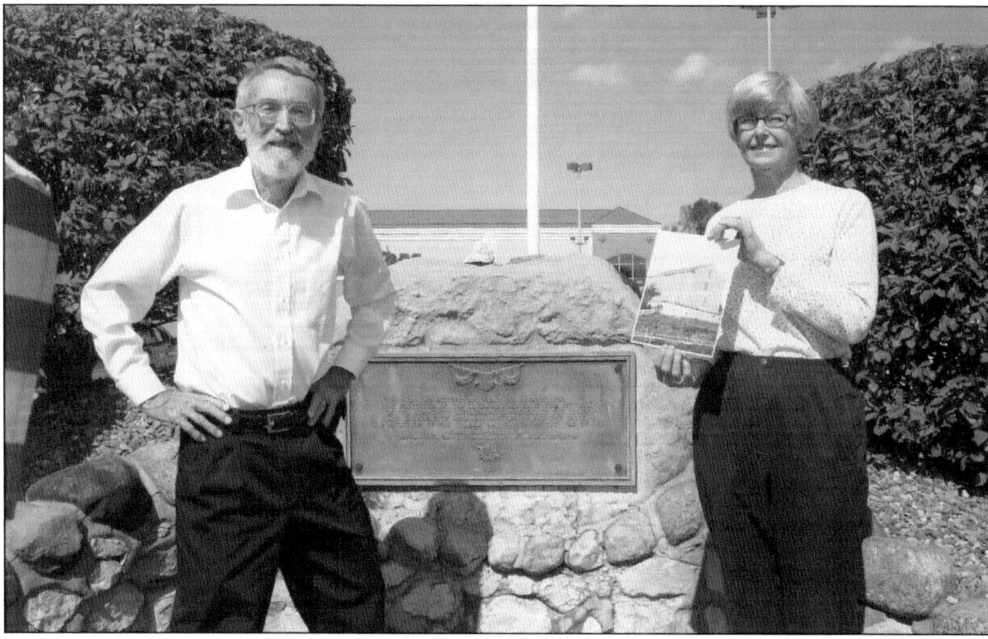

The author and his wife, Jerianne Barnes, are seen here standing before a marker where a stone arsenal once stood on West Main. The arsenal, shown in the picture held by Jerianne, was constructed during the War of 1812 when British troops threatened the area. In 1814, enemy forces burned Buffalo, and refugees fled east in search of safety. Fortunately Batavia remained unharmed. (Author's collection.)

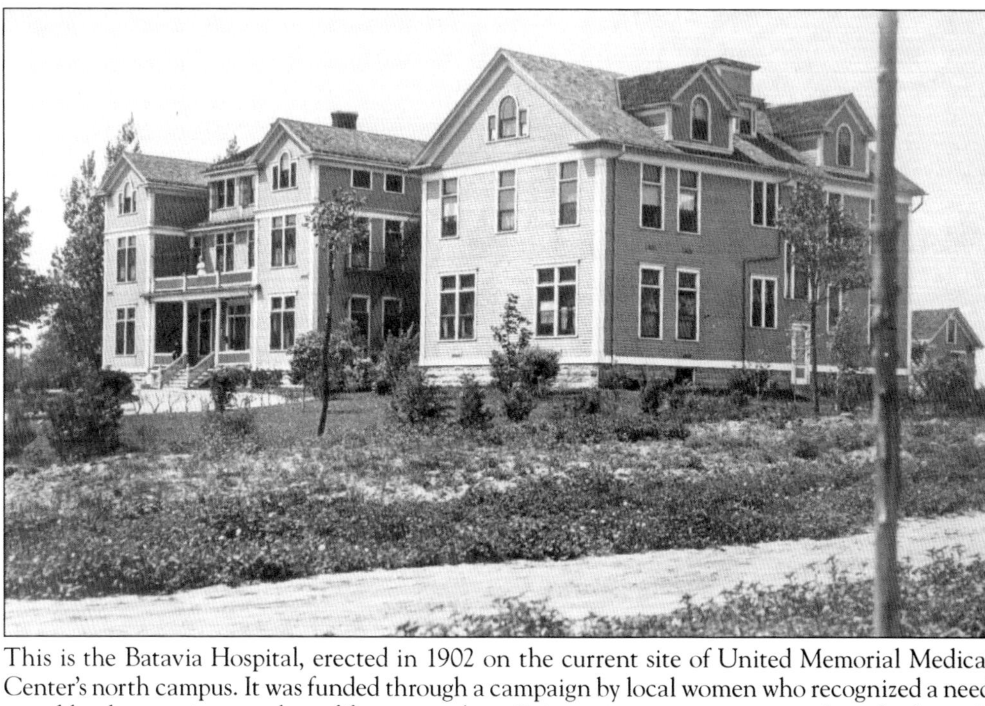

This is the Batavia Hospital, erected in 1902 on the current site of United Memorial Medical Center's north campus. It was funded through a campaign by local women who recognized a need posed by the growing number of factory workers. Prior to its construction, residents had to rely solely on the services of individual physicians. (Courtesy of GCHD.)

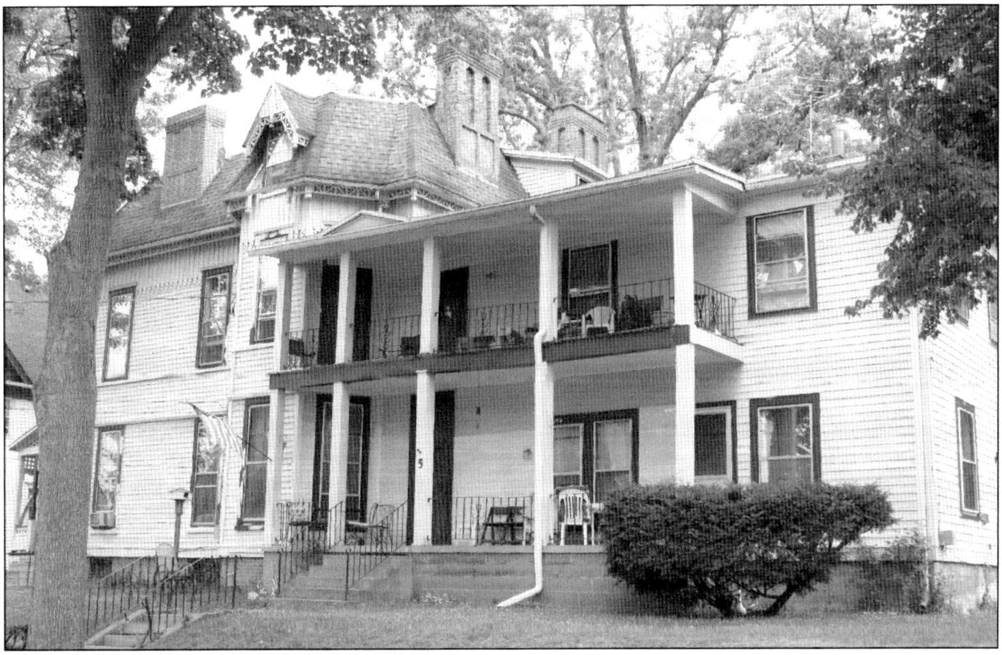

This building, located at 5 Thomas Avenue and now an apartment building, housed the Primrose Hospital from 1906 to 1918. It was operated by Dr. Clarence Gray and his wife until 1916 when a group of disaffected doctors from the Batavia Hospital took over. It closed soon after St. Jerome Hospital opened in 1917. (Courtesy of BCH.)

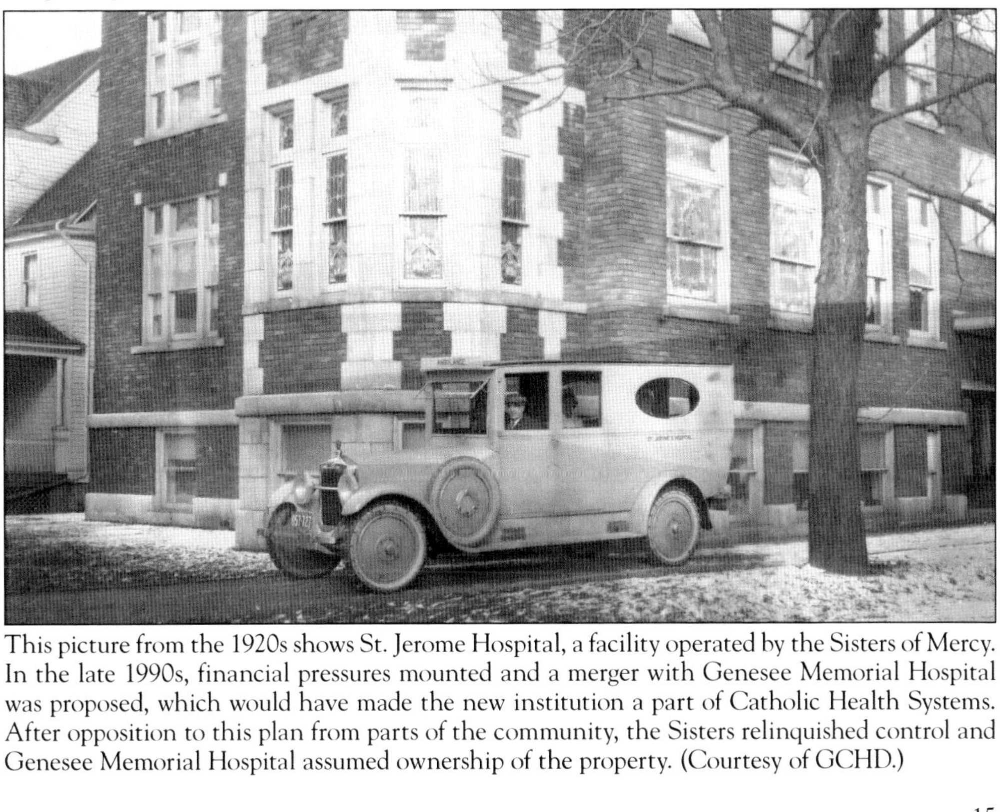

This picture from the 1920s shows St. Jerome Hospital, a facility operated by the Sisters of Mercy. In the late 1990s, financial pressures mounted and a merger with Genesee Memorial Hospital was proposed, which would have made the new institution a part of Catholic Health Systems. After opposition to this plan from parts of the community, the Sisters relinquished control and Genesee Memorial Hospital assumed ownership of the property. (Courtesy of GCHD.)

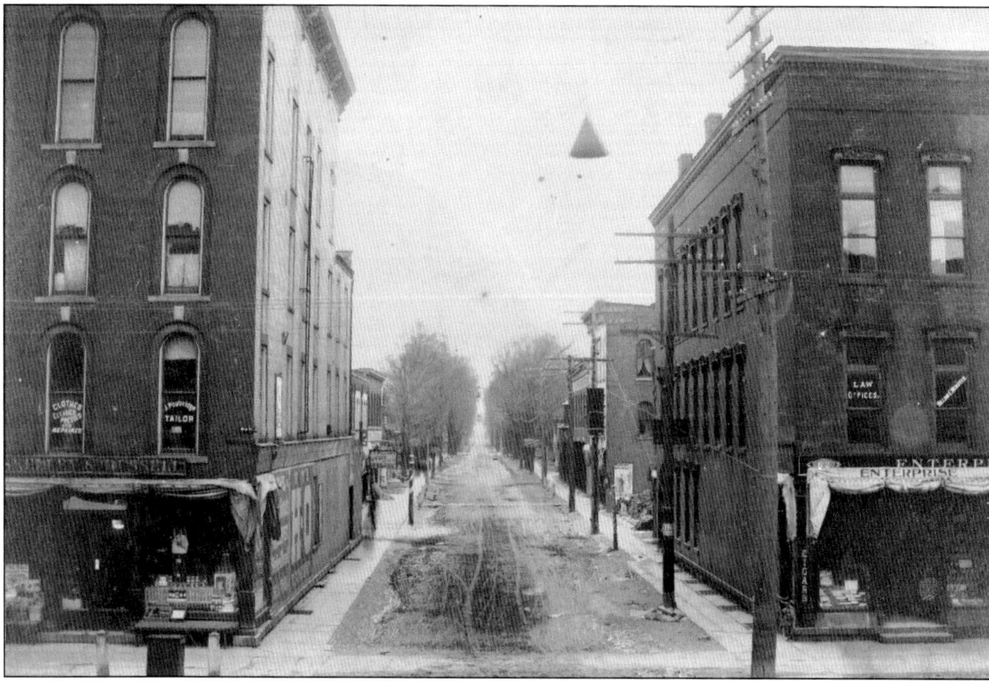

This photograph shows State Street, looking north from Main Street. It was taken in about 1900, when horses still outnumbered automobiles by a wide margin. Sheds on State Street, called farmers' sheds, provided shelter for the horses and rigs of shoppers who came to town from outlying areas. The object hanging over the street is an electric arc light. (Courtesy of GCHD.)

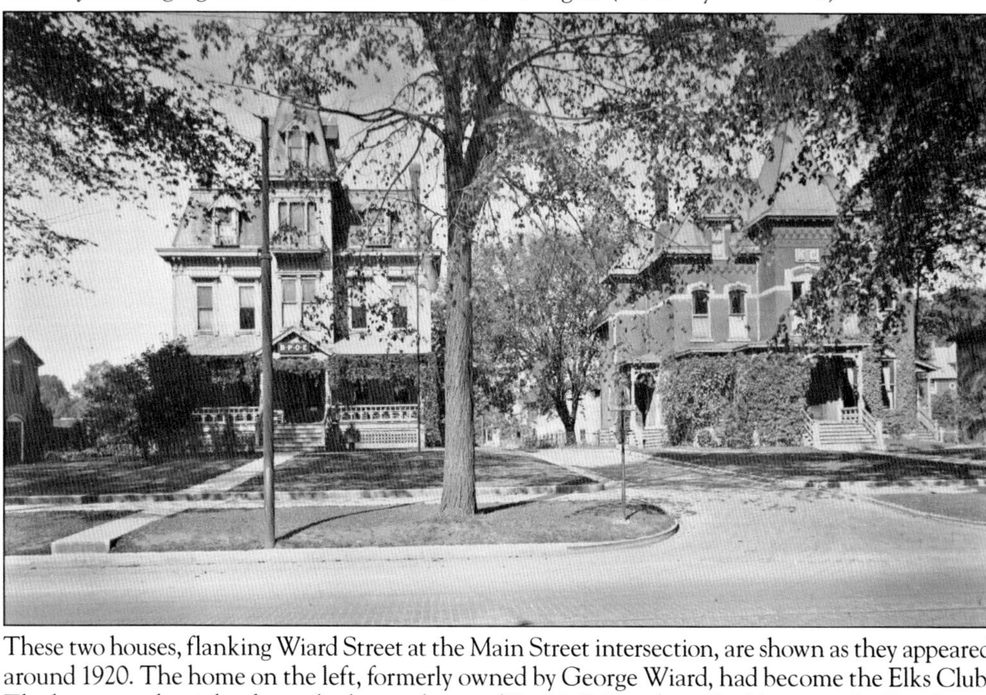

These two houses, flanking Wiard Street at the Main Street intersection, are shown as they appeared around 1920. The home on the left, formerly owned by George Wiard, had become the Elks Club. The home on the right, formerly the residence of Dr. H. S. Hutchins, had become the Knights of Columbus clubhouse. Wiard owned the Wiard Plow Company. (Courtesy of GCHD.)

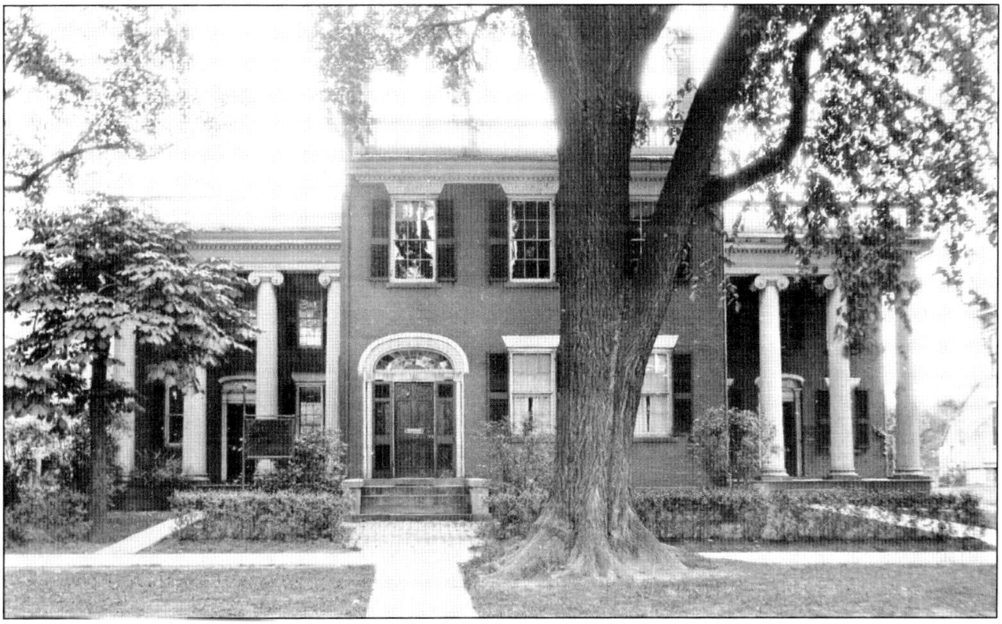

The mansion above, located just west of the Wiard house, was built in 1817 by Trumbull Cary for his bride, the former Margaret Brisbane. In 1934, George Cary, a grandson of the Trumbulls, gave the building to the City of Batavia with the intention that it be preserved as an example of an early colonial home. Shortly thereafter, the city returned the gift and over the years, the building was used for a variety of other purposes. As seen below, Pontillo's Restaurant was one of the businesses that occupied the structure. In 1959, St. Jerome Hospital purchased the mansion to use as a part of its nursing school. Maintenance costs proved excessive, and it was torn down in 1964. (Courtesy of GCHD.)

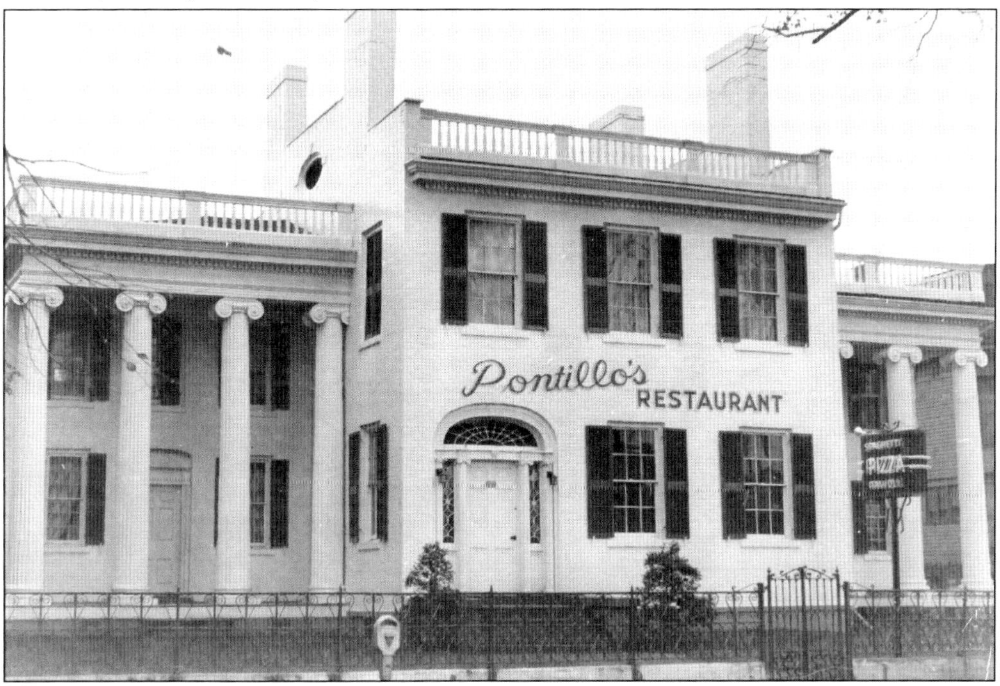

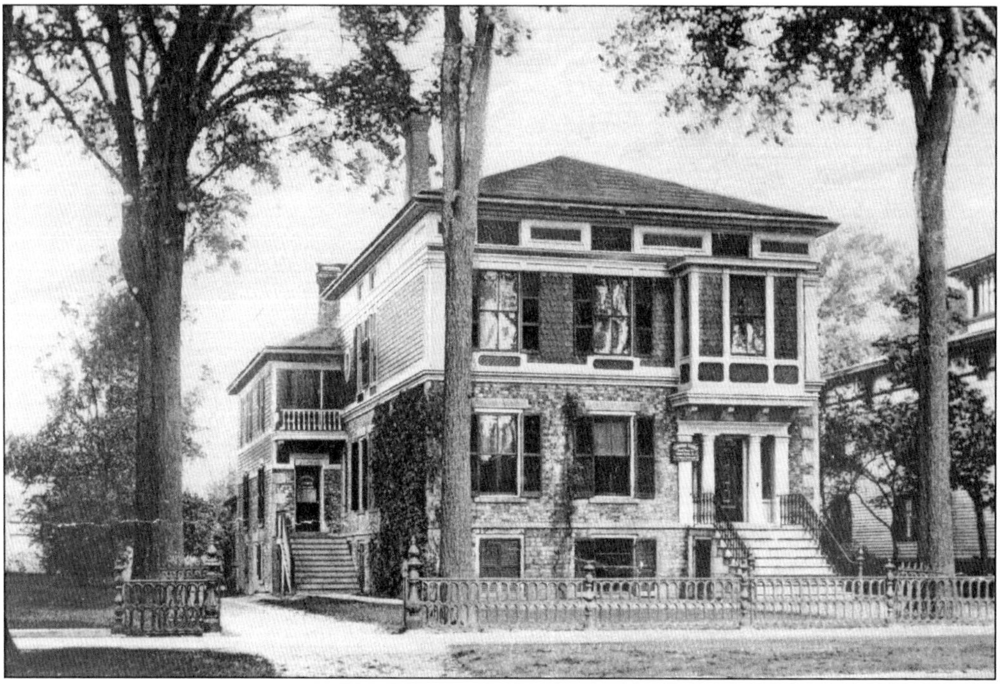

This 1911 photograph shows the building then used by the First Church of Christ Scientist. Located at 211 East Main Street between Wiard and Summit Streets, it was the former home of John Heywood. The Christian Scientists had purchased the structure and remodeled the interior of the building in 1907. (Courtesy of GCHD.)

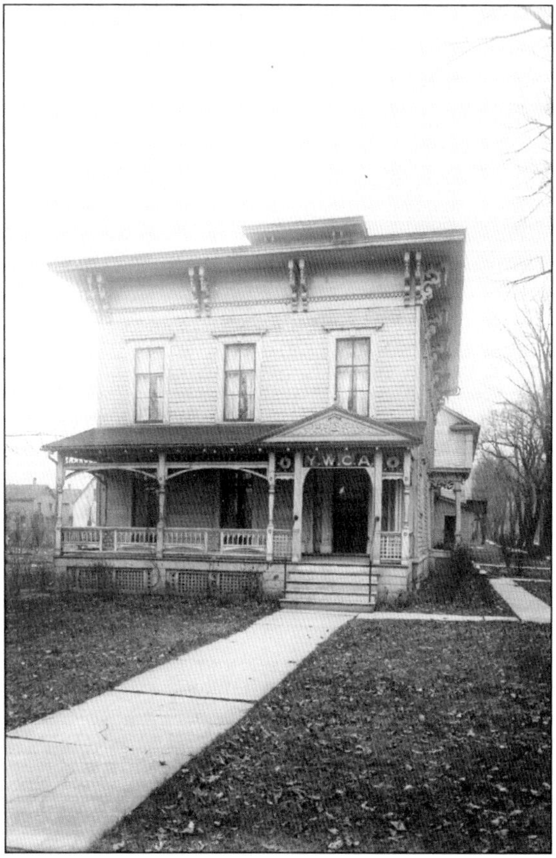

The YWCA was once on the northwest corner of Summit and East Main Streets, as documented in this picture taken around 1921. The building was the former home of Manley S. Bierce. The second floor served as a dormitory for roomers. The local branch of the YWCA was formed in 1903 by a group of women led by Frances G. Francis. (Courtesy of GCHD.)

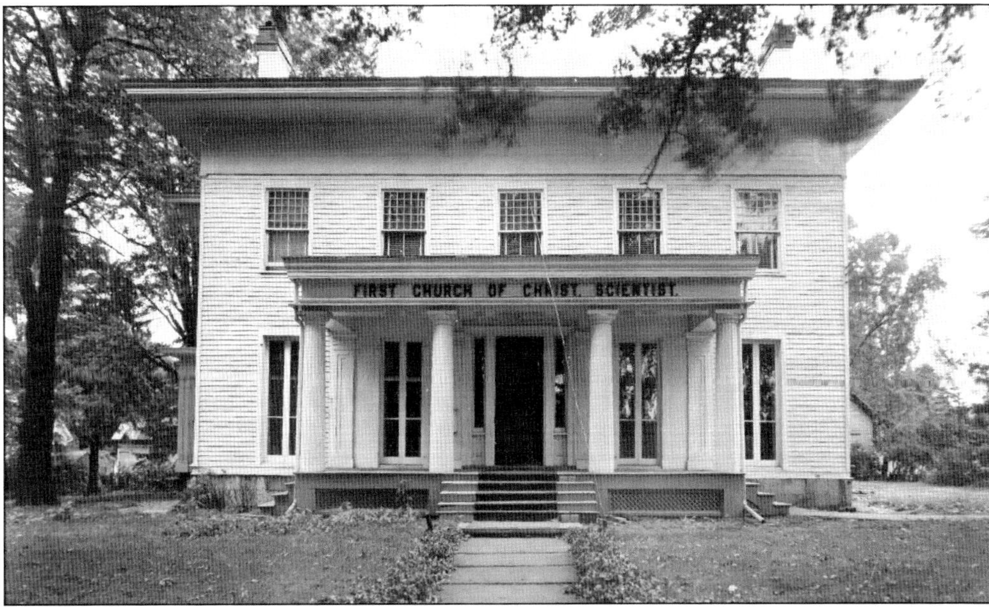

The First Church of Christ Scientist moved to this location at 427 East Main Street after the 1948 death of the building's previous owner, Kate Fisher McCool. The original building was built about 1811 and then underwent substantial alterations over the years, including the addition of an auditorium when it was purchased by the Christian Scientists. It was torn down in 1990. (Courtesy of GCHD.)

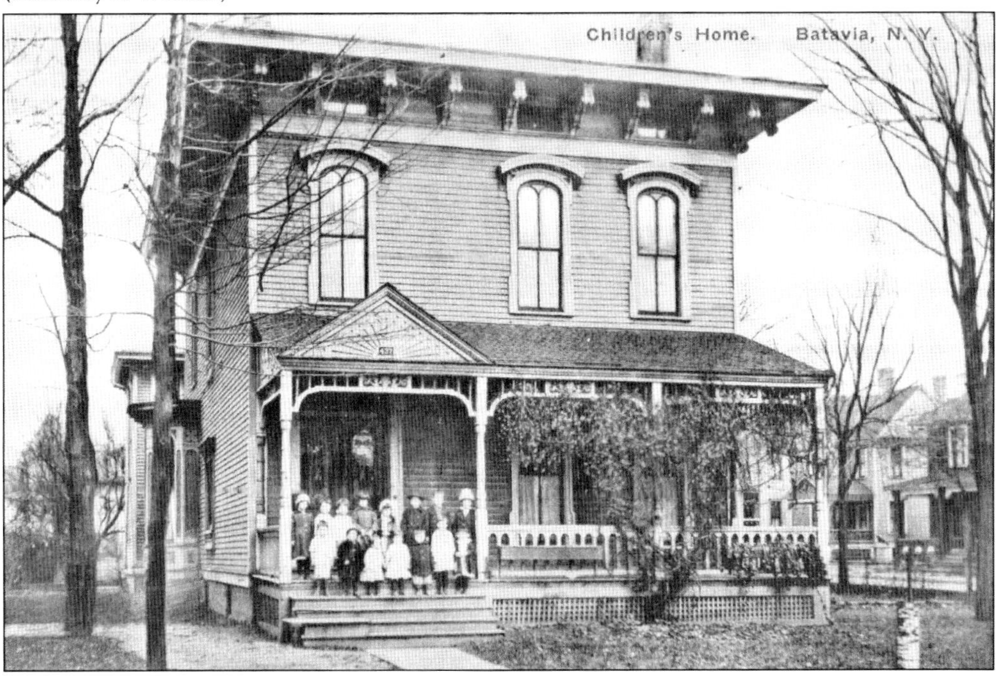

The Children's Home, as pictured here in the 1920s at 437 East Main Street, was housed in the former residence of George A. Farrall. It later moved to the Richmond Mansion. The Children's Home was founded in 1919 as a temporary refuge for children at risk or without parents. (Courtesy of GCHD.)

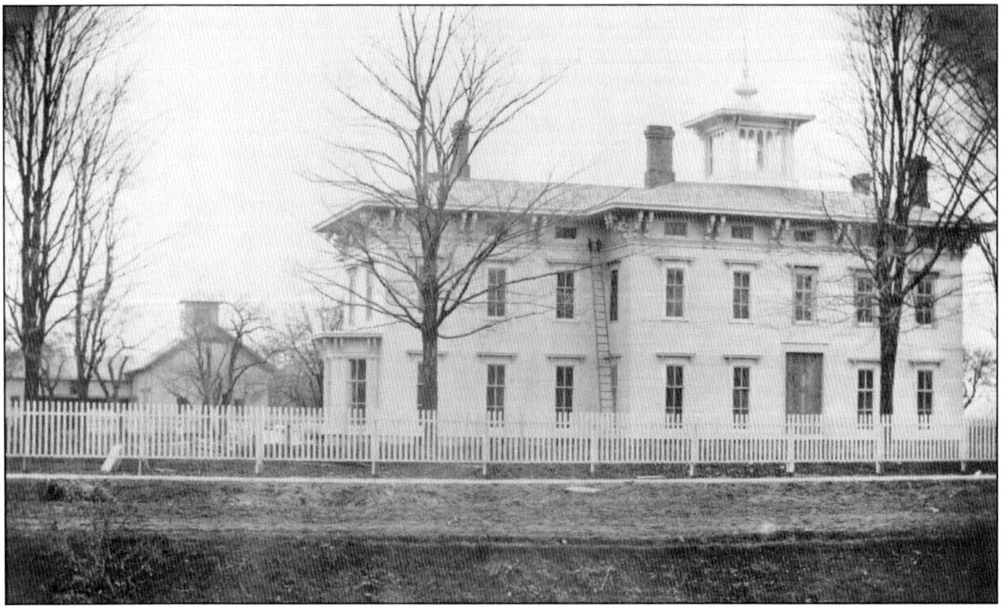

The Law Mansion, pictured above about 1865, was located at the intersection of Walnut and South Main Streets. It was built by George Law, a multi-millionaire in New York City, for his son-in-law and daughter, Maj. Laurence and Sarah Law Williams. The major was a descendent of Martha Washington. The mansion eventually passed through many other owners before becoming the property of John Pickert, a well-known builder in Batavia. Pickert originally planned to raze the whole structure, but eventually decided to divide it into three separate houses. Shown below are the two remaining buildings. The third appears to have burned. The house on the left is the former east wing, separated from the main structure and rotated 90 degrees. (Above, photograph by L. A. Phillipe, courtesy of Tudor Place Historic House and Garden, Washington, D.C.; below, courtesy of BCH.)

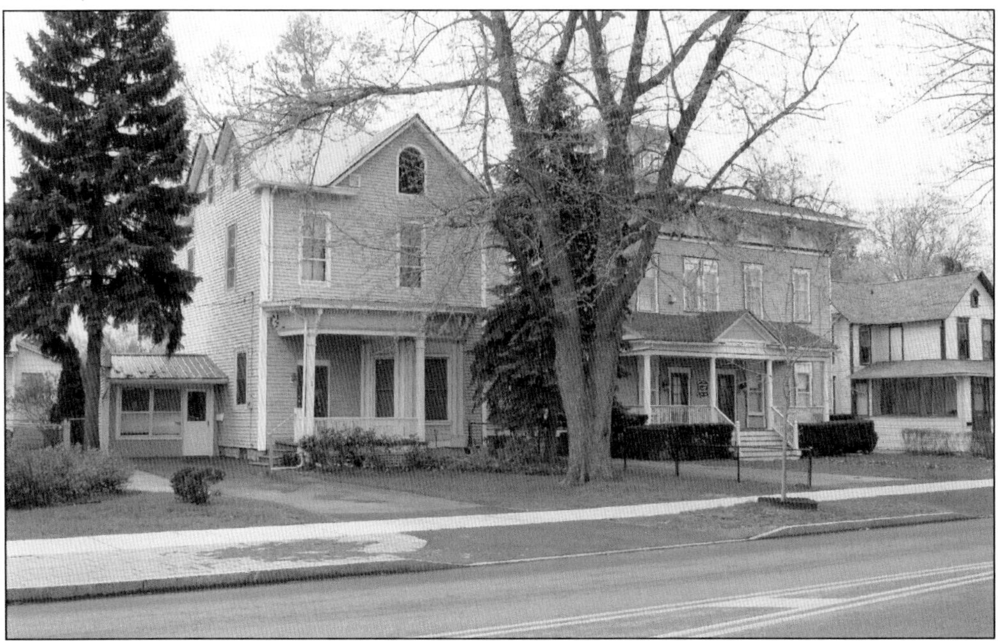

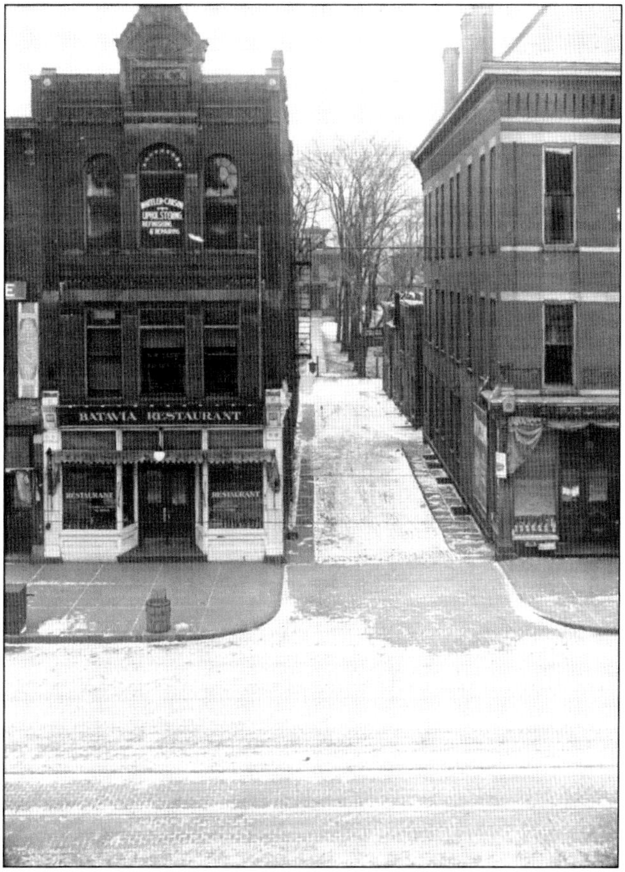

The view at right faces north up Park Place from the point where it intersected with Main Street. Park Place was located nearly opposite Jackson Street, but a little bit east. The picture was taken about 1920. Note the brick street surface and trolley tracks. Also note the mansion in the distance. Below is the Alva Smith Mansion at the end of Park Place, built about 1820. Over the years, it was occupied by the Park Place School, YMCA, and Odd Fellows. Local youngsters purportedly referred to it as "the ark." It was torn down about 1950 and replaced by a parking lot. (Right, courtesy of GCHD; below, courtesy of Elizabeth Rowsick.)

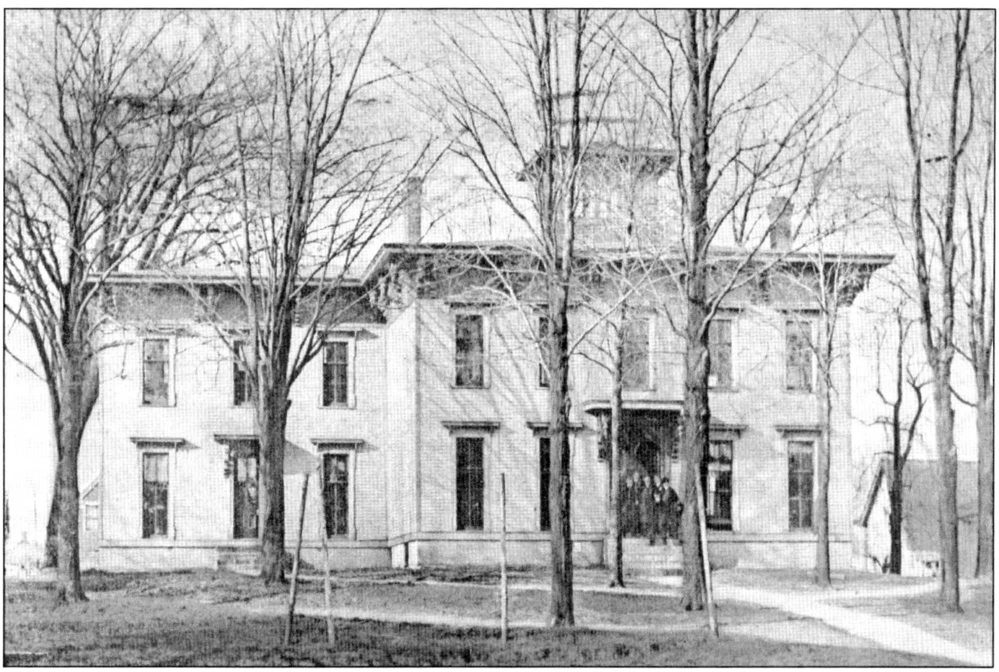

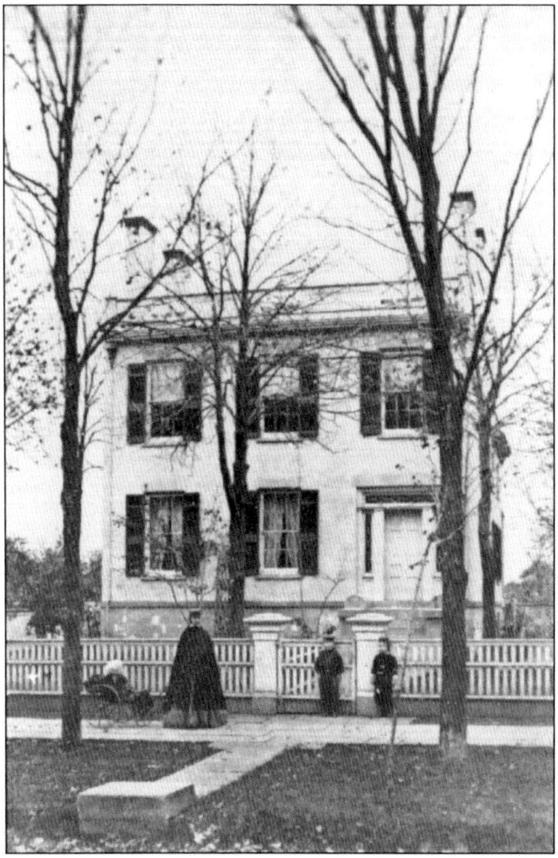

This is the Olmsted family home, located on the south side of East Main Street just east of where the Masonic Temple now stands. The unidentified persons standing in front of the house are probably Olmsted family members. Their dress suggests it was between 1840 and 1850. Note the stone block in front used to help enter and exit a carriage. (Courtesy of GCHD.)

The Olmsted home was purchased in 1902 by the Holland Club. This picture shows the building as it appeared about 1910. The Holland Club was a social organization for men similar to the Batavia Club across the street. At one time, it had 200 members. The annual Holland Club Ball reportedly was a major social event in Batavia. (Courtesy of GCHD.)

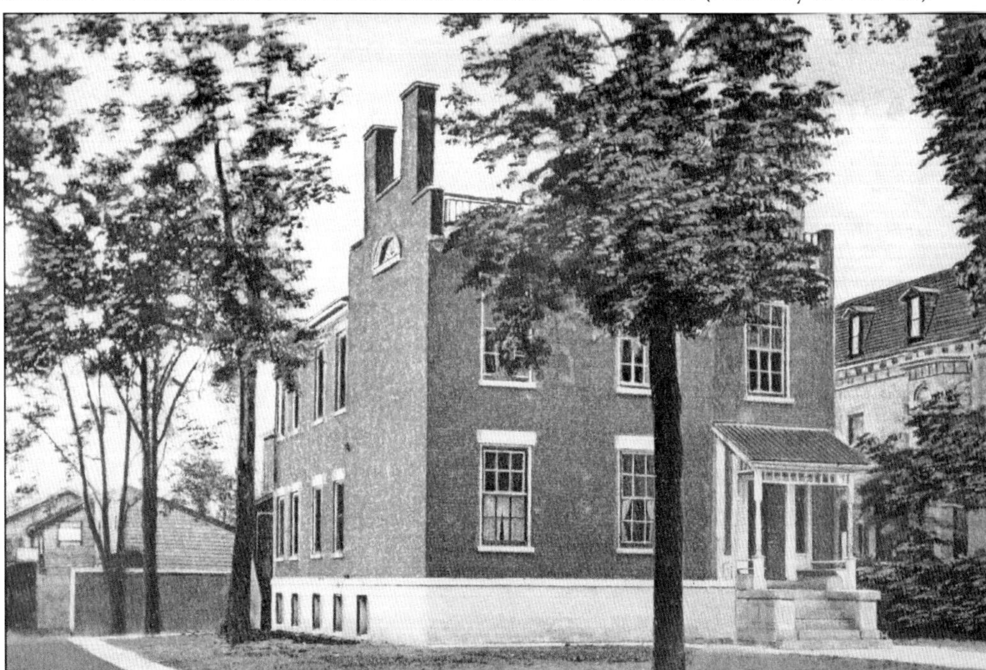

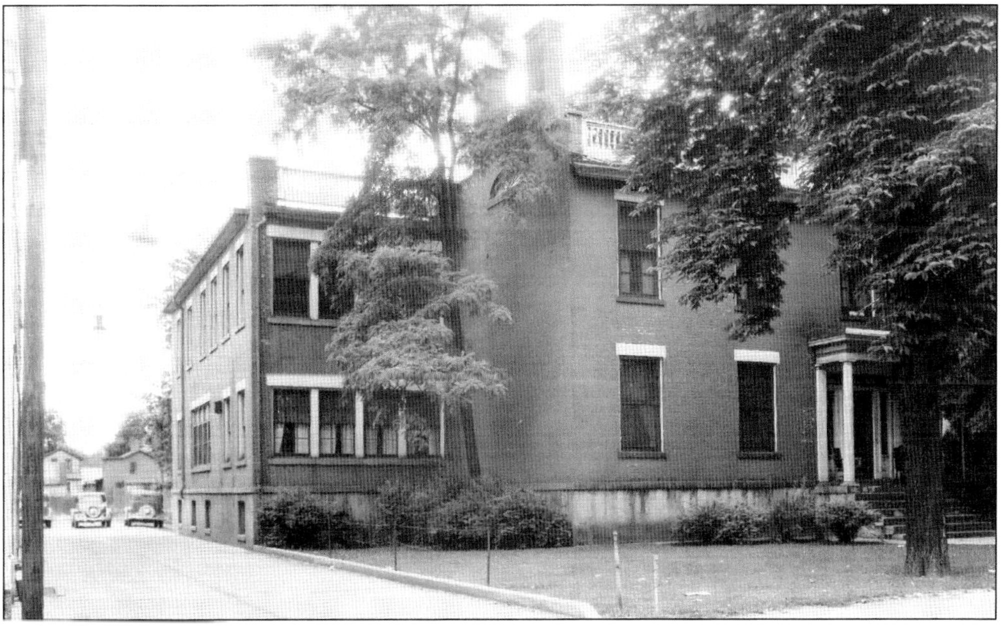

In 1912, John Pickert built the addition to the Holland Club visible in this picture from the 1930s. There were tennis courts in the rear and a shooting range on Law Street. However, the absence of a bar (unlike the Batavia Club, which had one) appears to have weakened the club's appeal. The organization disbanded in the mid-1930s. (Courtesy of GCHD.)

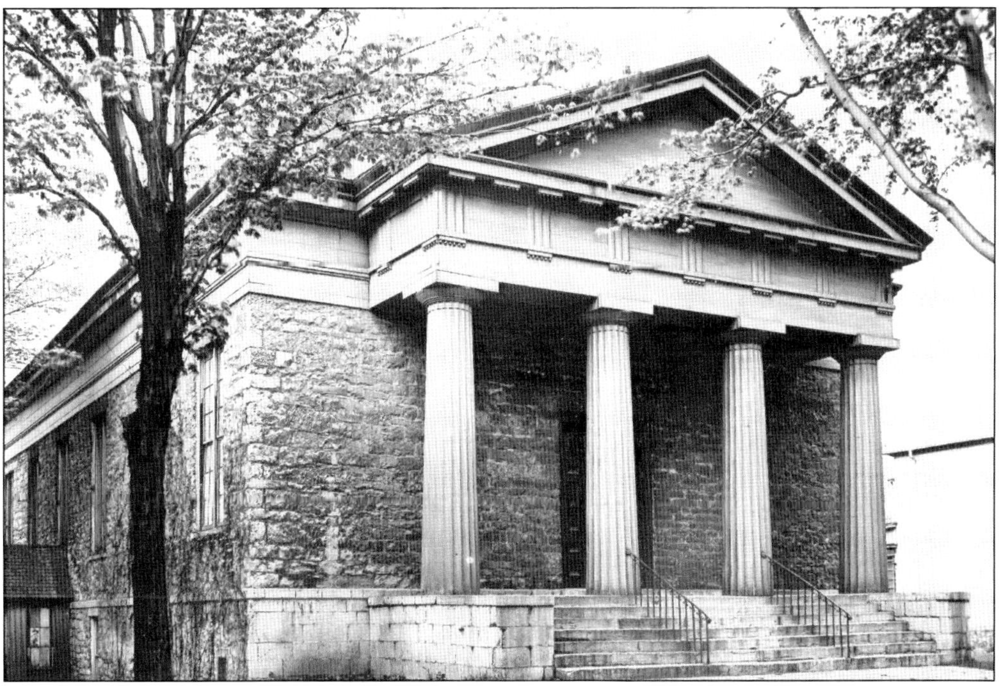

This undated photograph is of the St. James Episcopal Church when it was located on Ellicott Street across from the 1841 courthouse. Built in 1836, it was the second Episcopal church to stand at this location. An earlier brick structure, which had taken six years to complete, was occupied in 1822. (Courtesy of GCHD.)

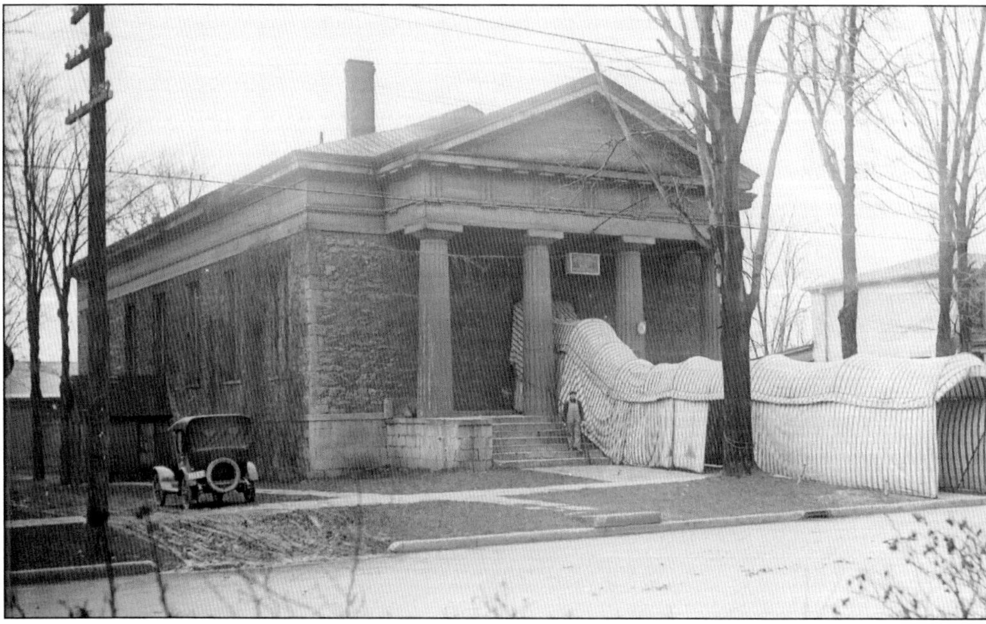

The new building was only six years old when the original roof and ceiling had to be torn off and replaced. However, it provided adequate service until 1909 when the Episcopalians built a third church, the one now on East Main Street. The Odd Fellows, seen above holding some sort of function, then became the new owners. (Courtesy of GCHD.)

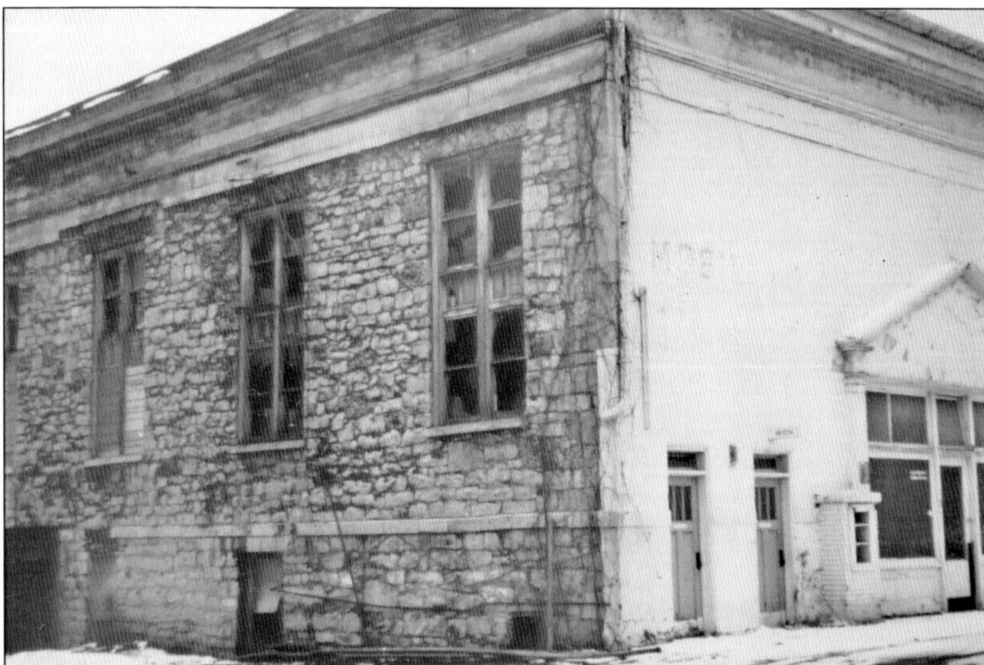

In the 1920s or 1930s, the structure became the property of William W. Buxton and was used as a garage and filling station. The last operator was Louis Moretto, who died in 1972. It stood unused after Moretto's death until 1975, when the building was razed and replaced by the Ponderosa Restaurant. (Courtesy of LSGC.)

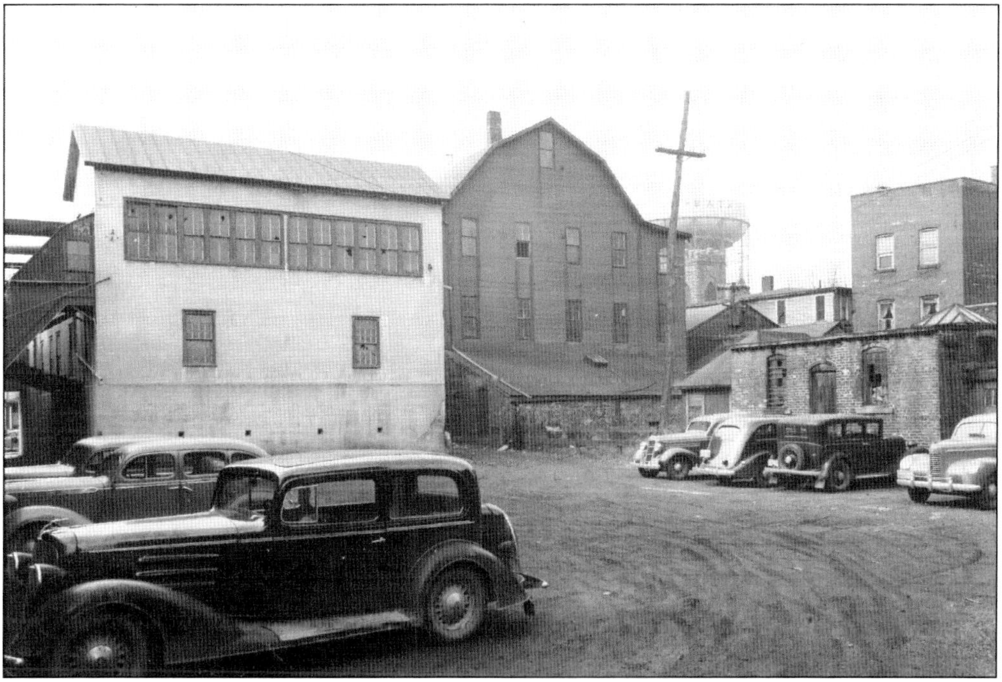

This is a view within the area that became the Court Street Plaza. In the distance is the water tower that hovered above downtown Batavia for more than 50 years. The automobiles suggest that this picture was taken in the early 1940s, but no earlier than 1939, since that is the year the tower was completed. (Courtesy of GCHD.)

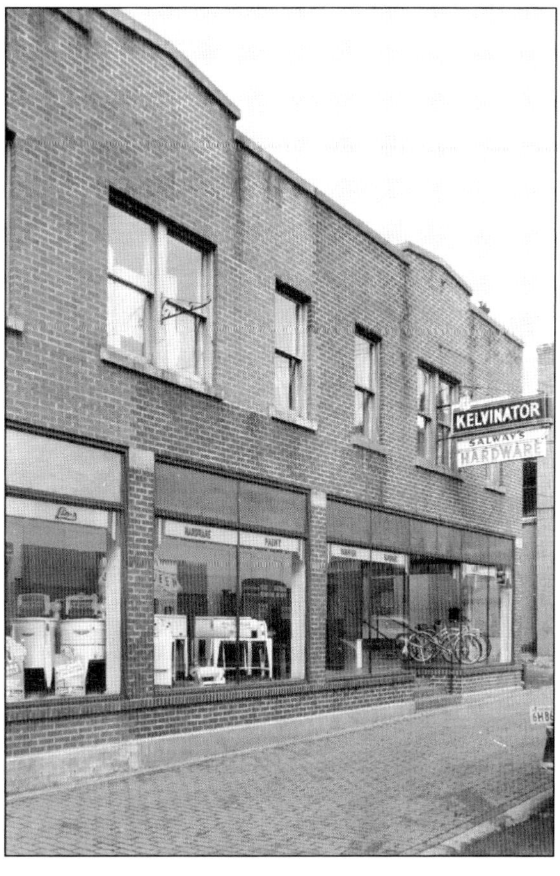

Salway's Hardware, shown here in 1954, was also in the area that became the Court Street Plaza. It was located on Exchange Place, a narrow thoroughfare that ran between Main and Ellicott Streets. The business later moved into the town of Batavia on West Main Street Road. Note the wringer clothes washers. (Courtesy of GCHD.)

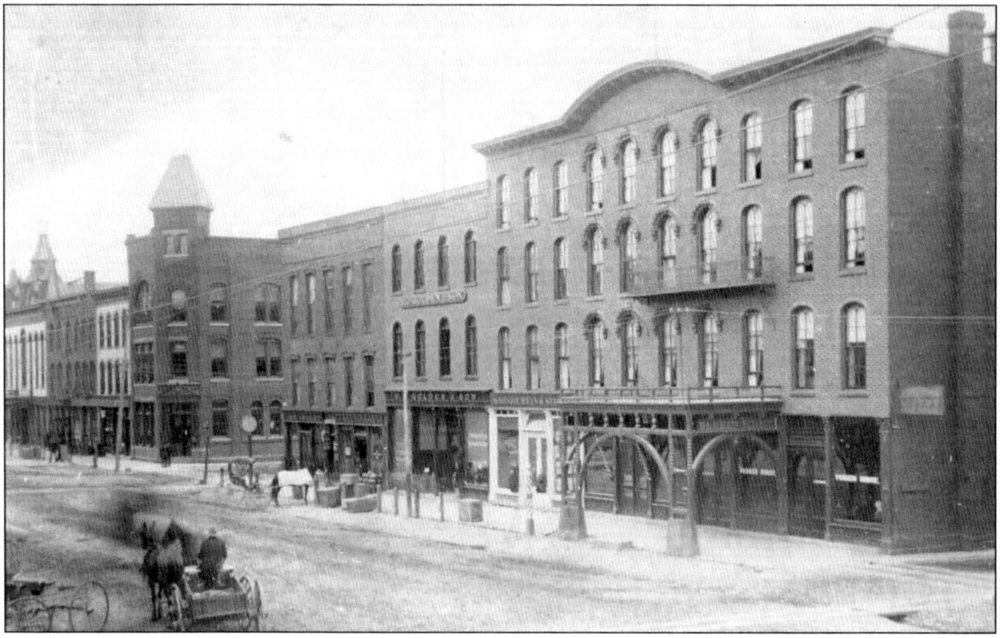

These two photographs are of the same general location and apparently from the same era, but it is unknown which is the earlier one. The above image shows the Doty Building in the distance, located on the corner of Main and Jackson Streets. It was built in 1890, so the picture was taken thereafter. There are no trolley tracks, which were laid in 1903, so the photograph must have been taken before that date. The nearest building, with the portico, is at the intersection between Main Street and Clark Place. The picture below shows the same building, but without a portico. The horse and buggy and safety bicycles suggest that this image was taken in either the late 1890s or early 1900s. (Courtesy of GCHD.)

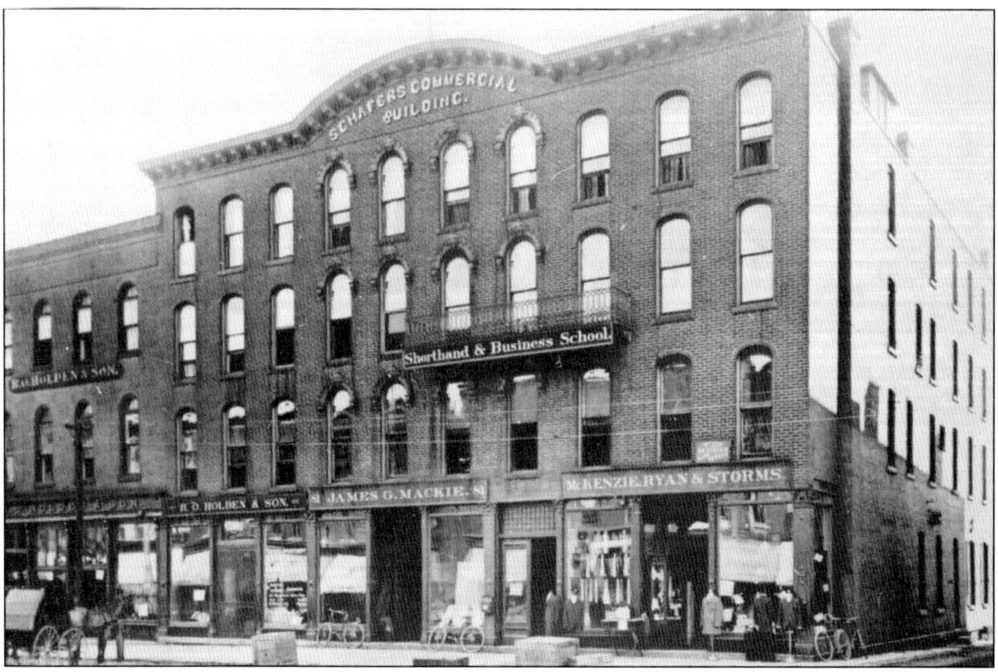

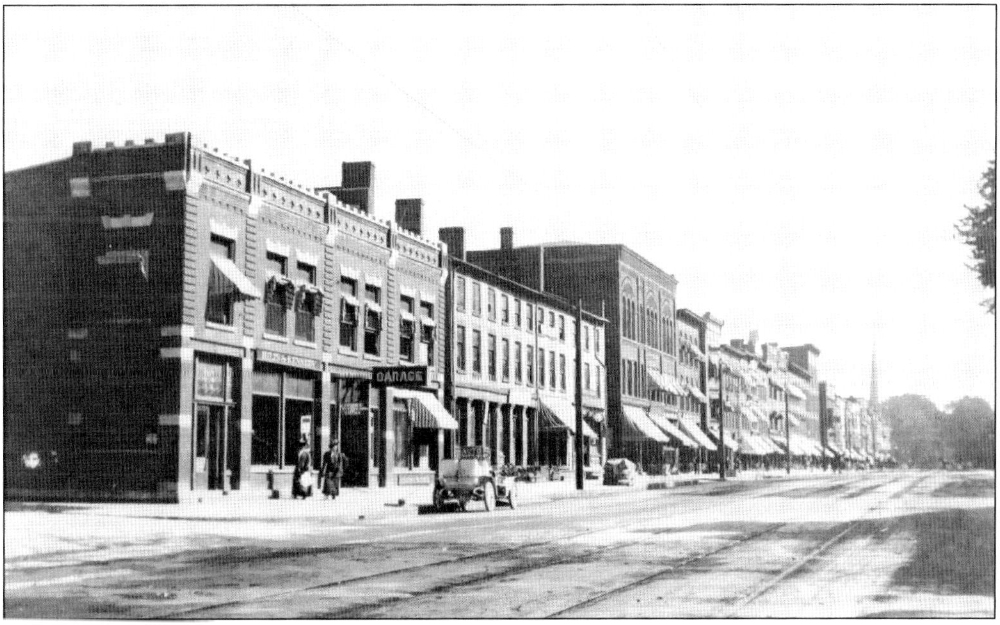

This photograph, taken around 1910, shows the north side of Main Street looking east from about the present location of the post office. Note the automobile dealership. Automobiles continued to be sold at this location until urban renewal leveled the area 60-some years later. Also note the awnings, used to help cool buildings prior to air conditioning. (Courtesy of GCHD.)

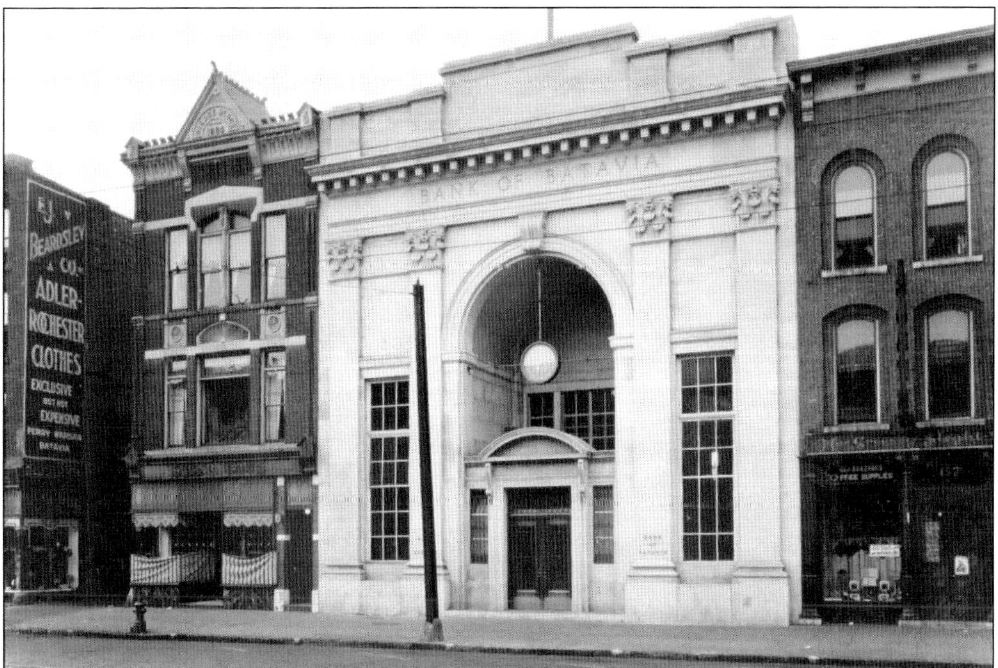

The Bank of Batavia was erected on the south side of Main Street roughly where its successor, HSBC, is now located. The picture is probably from the early 1920s. The vault had walls 27 inches thick that were reinforced with steel rails discarded by the New York Central Railroad. Note a popular establishment, the Sugar Bowl, located next door. (Courtesy of GCHD.)

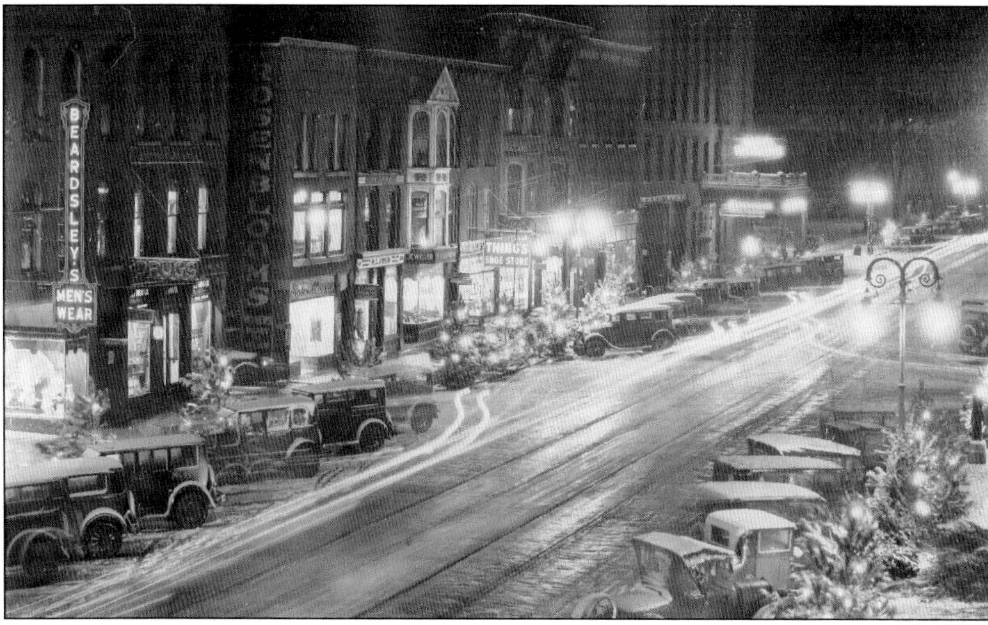

This rare nighttime photograph from the 1920s shows the south side of Main Street looking west. County Building One is in the distance. What appears to be an alley is Exchange Place. Observe the decorative street lamps, the lighted Christmas trees along the street, diagonal parking, and streetcar tracks. (Courtesy of GCHD.)

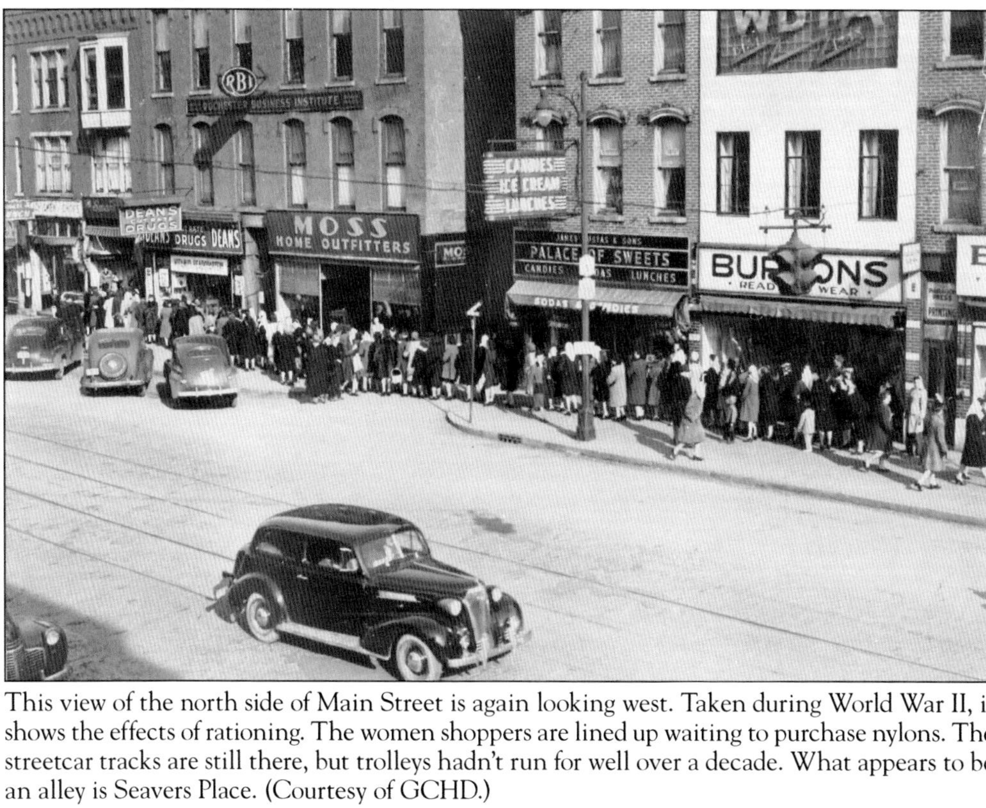

This view of the north side of Main Street is again looking west. Taken during World War II, it shows the effects of rationing. The women shoppers are lined up waiting to purchase nylons. The streetcar tracks are still there, but trolleys hadn't run for well over a decade. What appears to be an alley is Seavers Place. (Courtesy of GCHD.)

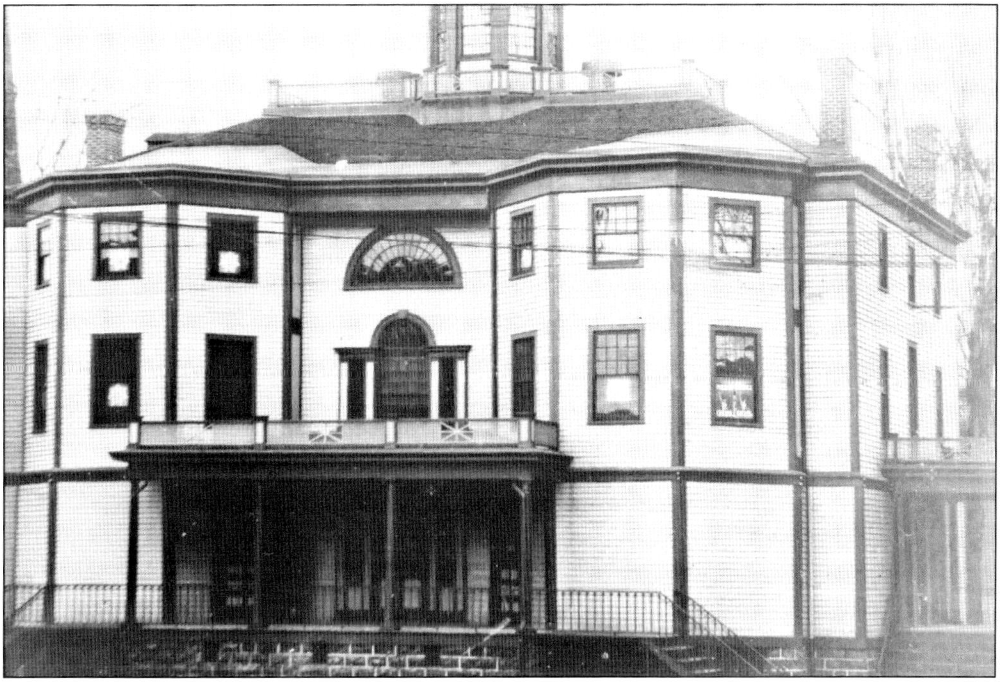

Ellicott Hall was built in 1802 by Joseph Ellicott to serve as a courthouse for the newly formed Genesee County. It was situated in the triangle formed by Main, Ellicott, and Court Streets. Above is the north side facing Main Street, and the view below shows the east side. Ellicott Hall featured not just the usual facilities associated with a courthouse, but half of the lower floor served as a tavern. When the county built a new courthouse in 1841, the one at the intersection of Main and Ellicott Streets, it leased Ellicott Hall to private individuals. Over the years, these individuals evidently forgot that they had leased the building and sold it to others. As more time passed, there was a succession of buyers and sellers who erroneously thought they owned the structure. (Courtesy of GCHD.)

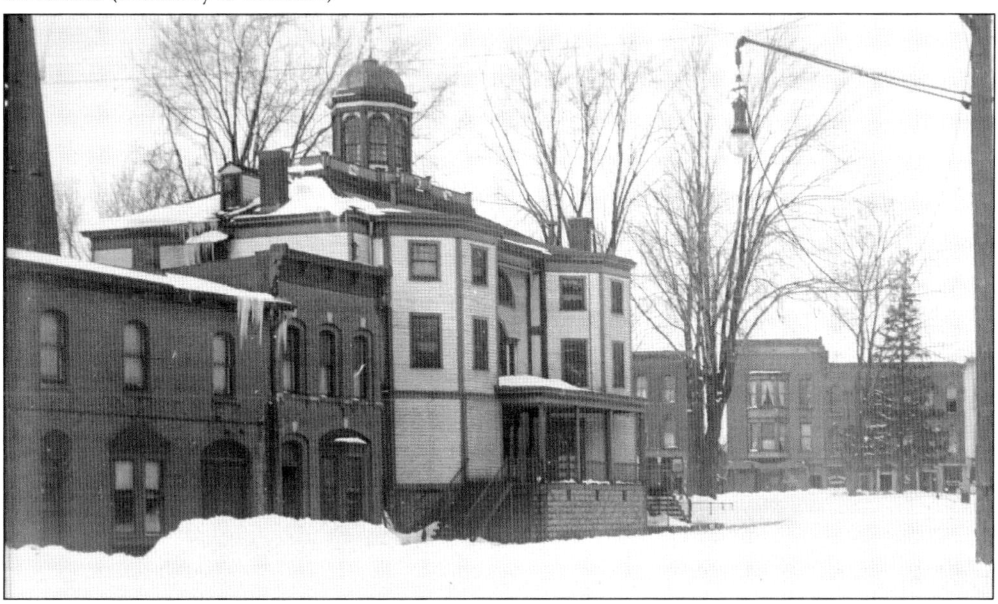

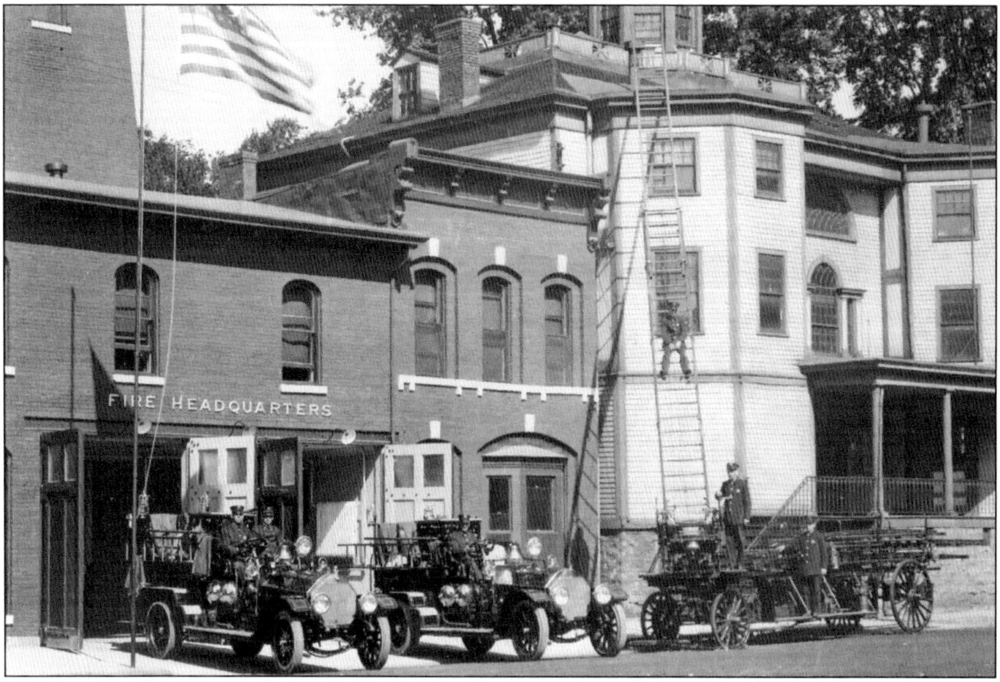

The photograph above appears to be of the firefighters of the semi-paid City of Batavia fire department established in 1916. This was the department's headquarters on Court Street, adjacent to Ellicott Hall. Its close proximity apparently didn't matter when fire broke out in the hall on a February night in 1918. The image below shows the result. The fire was attributed to an overheated furnace in bitterly cold weather. The city had been using the building and lost office furniture and equipment, voting machines, and a truck. However, to the relief of city officials, a vault holding important records survived despite the massive destruction. Insurance proceeds were used towards the conversion of the Brisbane Mansion into a city hall. (Courtesy of GCHD.)

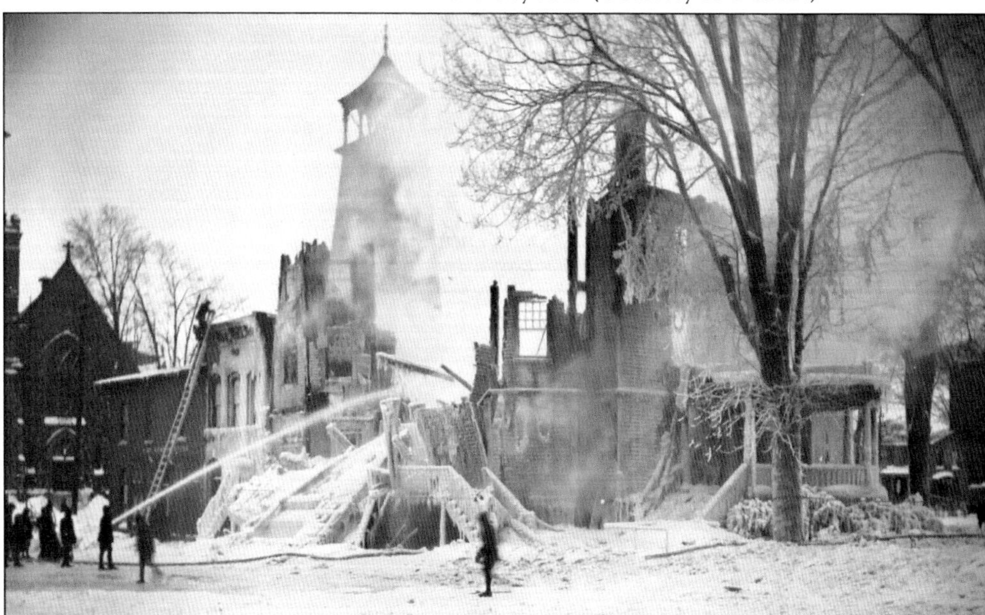

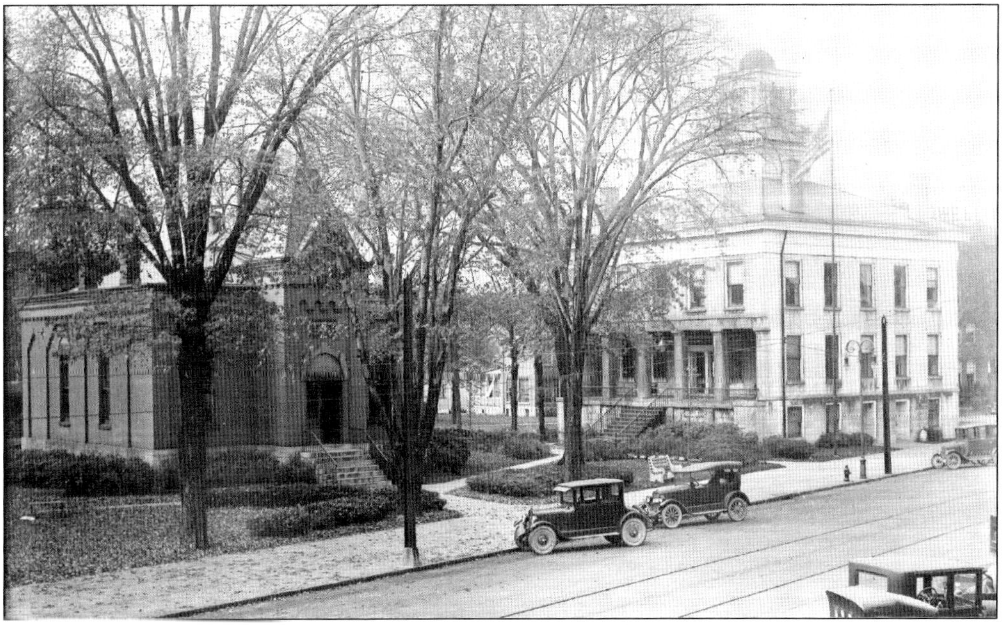

This picture was probably taken in the early 1920s. The building on the left is the surrogate court office. The east side of the 1841 courthouse is visible in the distance. Note the open porch area. Since it was enclosed in 1931 to provide more interior space, it is evident that the picture was taken before then. (Courtesy of GCHD.)

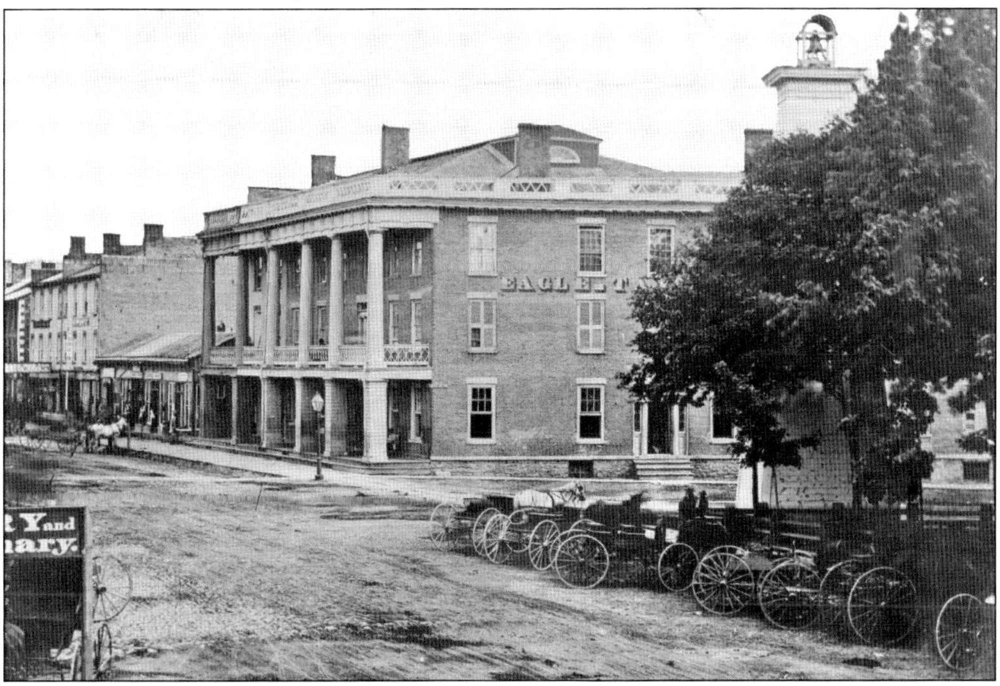

For a very long time, one hotel or another stood on the southeast corner of Main and Court Streets. It was an ideal location since major highway routes, railroad stations, and later an interstate bus terminal were all close by. The Eagle Tavern, shown here, was built in 1835. Note the fire bell on the tower to the right. (Courtesy of GCHD.)

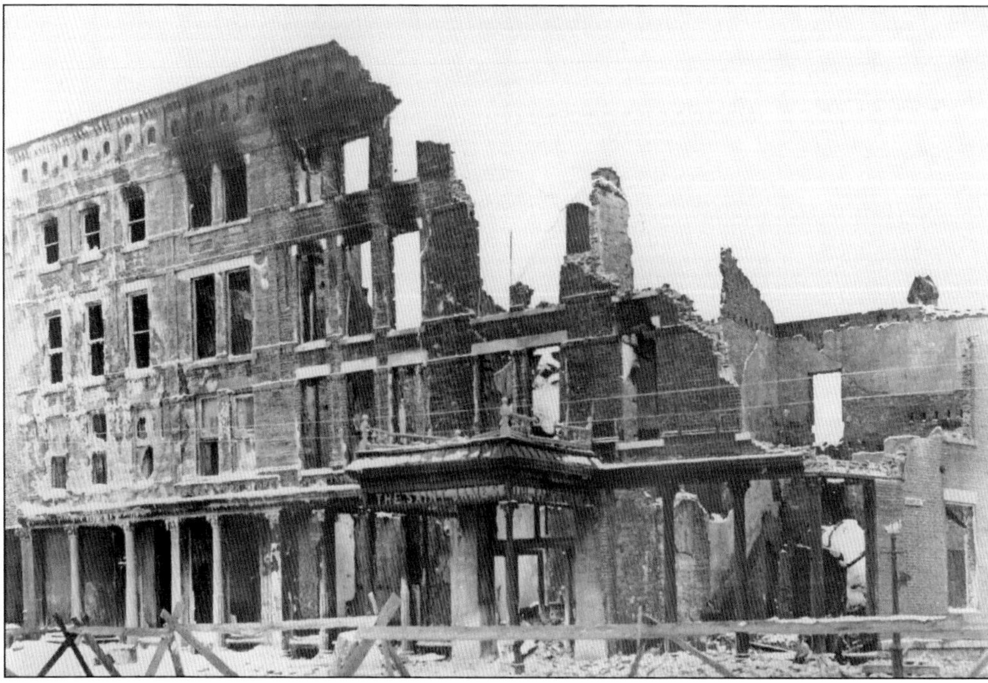

When the Eagle Tavern was acquired in 1869 by new owners, it was first renamed Hotel Richmond, but soon changed to St. James due to opposition from local citizens who didn't like the political associations. It was remodeled in 1884 into a four-story arcade. This picture was taken in 1886, after the building was destroyed by a fire. (Courtesy of GCHD.)

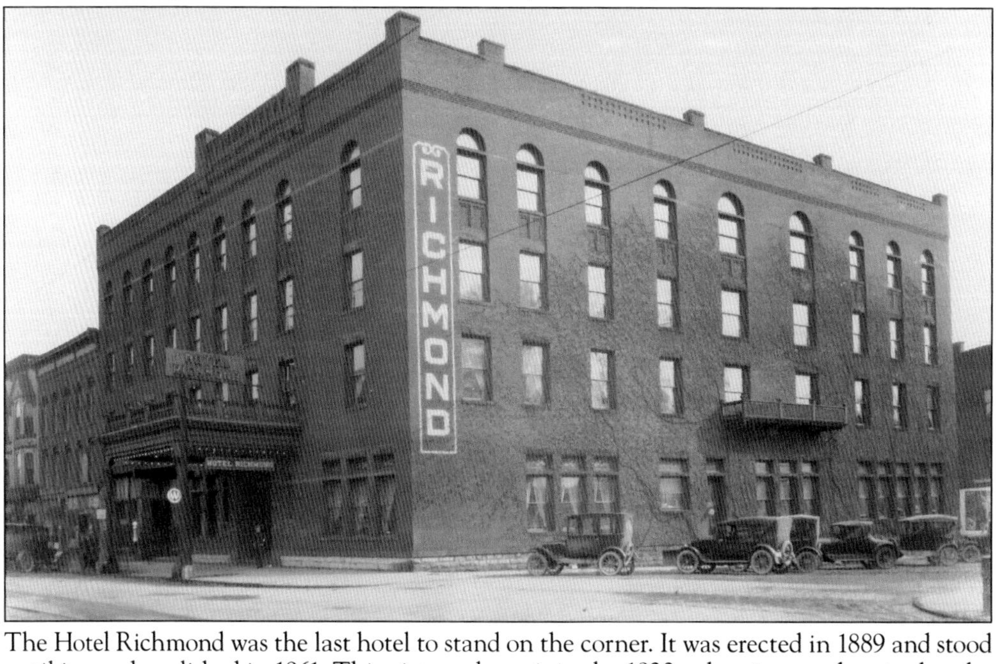

The Hotel Richmond was the last hotel to stand on the corner. It was erected in 1889 and stood until it was demolished in 1961. This picture shows it in the 1920s when it was advertised as the leading hotel between Buffalo and Rochester. It likely gained its name from Mary Richmond, a major stakeholder. (Courtesy of GCHD.)

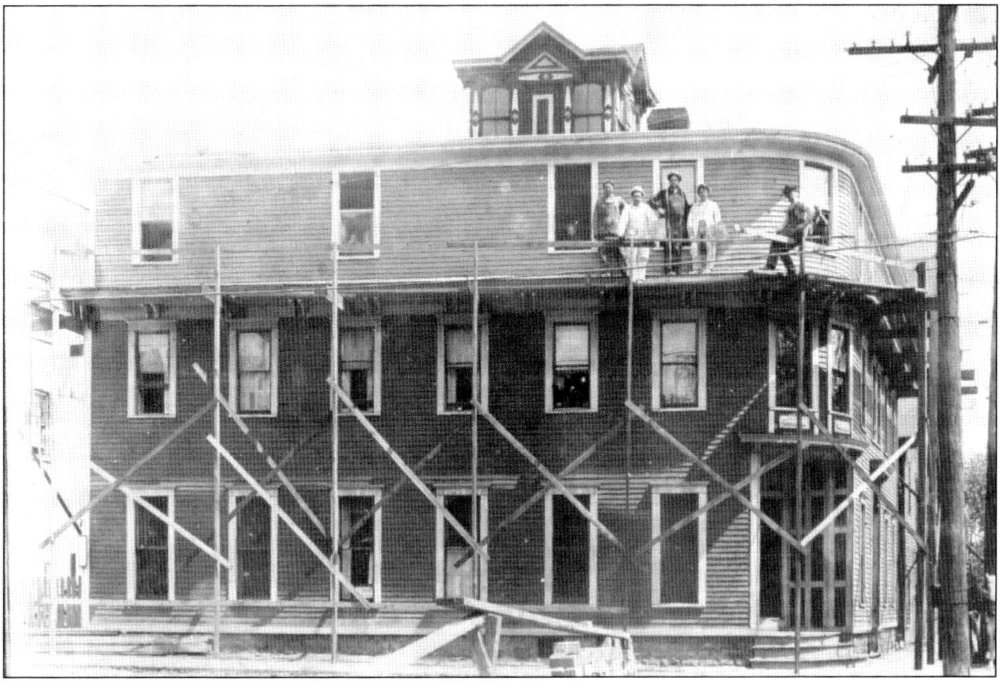

The above picture taken around 1919 shows the former Park Hotel on the northeast corner of Ellicott and Court Streets. It appears to be undergoing renovations. A hotel had been on this corner since at least 1866, but the building shown here was probably constructed about 1880. In 1919, this building became the Lafayette Hotel. In later years, the hotel reportedly served as an overflow annex for the Hotel Richmond. The photograph below shows the building many years after it had been sold to the Continental Motor Corporation. By the time the image was taken in the 1960s, it housed Trailways offices and terminal. The building was razed in 1965. (Courtesy of GCHD.)

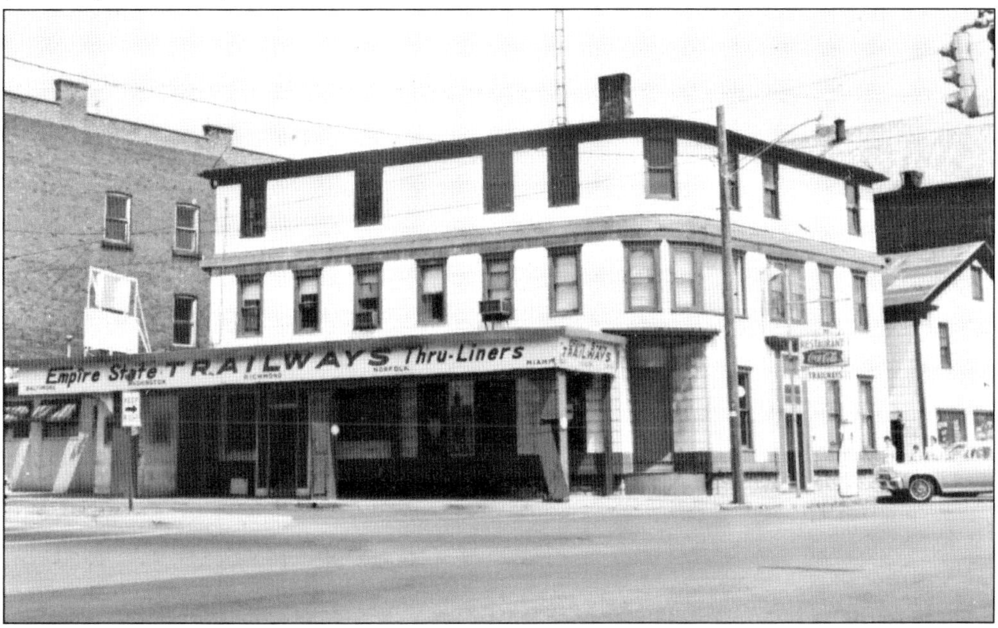

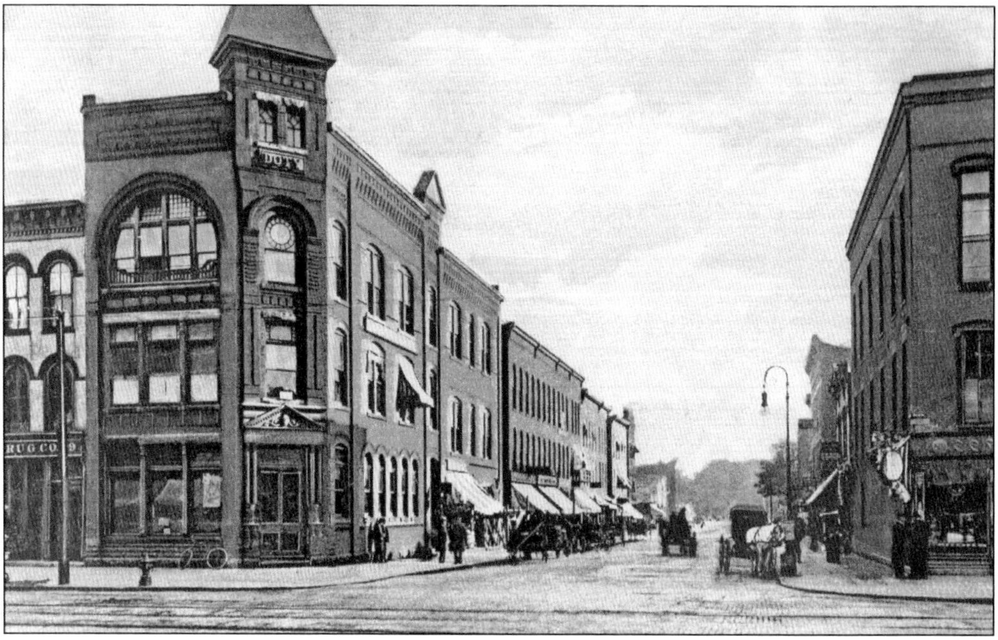

The above image shows the southeast corner of Main and Jackson Streets about 1911. The picture below is of the same corner in the 1920s. The building on the corner was built in 1890 by Leonidas Doty for the Farmer's Bank. For several years, the second and third floors were used by the YMCA. Eventually the Farmer's Bank went into bankruptcy, and the building became the property of the Bank of Genesee. Henry Homelius was hired to remodel the interior and design a new front. The new front included a clock, which was removed a few years later. In 1923, the building was expanded southward along Jackson Street. (Above, courtesy of Elizabeth Rowsick; below, courtesy of GCHD.)

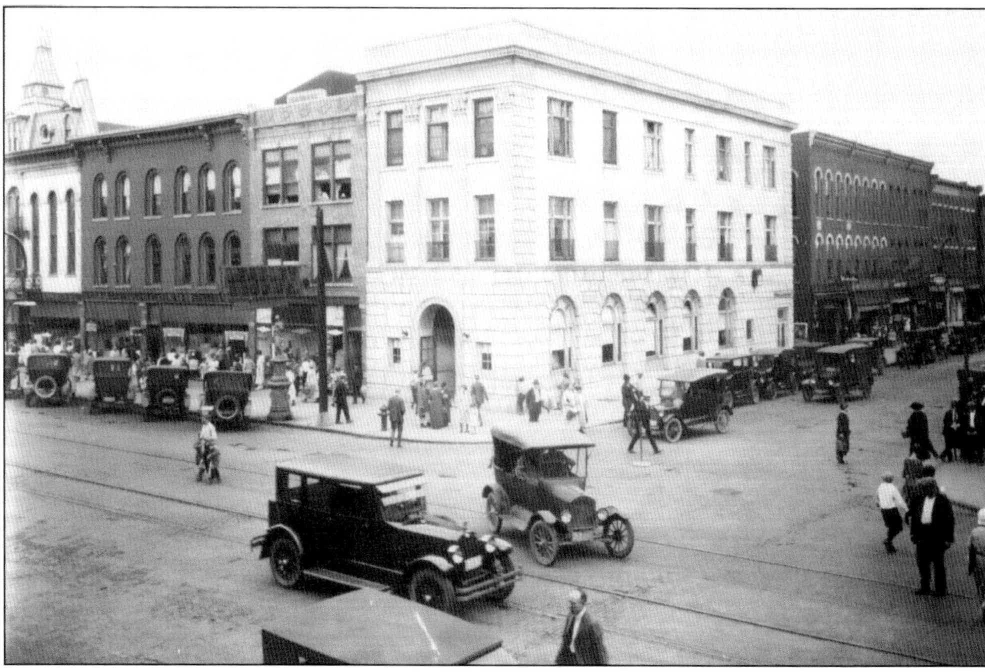

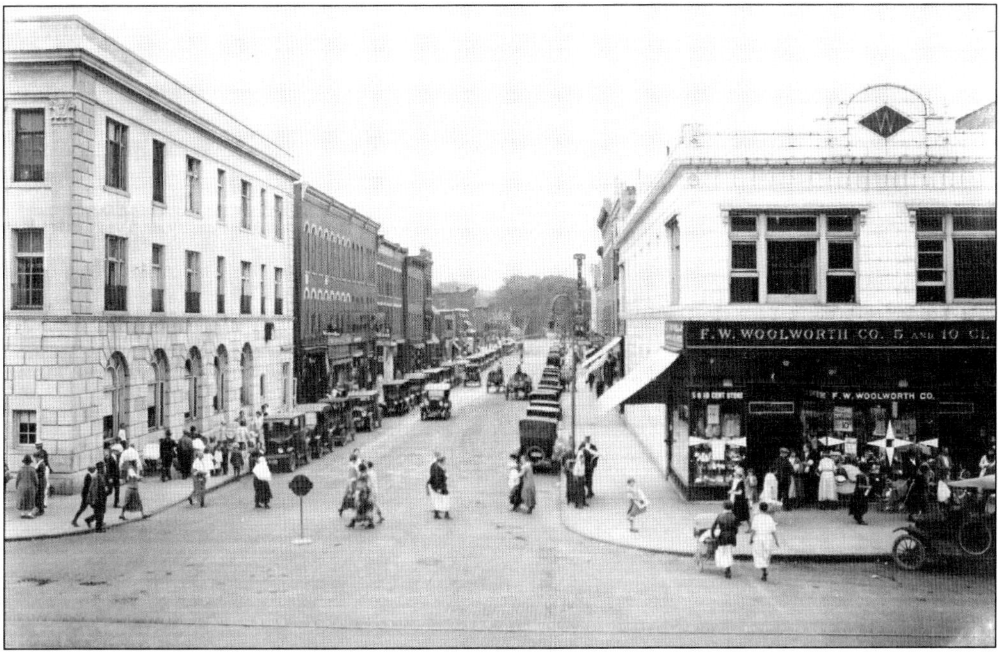

In 1924, this is what "Dollar Days" looked like on Jackson Street, facing south from Main Street. Note the large number of pedestrians, a sight common in the city of Batavia before its retail center moved out into the town of Batavia. The Woolworth 5¢ and 10¢ store on the right was a place where one really could make purchases for only a nickel or a dime. (Courtesy of GCHD.)

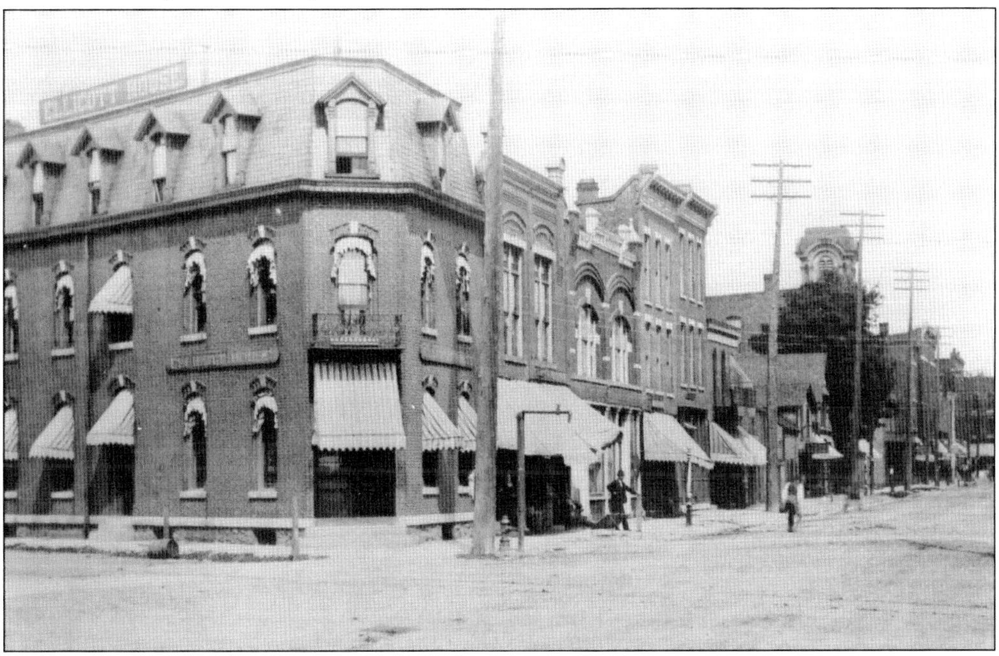

This is a considerably earlier view along Jackson Street, looking north from Ellicott Street. Since the street is still unpaved, it is likely from the 1890s. The pipe on the corner provided water to fill sprinkler wagons used to keep down the dust. Note the railroad spur in the foreground that ran along the north side of Ellicott Street. (Courtesy of GCHD.)

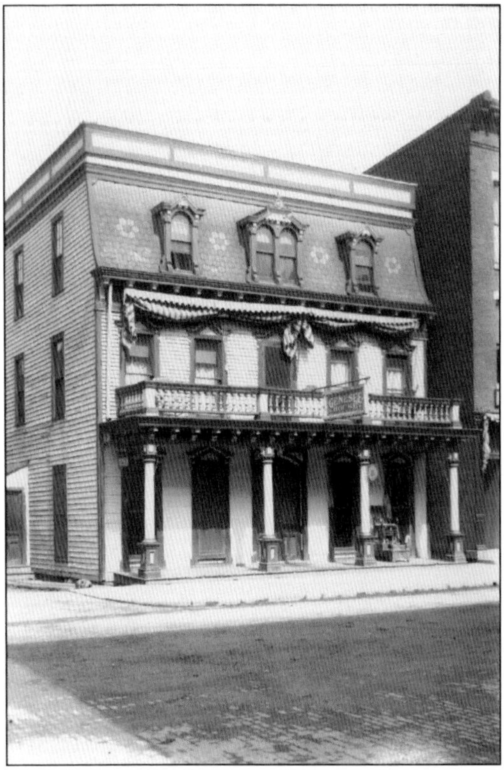

These two pictures show the Genesee House at 18 Jackson Street. That location is roughly across Jackson from today's entrance to Jackson Square. It was just north of the Family Theatre. The photograph at left shows its appearance in around 1920 and below is how it looked shortly before demolition in 1940. The best guess places its construction in 1819. An owner by the name of Timothy Lynch expanded it considerably shortly after the Civil War. When he rebuilt the porch in 1896, a newspaper account said the building was 77 years old. Lynch's widow still owned the building in 1939. In 1940, Irving Krieger bought it in a tax delinquency sale and tore it down. (Courtesy of GCHD.)

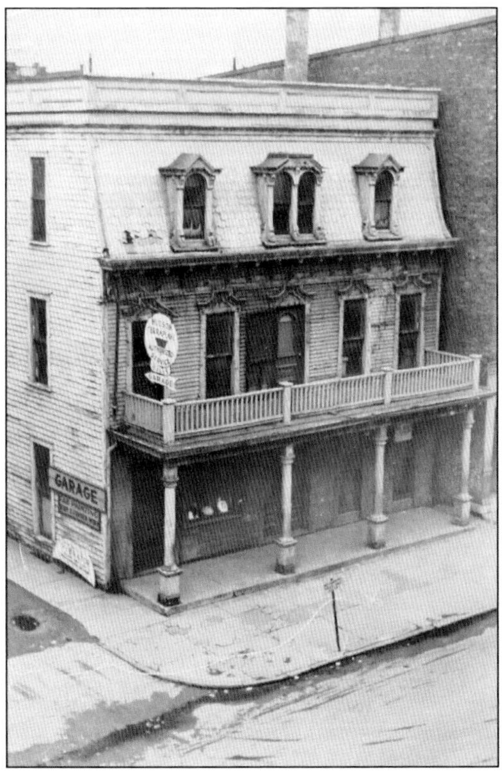

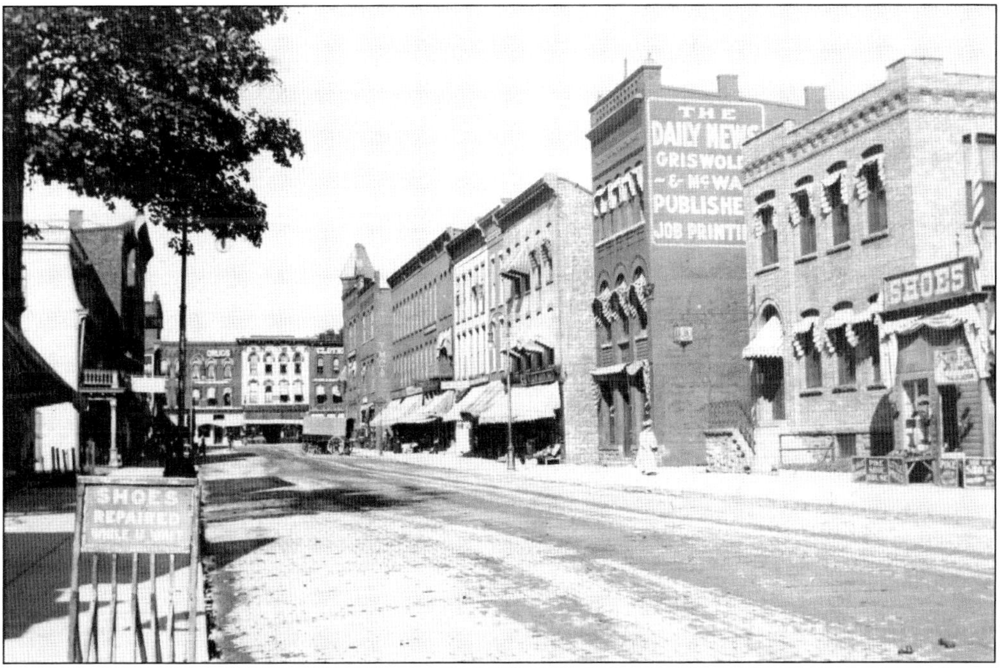

This is another view facing north on Jackson Street, probably photographed about 1910 or soon after. In the distance on the far right at the intersection with Main Street is the Doty Building, erected in 1890. On the left, the porch of the Genesee House is visible. The structure between the Daily News Building and the shoe shop was built in 1907 by the New York Telephone Company. (Courtesy of GCHD.)

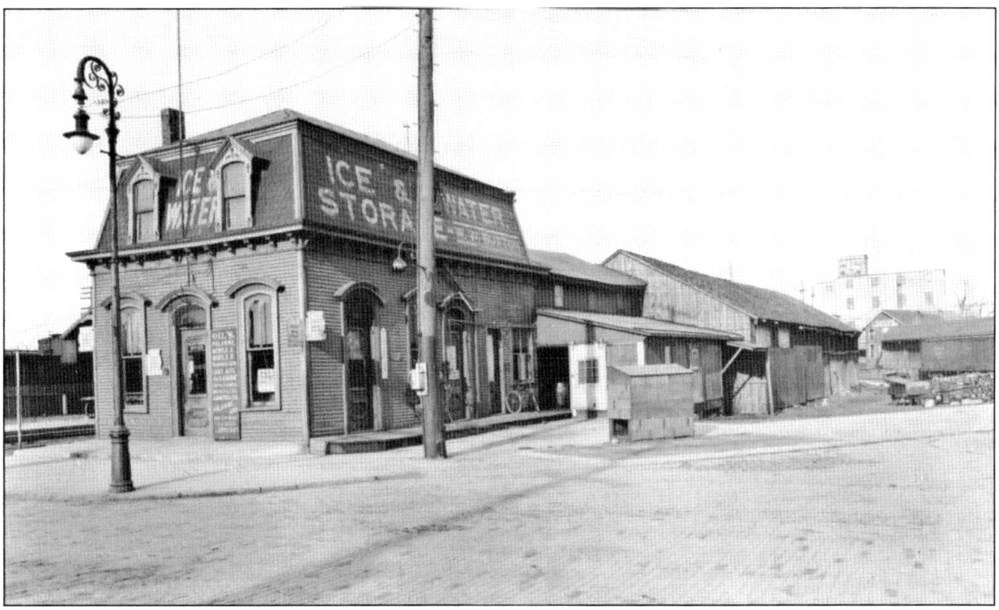

This business operation, located on the south side of Ellicott Street between Evans and Jackson Streets, was owned by William W. Buxton. The picture dates from about 1905. The ice he sold would have been harvested from lakes and ponds, since refrigeration was not yet available for producing it. (Courtesy of GCHD.)

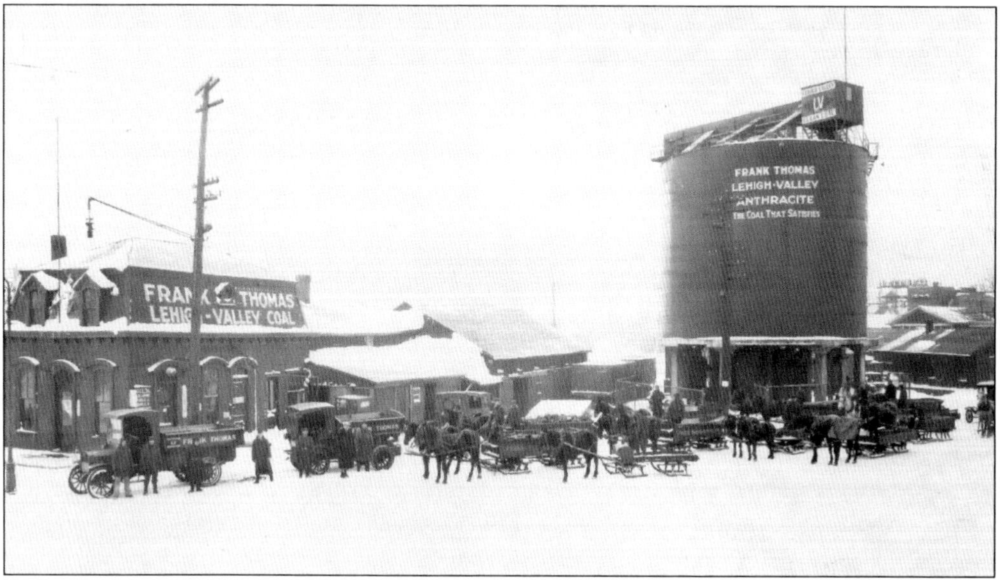

Note that the building in the previous picture also appears in this one, but with a different name on it. Buxton sold it to Frank Thomas in 1919, around the same time as the photograph was taken. Observe the reference to anthracite coal on the coaling tower. This type of coal was popular because it burned cleanly. (Courtesy of GCHD.)

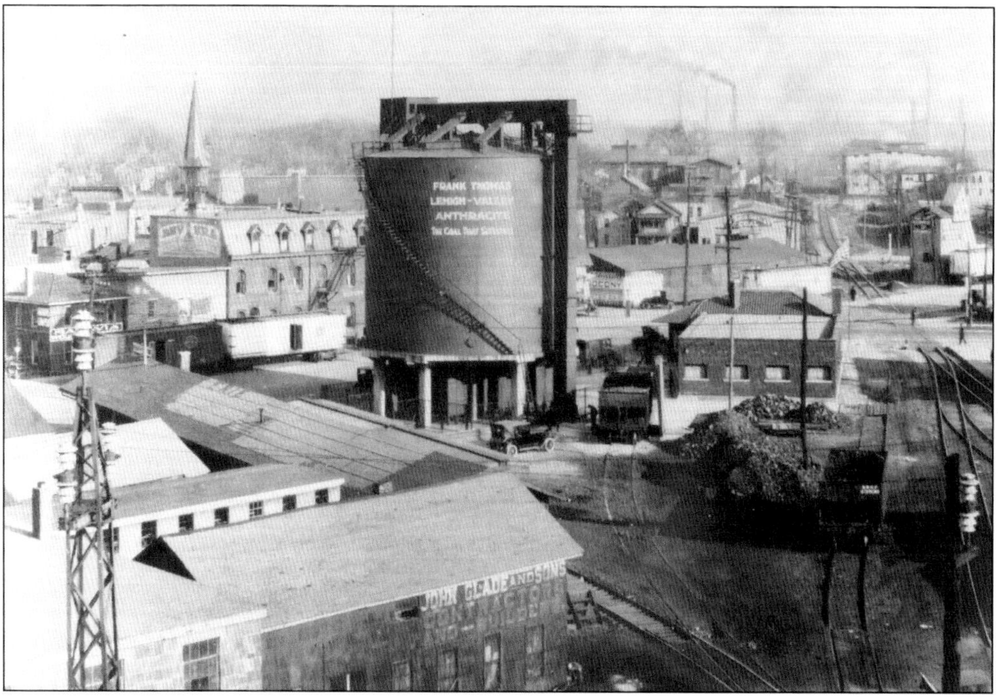

Frank Thomas married Adelaide Richmond, the granddaughter of Dean Richmond, and lived in the Richmond Mansion until her death in 1925. Frank died in 1938 in a tragic accident. After surviving an automobile mishap without injury, he was struck by another motorist while walking to summon aid. This view looks north across Ellicott Street. Note the Ellicott House just left of the coaling tower. (Courtesy of GCHD.)

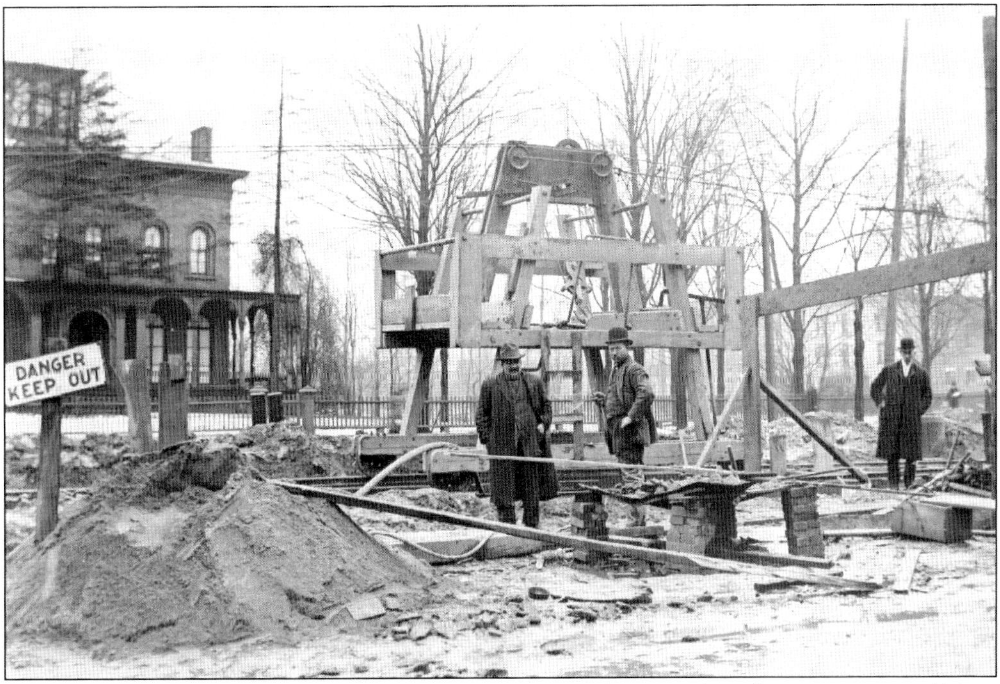

Tracks for Batavia's trolleys were laid in 1903. This image shows work at the intersection of Main and Ellicott Streets. This is the only photograph known to the author that shows the Brisbane Mansion prior to it becoming city hall. Note the veranda extending across the front of the building, a feature later removed. (Courtesy of GCHD.)

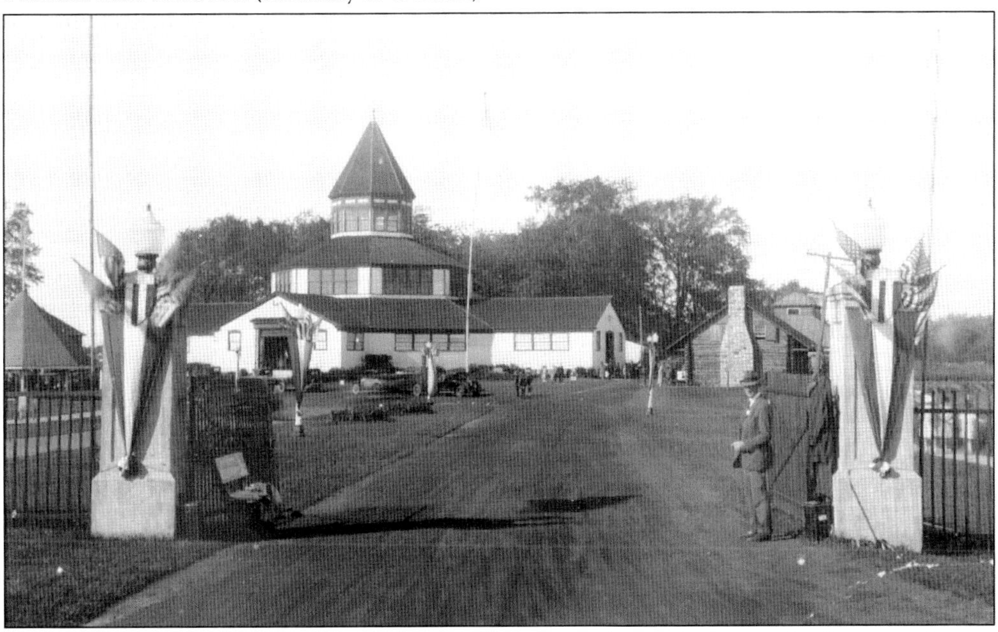

The trolley tracks ran from a barn and powerhouse on Clinton Street to the Genesee County Fairgrounds on West Main Street. This picture shows the fairgrounds in the late 1920s. The Buffalo firm that built the line planned to lay tracks all the way from Williamsville to Rochester. (Courtesy of GCHD.)

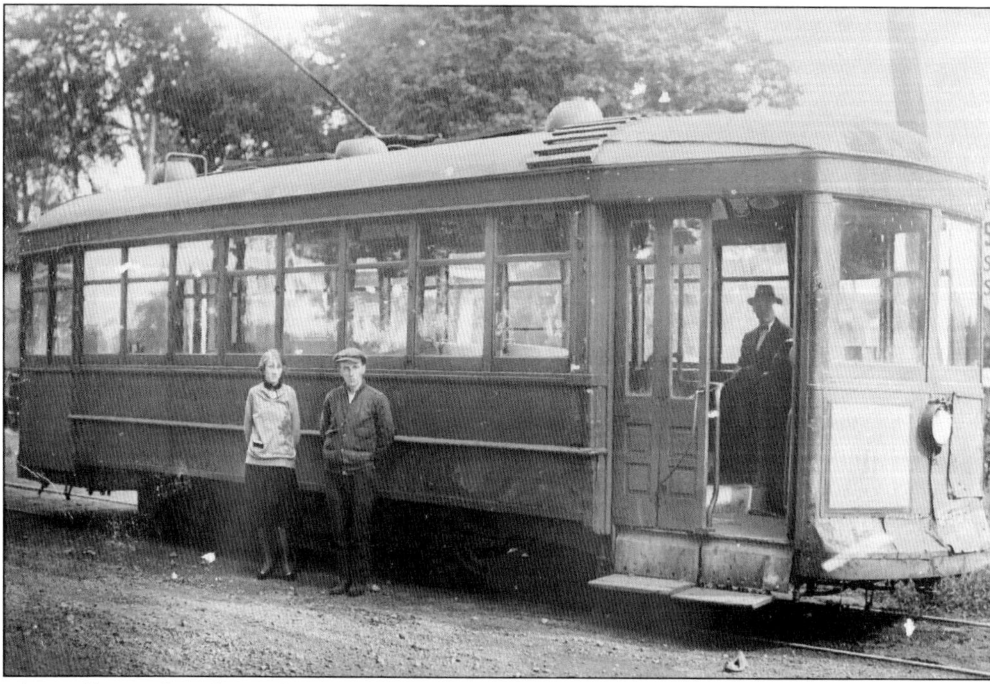

This trolley car has obviously seen better days. Judging by the clothing of the unidentified persons, this photograph was taken sometime in the 1920s. Local investors assumed ownership of the trolley line in 1915 in an unsuccessful effort to turn it into a moneymaker. Operation ended in 1927. (Courtesy of GCHD.)

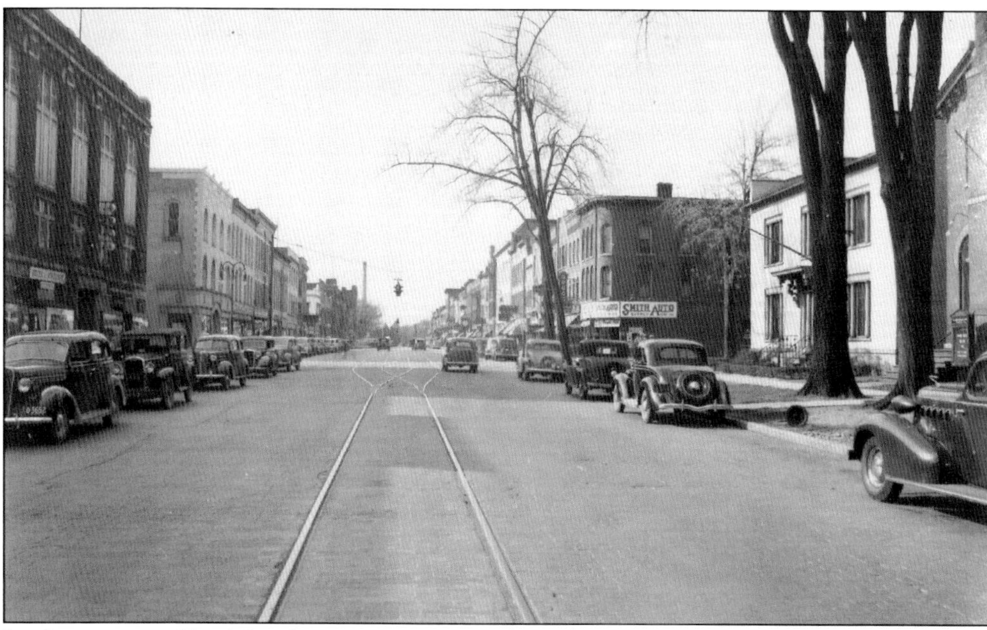

Looking west on East Main Street, one can see where the trolley tracks split to allow trolley cars to pass one another. Note that although the picture was made in the 1930s after trolley service had ceased, the tracks still appear functional. Some sections of track survived into the 1960s. (Courtesy of GCHD.)

Two

Moving the Railroad Tracks

Lacking navigable waterways, when Batavia was founded, the only means of cross-country travel was on foot or by horse and horse-drawn vehicles. This limitation was dramatically altered with the arrival of railroads. The first railroad line to reach Batavia appeared in 1836 when track was laid between the village and Rochester. Before many years passed, railroad lines connected Batavia to communities all over western New York. Travel by rail became the normal manner of coming and going to such nearby places as LeRoy, South Byron, Corfu, Alexander, and Linden. It was also the preferred means of travel to more distant cities such as Buffalo, Rochester, and Syracuse. Travelers could catch trains to and from these places several times a day.

In the 1800s, most people got around Batavia by walking; therefore, it made sense for the railroads to run through the center of the village and for passenger stations to be located downtown. Eventually downtown Batavia was traversed by a large number of tracks including the four that defined the main line of the New York Central Railroad.

So much rail traffic in a densely populated area created danger. Papers from this time were full of accident reports involving collisions with passing trains, despite crossing guards and other precautions. A fire station on either side of the tracks had to be built to insure that trains did not prevent fire fighters from quickly reaching a fire. Consequently, when automobiles eventually became the preferred mode of travel and passenger service on the railroads started to disappear, a movement began to relocate the main tracks to the periphery of the city.

Progress in moving these tracks proceeded slowly. Decisions on exactly where to run the new tracks and how to pay for the relocation took several years to work out. The Great Depression, followed by World War II, also slowed progress. Finally in the early 1950s, the work began and tracks carrying trains through Batavia were shifted southward. Today tracks in the downtown area exist only to serve the limited needs of local industry.

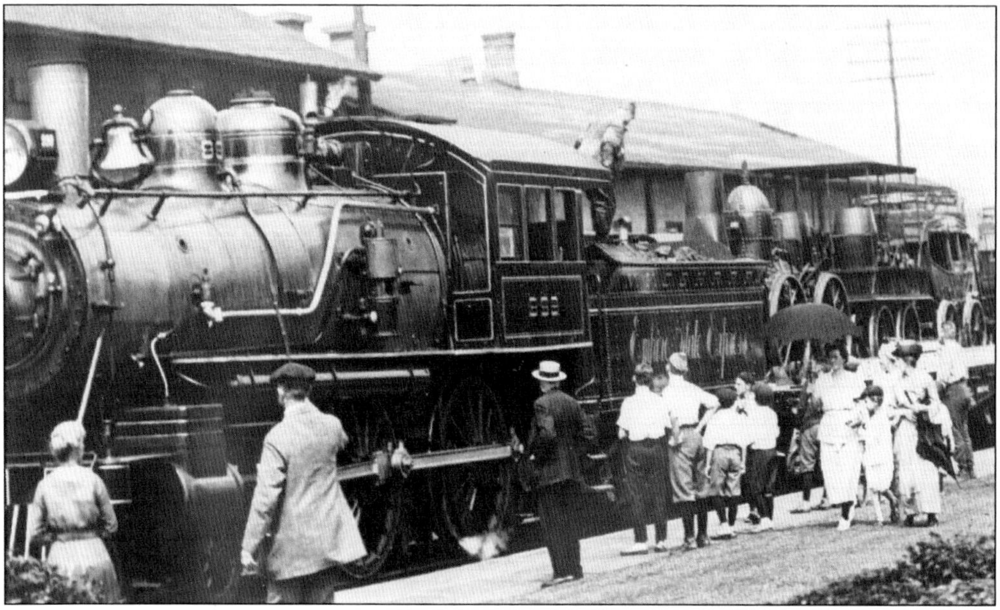

Batavia and railroad lore have long been closely intertwined. The grade coming in from the east is said to have been the steepest climb on the New York Central between New York and Chicago; however, the tracks running west to Buffalo were nearly dead level and perfect for setting speed records, as this engine did in 1893. Built for speed with unusually large driving wheels, it succeeded in reaching 112 mph a few miles west of Batavia. The above picture shows the engine on a commemorative visit to Batavia in 1921. The last visit to Batavia occurred in 1962, as shown below, when it was being towed by a modern diesel to its final resting spot, a railroad museum. (Courtesy of GCHD.)

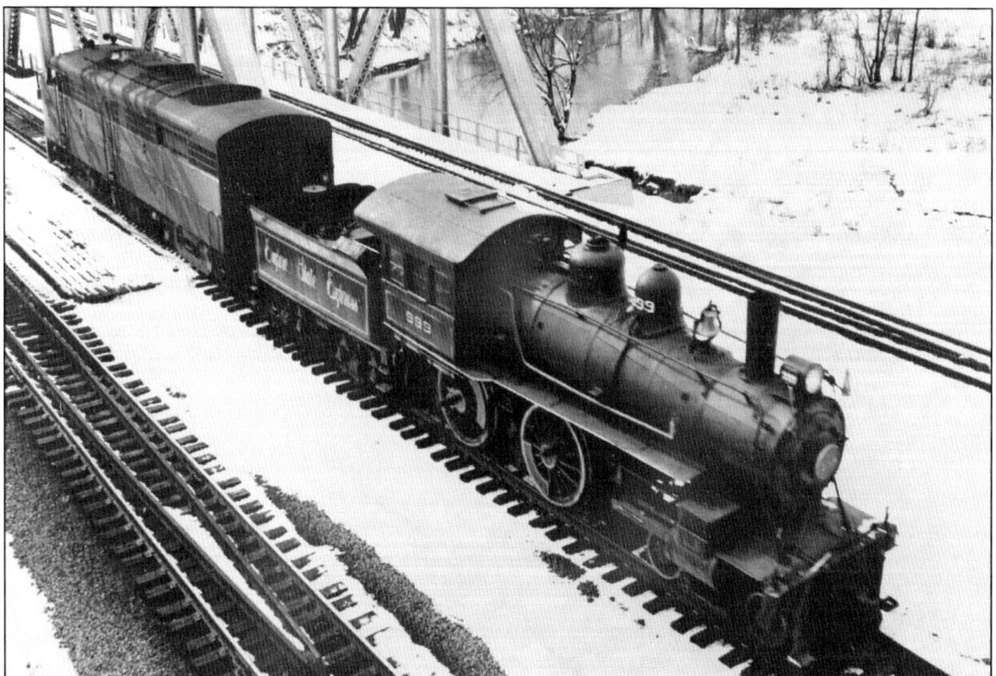

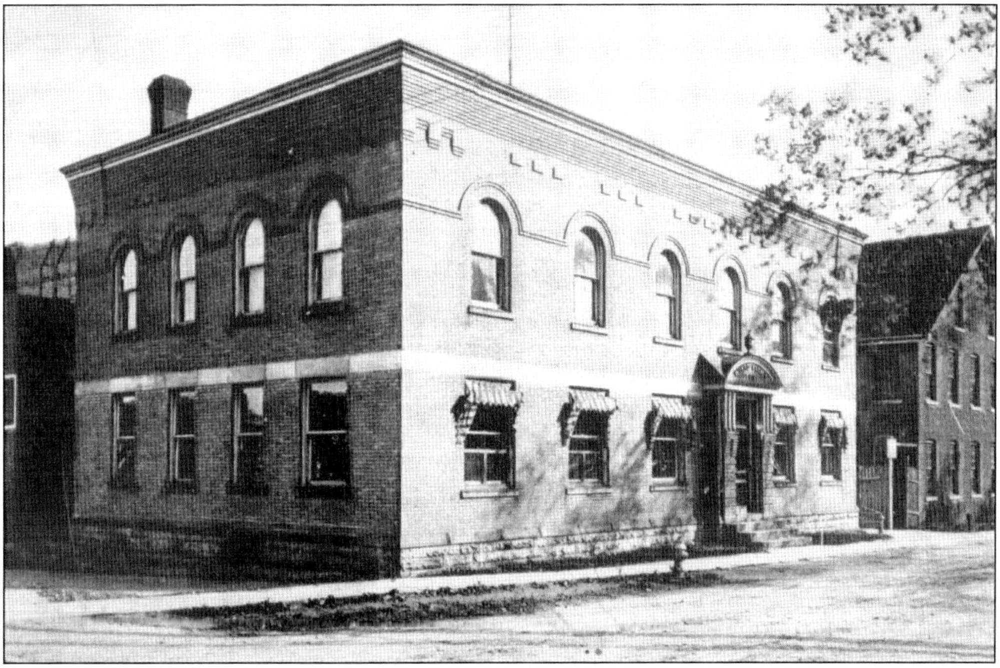

The importance of the railroads to Batavia was particularly great when the community had many large manufacturing firms that made heavy use of the rails. This relationship is illustrated by the photographs seen here. Above is the Wiard Plow Company offices. George Wiard and his partner moved the company from East Avon to Batavia specifically because of Batavia's excellent rail connections. The below picture shows the Massey Harris Harvester Company with tracks and three trains in view. It grew from a company that similarly moved from Brockport to Batavia in order to take advantage of Batavia's several railroad lines. (Courtesy of GCHD.)

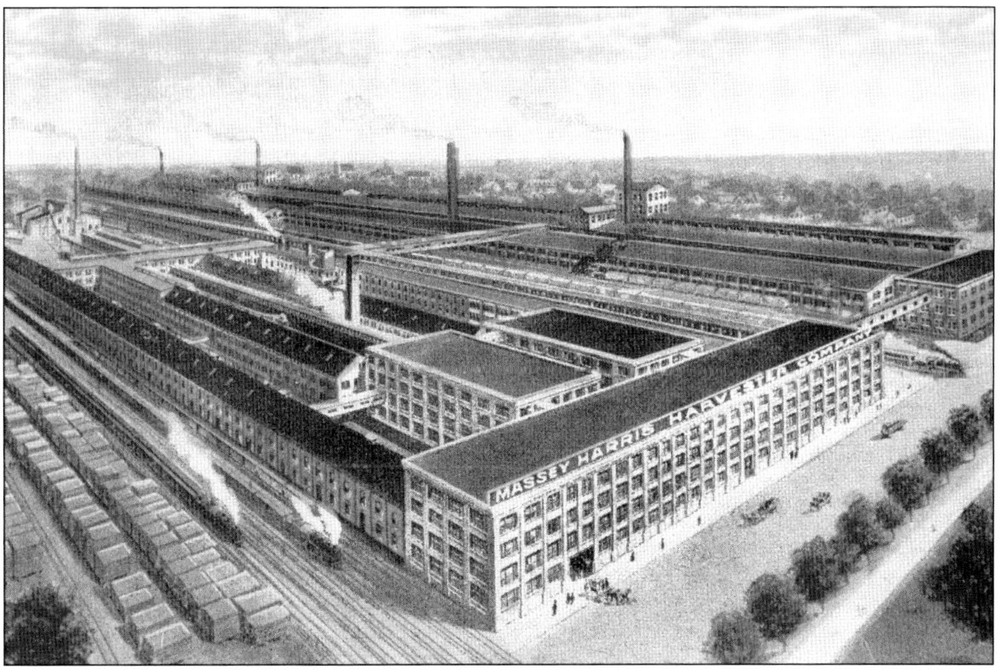

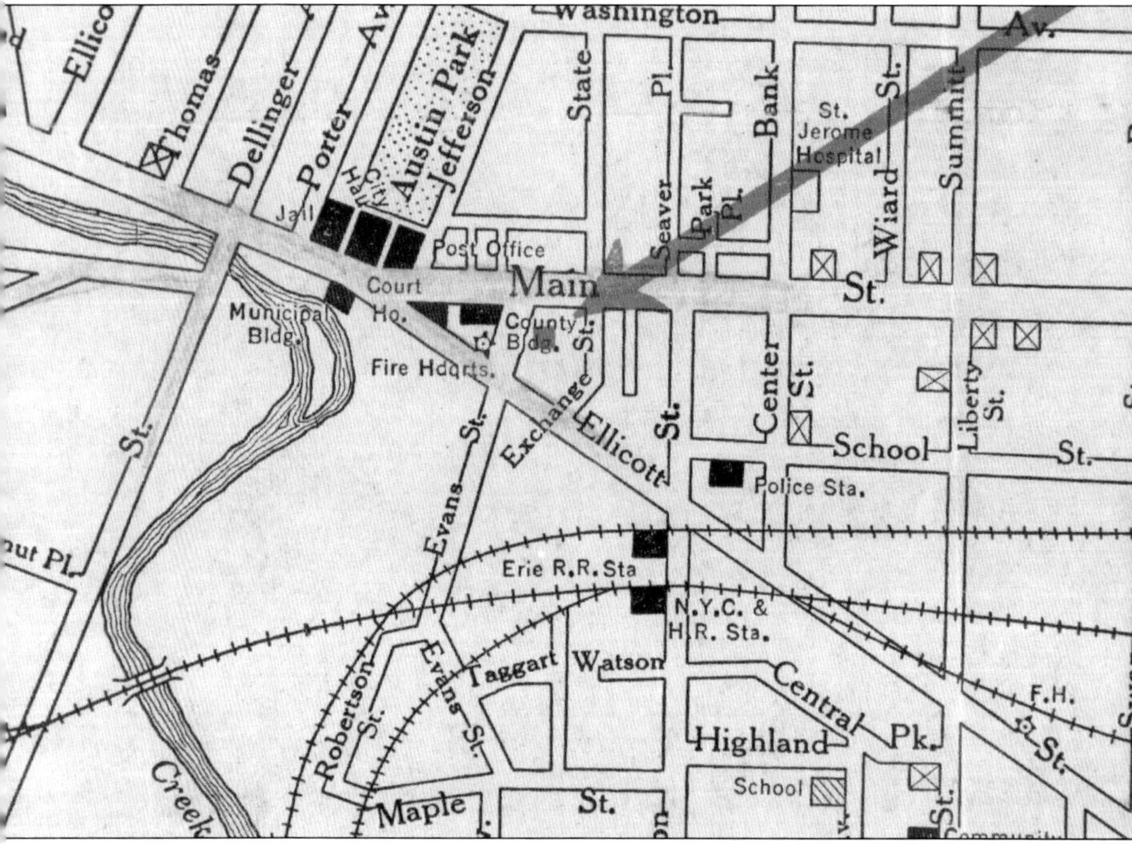

This map, published in the 1930s for distribution by local businesses, shows the main tracks running through central Batavia. Note that spurs, such as the one that ran northwest up Ellicott Street, have been omitted. Observe the locations of the New York Central and Erie railroad passenger stations. On this particular map, the arrow was added to identify where the Hotel Richmond was located. The rectangles with Xs are churches. From the day of the first railroad, tracks passed through the central area of the community. One can readily see the dangers posed by these tracks when they crossed so many busy streets and why it was common for collisions to occur between trains and pedestrians, horse-drawn rigs, and, later, motor vehicles. Early newspaper accounts described these accidents in gory detail, describing bashed brains, crushed torsos, and severed limbs. (Courtesy of GCHD.)

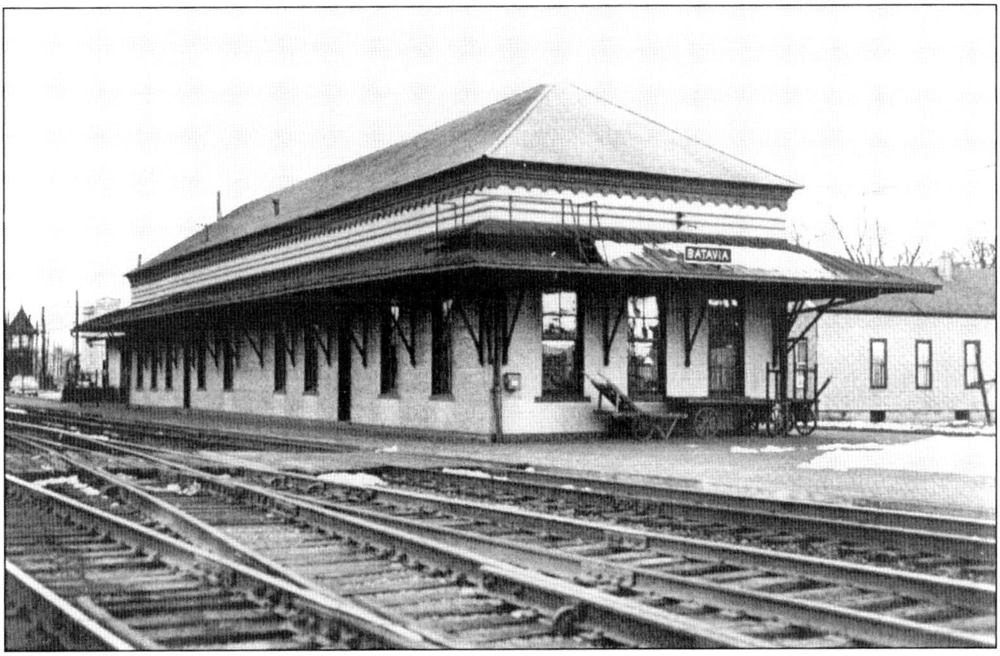

Seen here is the New York Central passenger station as it appeared in the 1950s, shortly before realignment of the main line began. The above picture shows the station viewed from the west. The photograph below is of the station viewed from the east. A new station was built on Lehigh Avenue, a location far less accessible to rail passengers. In the 1950s, passenger traffic was dramatically lower than at the turn of the century and railroads were no longer interested in catering to this part of their business. The New York Central ended regular passenger service to Batavia in 1962. (Courtesy of GCHD.)

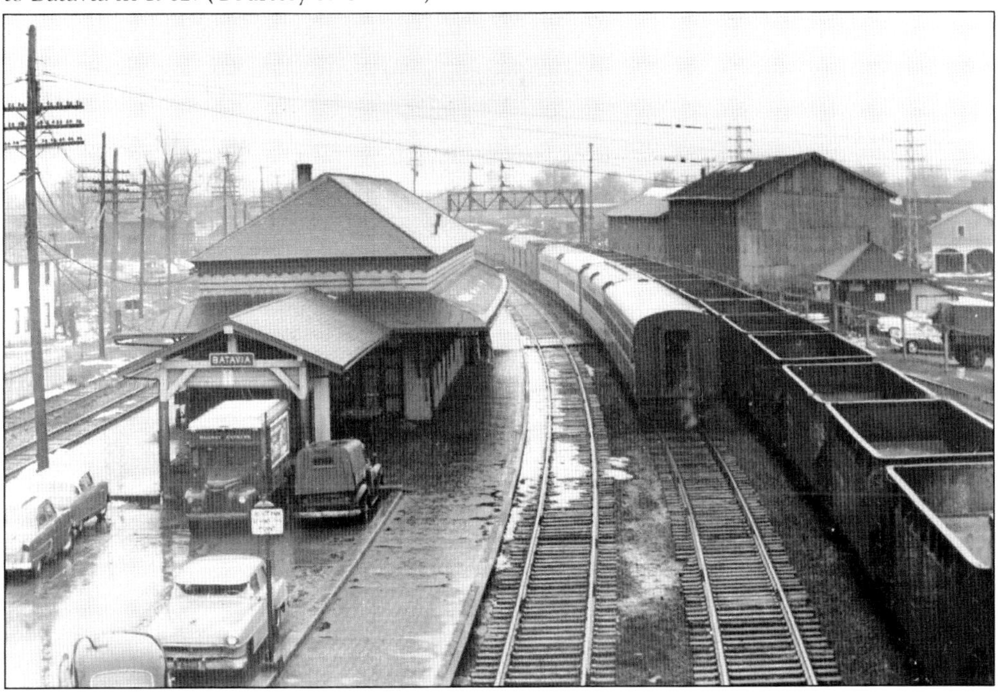

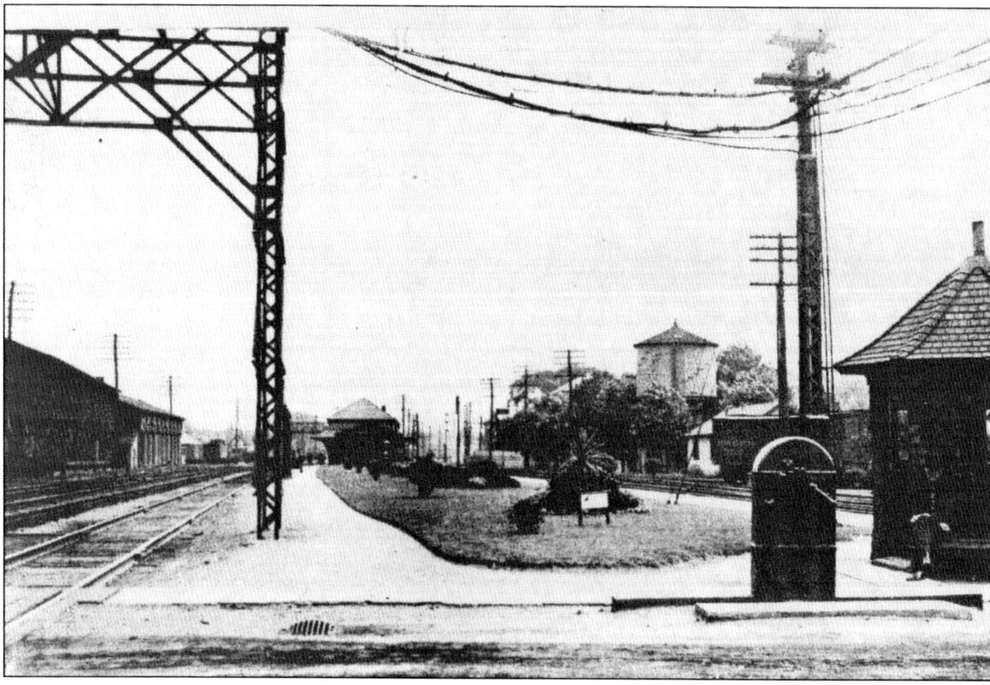

A crossing on Evans Street is shown in the photograph above. On the right is a shanty for the crossing guard. Also on the right is a crossing gate, which was raised and lowered by a crank. Safety at the crossings obviously was dependent on the crossing guard's alertness to oncoming trains. (Courtesy of GCHD.)

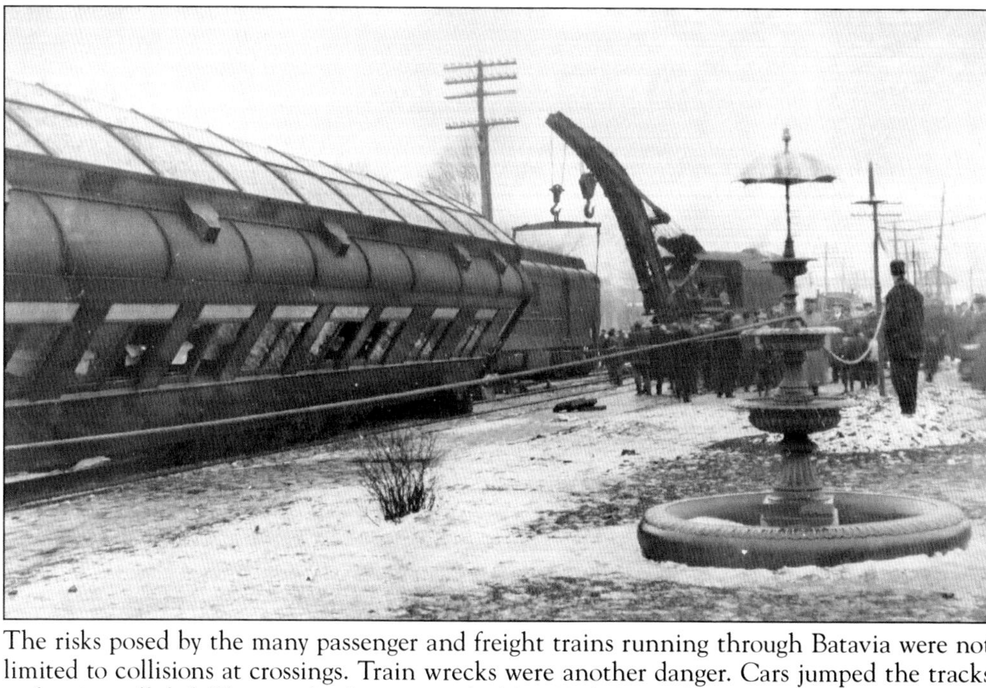

The risks posed by the many passenger and freight trains running through Batavia were not limited to collisions at crossings. Train wrecks were another danger. Cars jumped the tracks and trains collided. This wreck of a train at the New York Central station in 1911 caused seven deaths. (Courtesy of GCHD.)

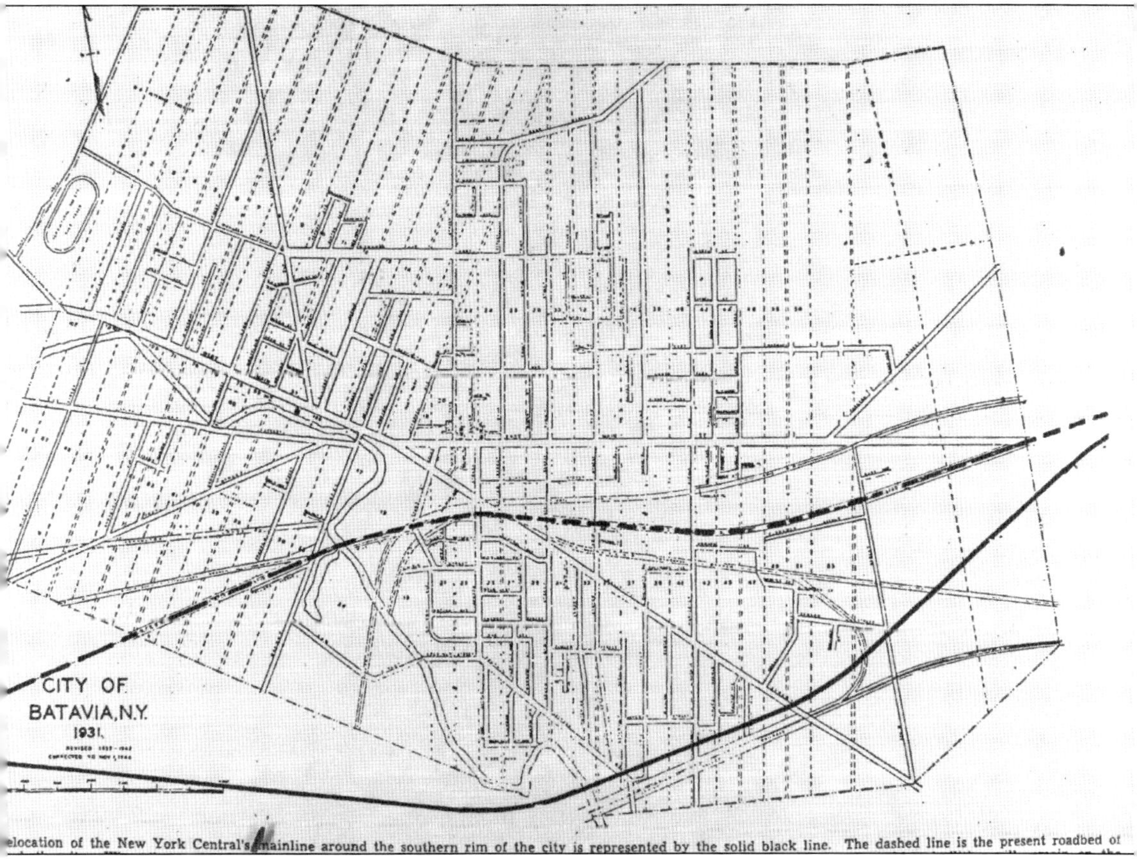

This map, initially drawn in 1931, shows the proposed realignment of the New York Central tracks at that time. The heavy broken line is the old route through the city. The heavy solid line was the proposed new route running in a more southerly manner. It is pretty much identical to the final plan. Whether to move the tracks and where to relocate them was debated for many years. As noted in the chapter introduction, even after a decision to go ahead was made, the Depression and World War II delayed action. Finally in 1951 work began, prompted in part by a horrendous accident that aroused the public. It was a major undertaking and was considered the biggest Batavia saw prior to urban renewal. The last train to use the old roadbed, a freight, passed through the city on April 12, 1957. (Courtesy of GCHD.)

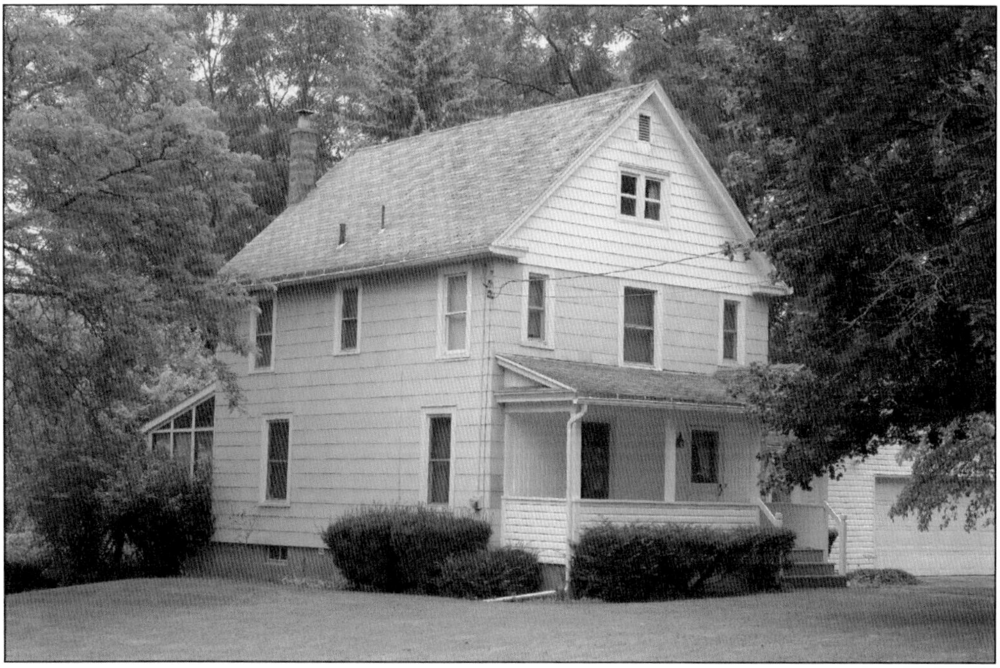

A large number of buildings, including 31 dwellings, stood in the way of the new railroad tracks. A significant number of the homes were moved to new locations. Shown here are two houses relocated about 1955. The above picture shows the Broderick residence, now at 4 Edwards Street, but formerly on Ellicott Street. The below picture is a photograph of the Smith home, now at 3 Lehigh Avenue, but also once standing on Ellicott Street. Sometimes the move did not go smoothly. For example, the foundation that had been prepared for the Smith house did not fit initially. (Courtesy of BCH.)

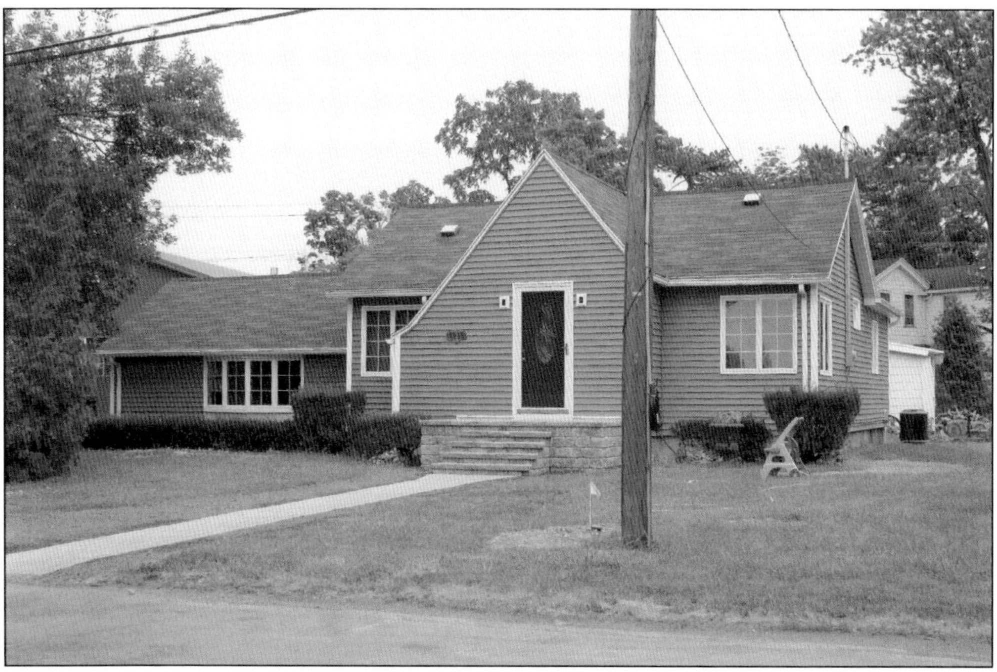

Three

BUILDING THE OAK STREET BRIDGE

Another relatively quick but major change to the city also occurred in the 1950s with the construction of a new bridge across the Tonawanda Creek just west of downtown. This is the bridge running directly south of the intersection of West Main and Oak Streets.

In the earliest years of the community, the only bridge across the creek was the Walnut Street Bridge, which carried traffic directly between Walnut and West Main Streets. It was situated where the wooden pedestrian bridge now stands. As time passed, three other bridges were built across the creek: the South Lyon Street Bridge, the Law Street Bridge, and the River Street Bridge. However, the Walnut Street Bridge continued to be the chief means of crossing the Tonawanda.

As traffic increased and vehicles became larger and heavier, the bridge's inherent features became a significant problem. One such problem was the steepness of the approaches to the bridge proper. A new bridge a short ways downstream was determined to be a better location. The design of the new bridge also called for a wider structure.

Construction of the new bridge required removal of seven or more buildings on West Main, South Main, and Pearl Streets. Perhaps the best known of these was the Flatiron Grocery at the intersection of Pearl and South Main Streets. Many of these buildings, including the grocery, were moved elsewhere in the city. In addition, a short connector street, Oak Street Extension, was built between West Main and Pearl Streets.

The new bridge significantly changed the appearance of the neighborhood and the traffic patterns in that area of the city. For the most part, the new bridge appeared to be an improvement; however, the new intersections at the south end of the bridge proved problematic. In particular, traffic traveling east on South Main Street and continuing through or turning north often ran into difficulty. Pedestrians also found negotiating the intersections to be a challenge. In 2009, a roundabout was constructed to smooth the flow of vehicles and facilitate pedestrian traffic.

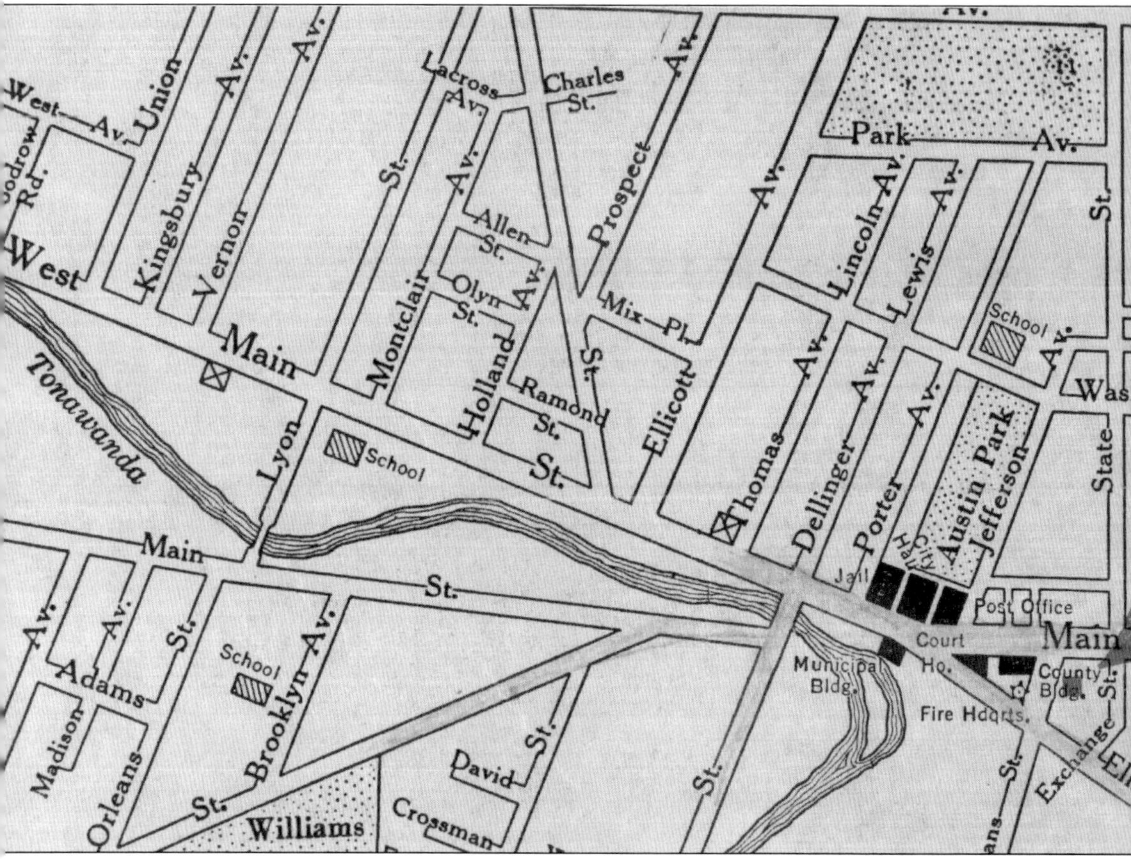

This map from the 1930s shows an area of Batavia west of downtown. West Main Street runs roughly east and west north of Tonawanda Creek. South Main Street, not fully labeled, also runs in an approximately east and west direction, but does so south of the creek. Oak Street (unlabeled) approaches from the north and intersects West Main Street just west of Ellicott Avenue. Walnut Street (unlabeled) approaches West Main Street from the south and intersects West Main Street opposite Dellinger Avenue. Pearl Street (unlabeled) approaches from the southwest and intersects South Main Street about a block west of Walnut Street. The one-lane South Lyon Street Bridge and the inadequate Walnut Street Bridge are the only ways across the Tonawanda in this general area. South Main Street was once named Tonawanda Street. (Courtesy of GCHD.)

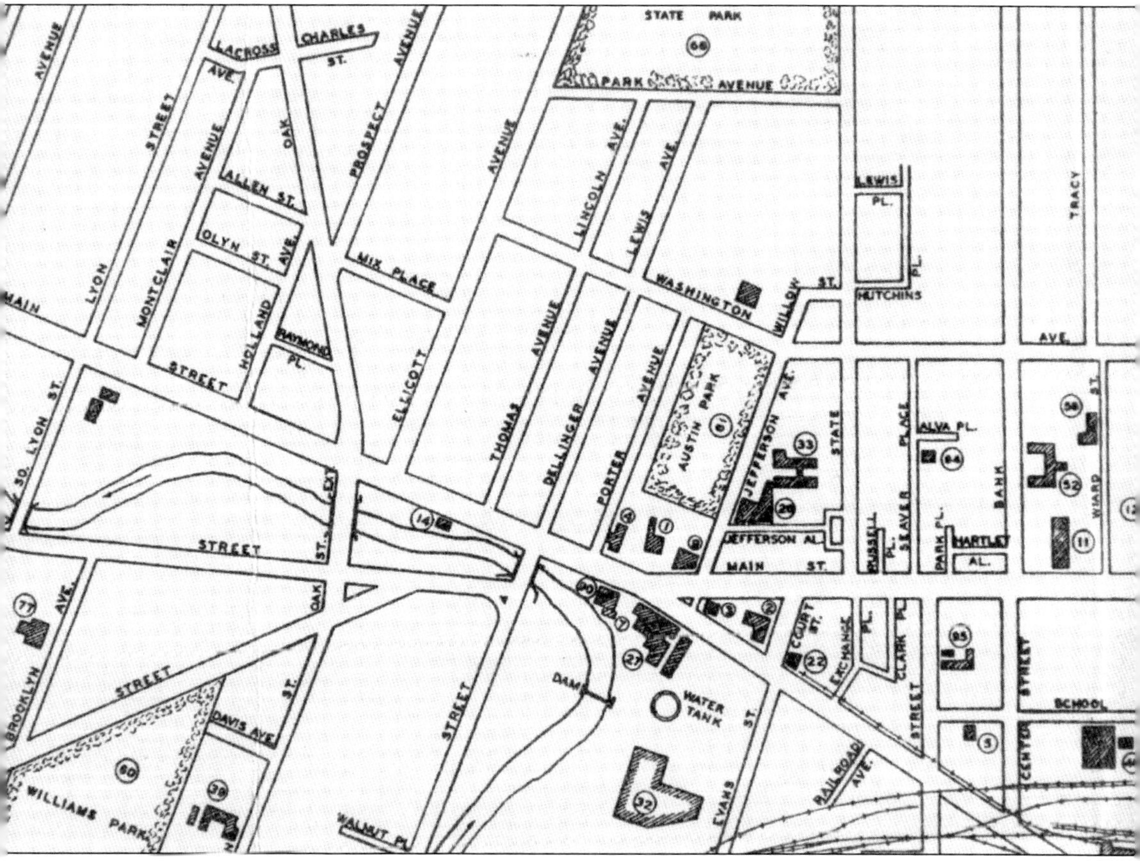

This map dates from the 1960s. A new street, Oak Street Extension, crosses a multi-lane bridge and then intersects with South Main Street, Pearl Street, and an unlabeled Franklin Street that enters from the south. This rearrangement of the landscape required the removal of many structures on West Main, South Main, and Pearl Streets. At the time this map was printed, the original Walnut Street Bridge still stood, but it was later replaced by a pedestrian bridge. The Oak Street Bridge proved to be an improvement, especially for large vehicles, but the multiplicity of new intersections introduced new problems as both drivers and pedestrians frequently found them tricky to negotiate. It was soon obvious that some means was needed for traffic to travel either way on South Main Street without interference from the cross traffic using the Oak Street Extension. (Courtesy of GCHD.)

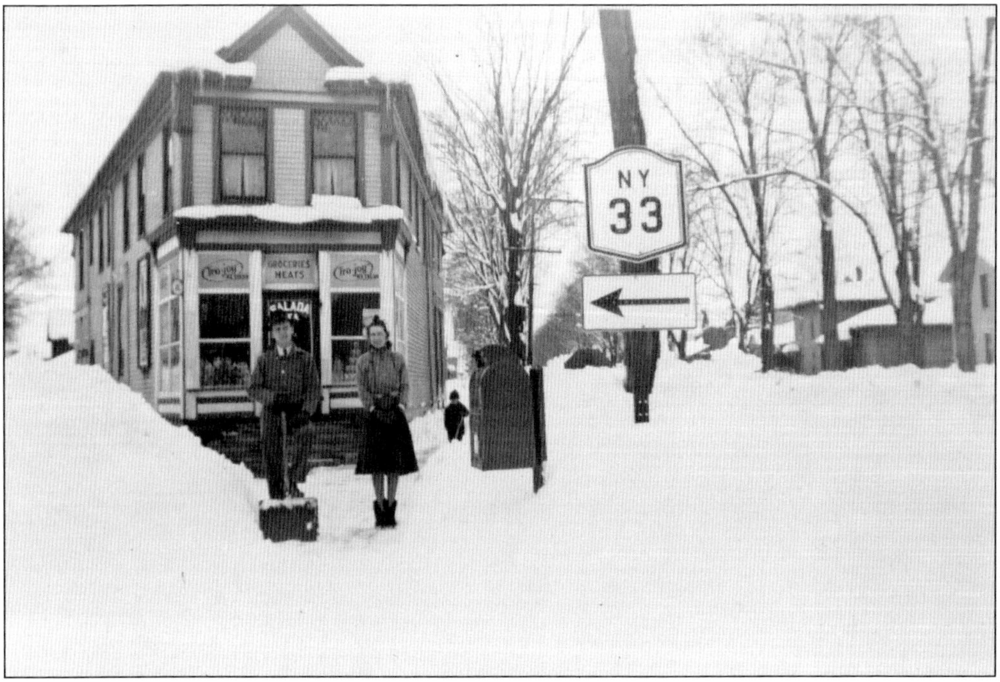

In the image above, an unidentified couple stands with a snow shovel in front of a grocery store where South Main and Pearl Streets intersected. Its wedge-like shape was dictated by the angle of the intersection. At one point, the store was Flatiron Cash Grocery. In a move that took the best part of a day, the building was relocated west to 142 Pearl Street. The view below shows the relocated building when it housed a realty business. The building was also once used as a florist shop by the Stroh family. (Above, courtesy of Michael Smith; below, courtesy of BCH.)

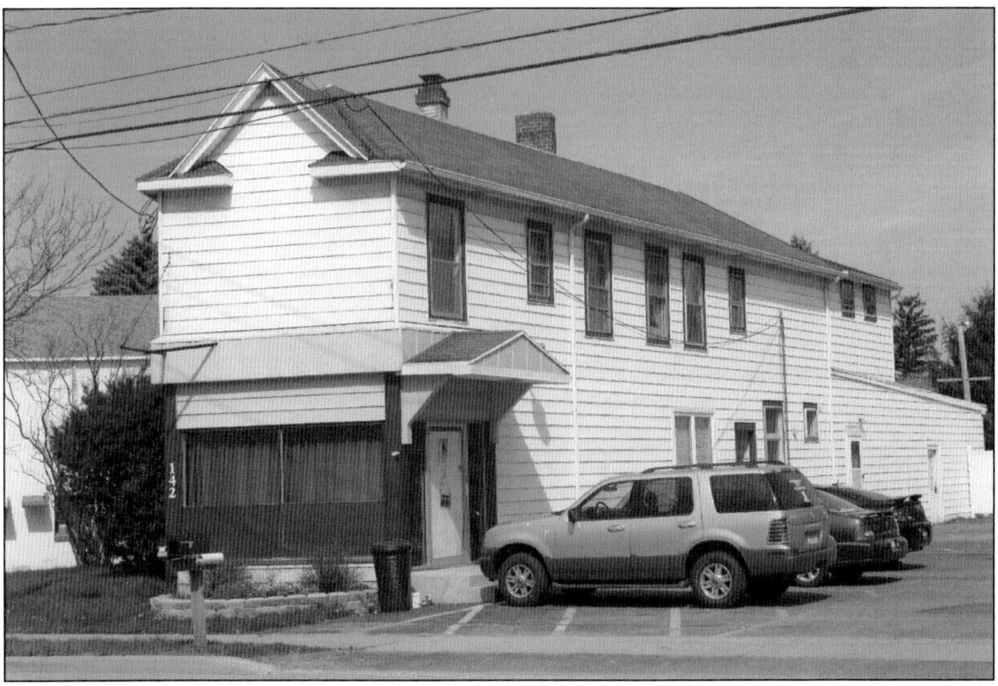

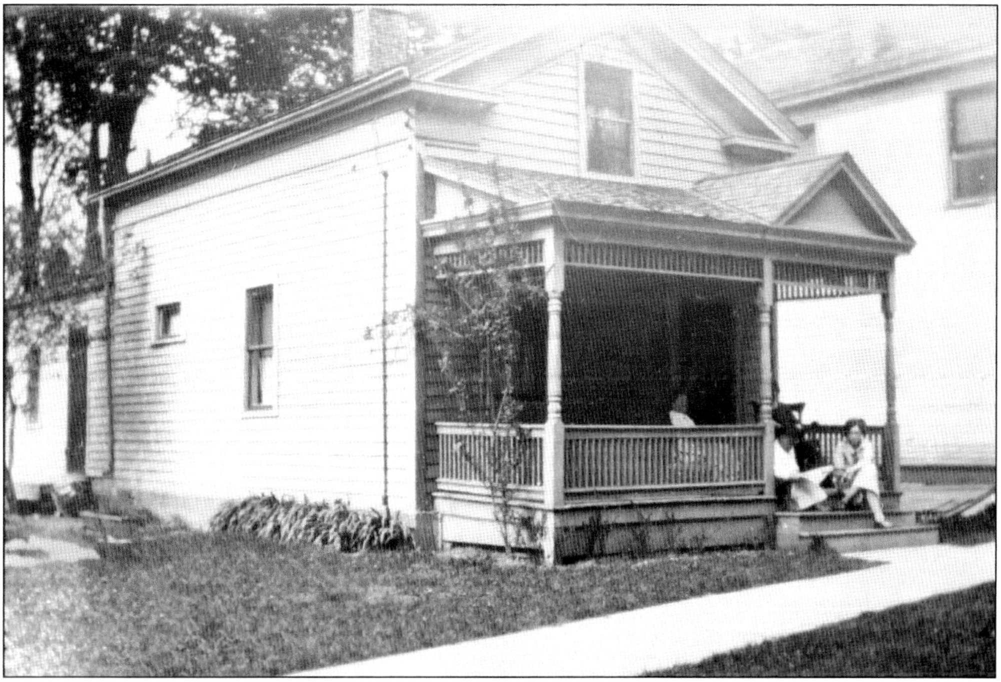

This picture, thought to be taken around 1920, shows the house that was at 4 Pearl Street. It was immediately west of the Flatiron Cash Grocery. The latter can be seen in the background. For subsequent comparative purposes, note the structural details of the building. (Courtesy of Michael Smith.)

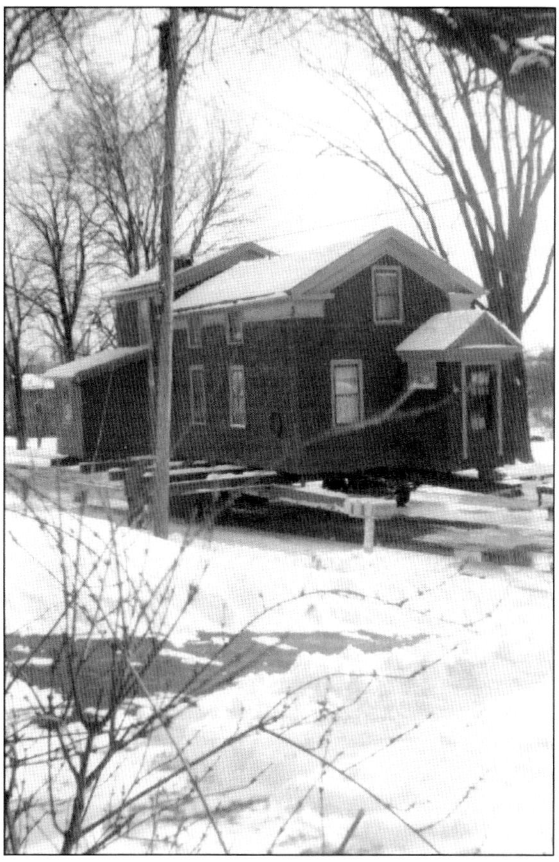

In 1953, the house in the above photograph was moved to 125 Pearl Street. A number of steel beams placed underneath the building provided support as it was towed on multiple sets of rubber tires. Observe how much the appearance of the house had been altered since 1920. (Courtesy of Michael Smith.)

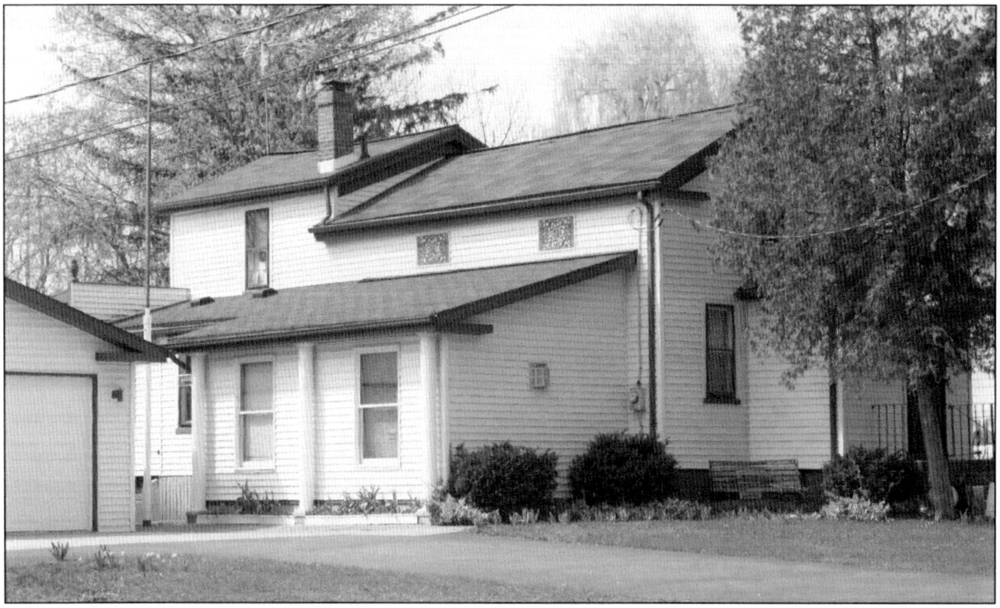

Here is the house on the previous page as it appears in more recent times. One clue that a building has been moved can be found in examining the foundation. This house, for example, has concrete blocks and a poured wall, which are forms of construction that postdate a structure obviously dating to the 19th century. (Courtesy of BCH.)

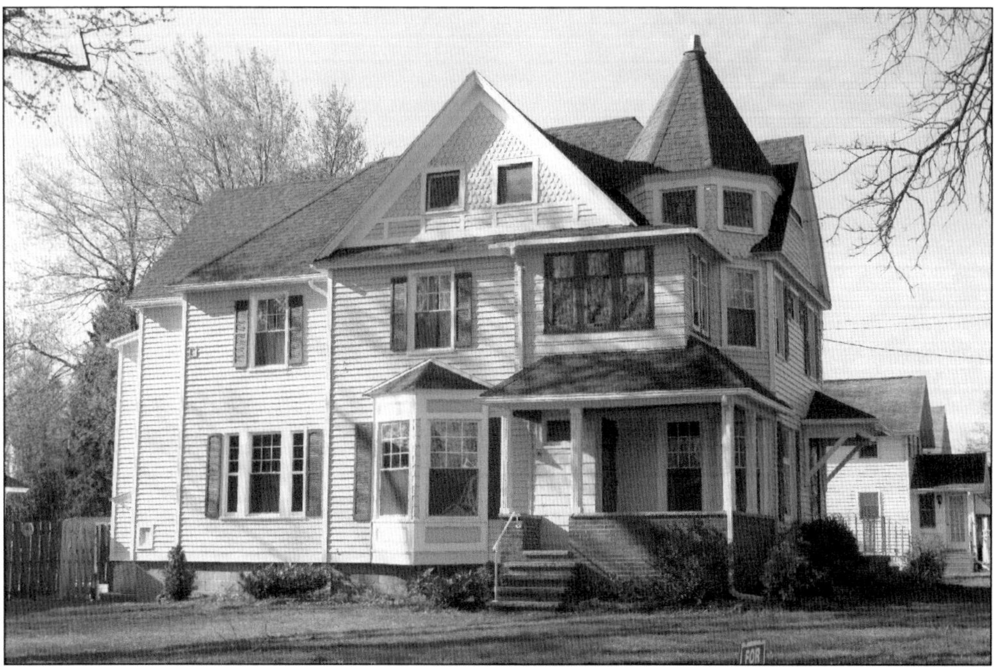

This house, now at 23 Roosevelt Avenue, was the largest home relocated to make way for the Oak Street Bridge. Originally located opposite Franklin Street, the house faced South Main Street, but its garage in the rear was accessed from Pearl Street. Before starting, the work crew placed a bouquet of flowers on a table and guaranteed it would remain undisturbed at the end of the move. They were successful. (Courtesy of BCH.)

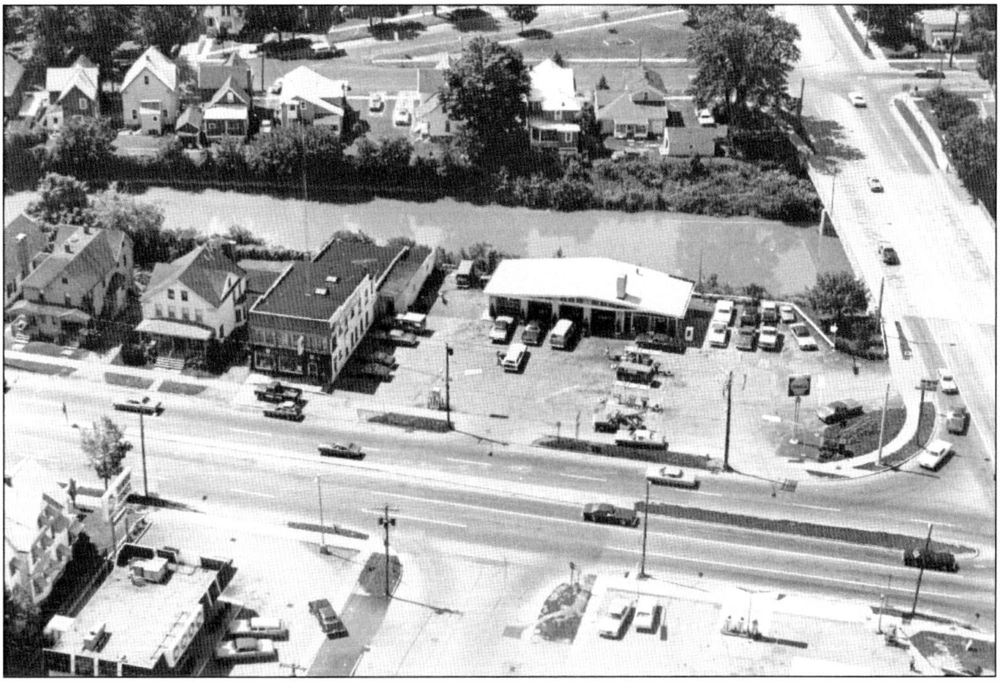

This aerial view was taken not long after the bridge was completed. South Main Street runs across the top of the picture and West Main Street across the bottom. The long, narrow building just east of the bridge still stands, but most of the other buildings between the creek and West Main Street were razed during the 1970s. (Courtesy of GCHD.)

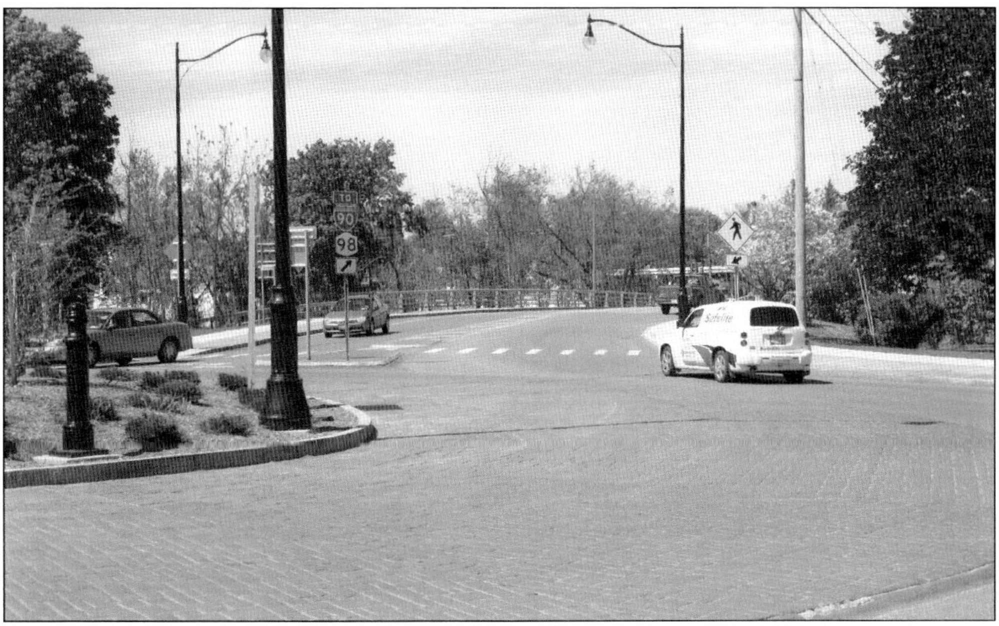

This is a roundabout recently built to replace the troublesome intersections created by Oak Street Extension. In the distance is the south end of the Oak Street Bridge. Traffic ordinarily negotiates a single-lane asphalt surface, but large vehicles can utilize a brick apron provided to accommodate their size. (Author's collection.)

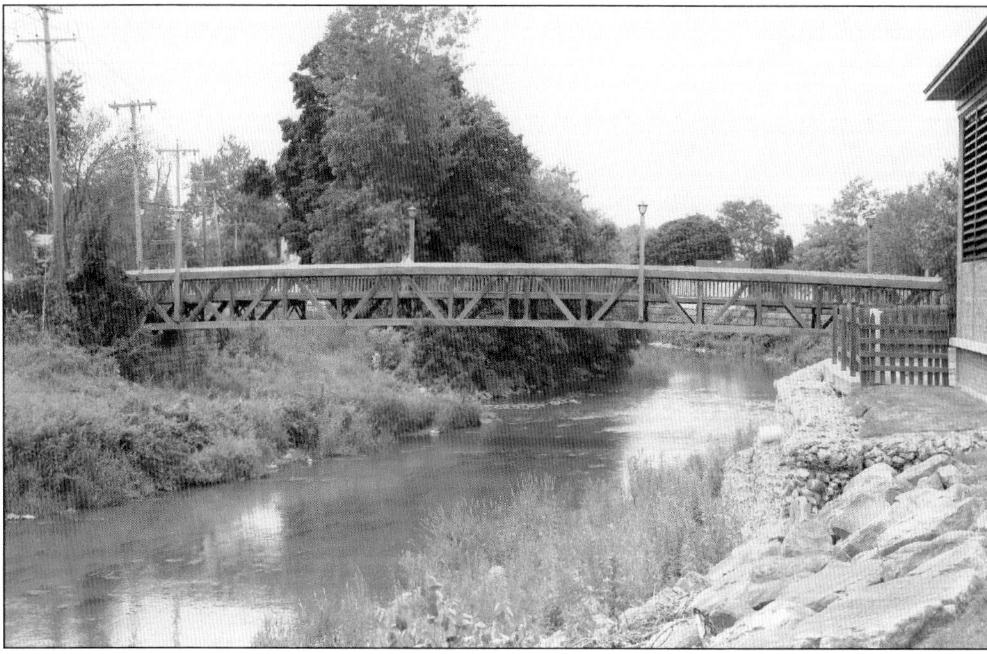

This pedestrian bridge replaced the Walnut Street vehicle bridge in 1989. It was built in two sections and shipped to Batavia by the Cecco Trading Company of Milwaukee, Wisconsin. The sections arrived by truck and then were lifted into place by cranes. County highway department employees assembled the structure. The bridge is made of bongossi wood, an African hardwood that is four times harder than oak. The bridge is eight feet wide and 109 feet long. The photograph above is of the bridge from upstream near the sewage pumping station. The view below faces southward from the north end. (Courtesy of BCH.)

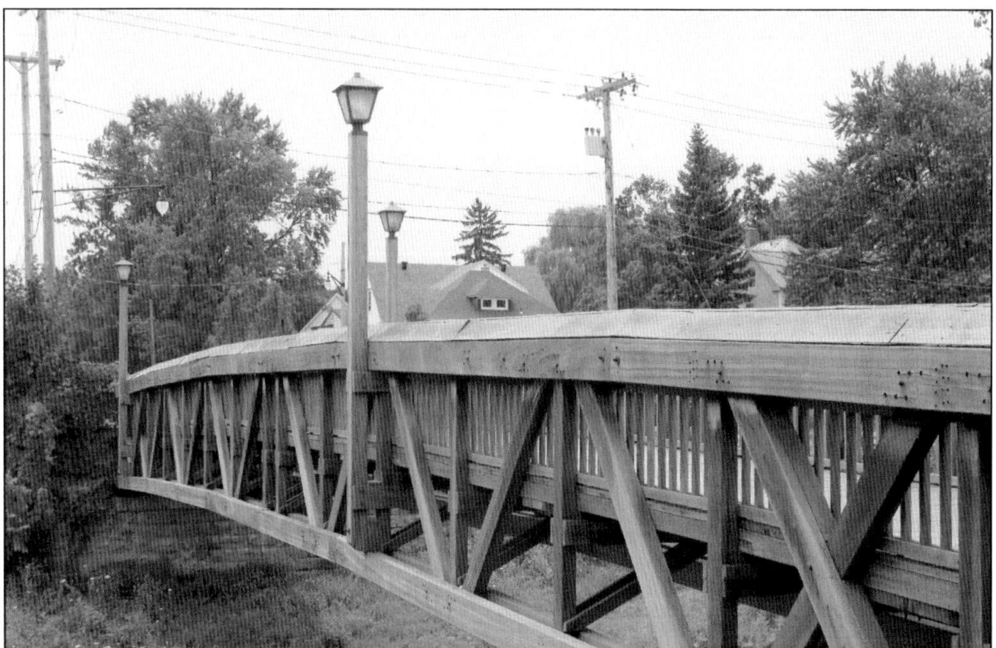

Four

Urban Renewal and Batavia

In the middle of the 20th century, there was growing concern about the health and future of America's major cities. Buildings, particularly in the inner cities, were falling into disrepair and were often abandoned outright. Urban blight was becoming more and more evident. In an effort to deal with the situation, Federal funds became available to renew these areas. The program under which they were administered came to be known as urban renewal.

Although not part of a big city, the downtown area of Batavia was also showing signs of urban blight. Many buildings were in poor shape. Development over the years had produced a jumble of structures along narrow streets and alleys running both north and south from Main Street. To a large extent, the area was physically unattractive.

The new federal program looked like a way out of this situation and in 1962, Batavia's city council successfully applied for urban renewal funding. A year later, funding began. The first phase involved the area south of Main Street. Later in the second phase, the area north of Main Street was addressed.

A group of 20 local citizens was formed to act as an advisory committee working together with the director of urban renewal. One of the issues it faced was whether to save any of the existing buildings in the affected areas. There were arguments for doing so. Some buildings, such as the former Bank of Batavia, were architecturally significant. Others, such as the Salvation Army Building, were nearly new. Ultimately it was decided to level virtually everything to make it easier to rebuild.

In hindsight, perhaps the most far-reaching action was the frequently regretted decision to erect a downtown mall on the north side of Main Street. The Genesee Country Mall officially opened in 1978. Unfortunately, the vibrant retail operation that was hoped for has never developed as shopping centers in the town of Batavia have drawn increasingly greater numbers of stores and customers. What to do with the mall, now known as the Batavia City Centre, remains an open question.

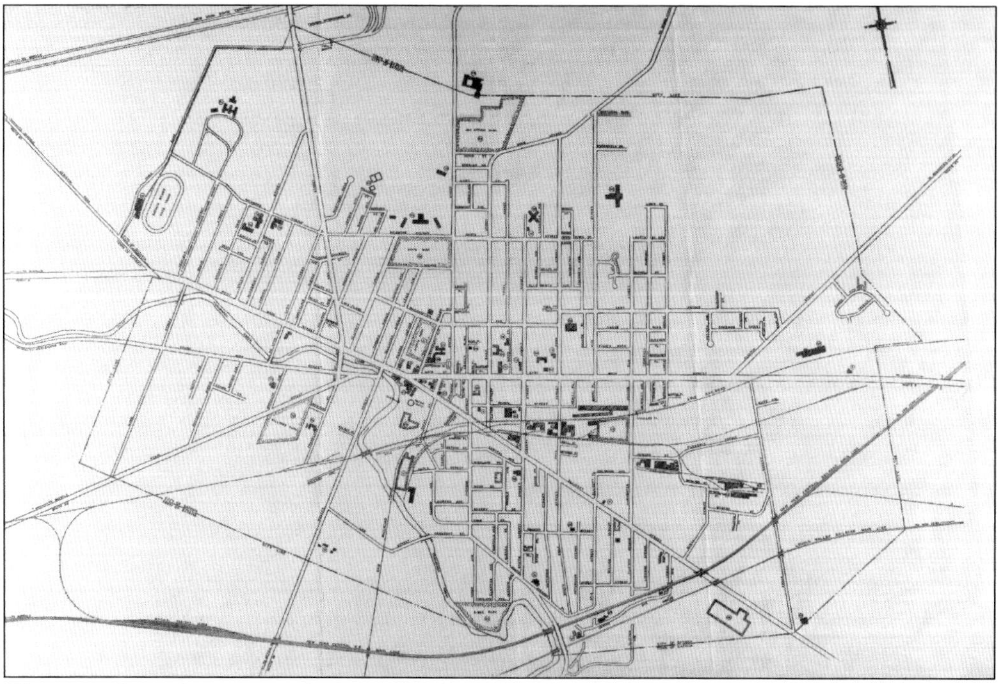

This map shows Batavia in about 1960. The railroad tracks have been moved. The Oak Street Bridge has been built, but urban renewal has not gotten underway. North Street does not extend fully eastward. The high-end housing in the area of Naramore Drive hasn't appeared in the northeast quadrant either. (Courtesy of BCH.)

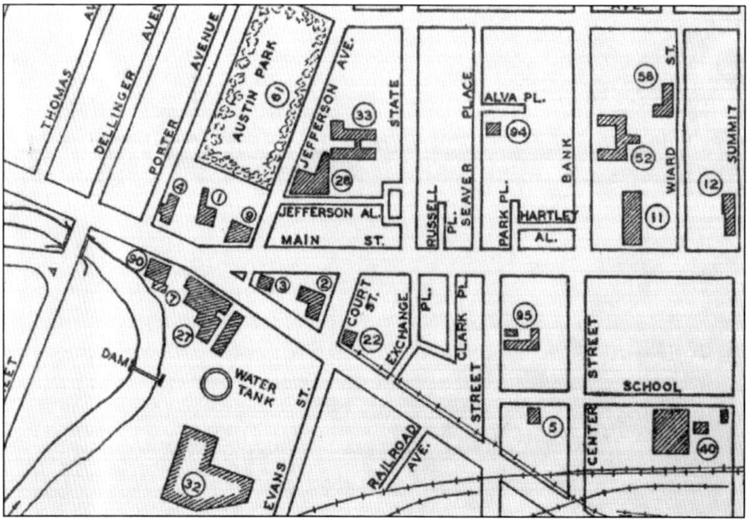

This different map offers an illustration of downtown Batavia in the decades prior to urban renewal. Note all the narrow little streets or alleys that ran north and south off Main Street. Building 23 was the P. W. Minor Shoe factory. Buildings 27 and 28 were E. N. Rowell factory buildings. (Courtesy of BCH.)

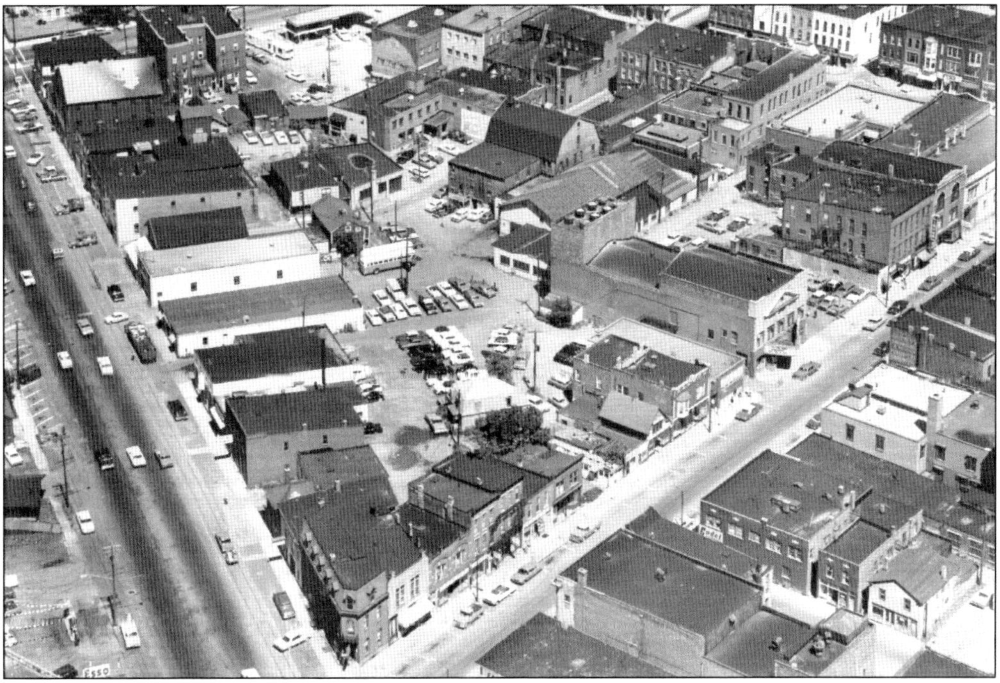

The area that became Court Street Plaza is shown here about 1960. The intersection at the bottom of the picture is that of Ellicott Street on the left and Jackson Street on the right. Notable structures include the Panzone Hotel on the corner and the Family Theatre halfway up Jackson Street. (Courtesy of GCHD.)

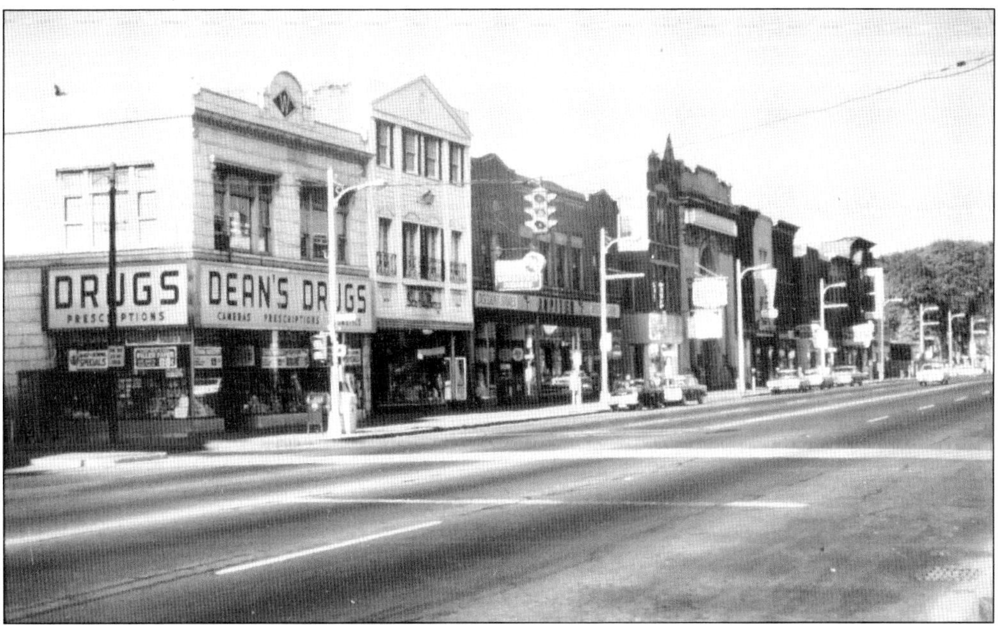

In this and the next several photographs, the reader will be taken on a virtual walk around the perimeter of the future Court Street Plaza area. All the pictures in this series were taken in the decade leading up to urban renewal. Here is an early morning view of the south side of Main Street from Jackson Street west to Court Street. (Courtesy of LSGC.)

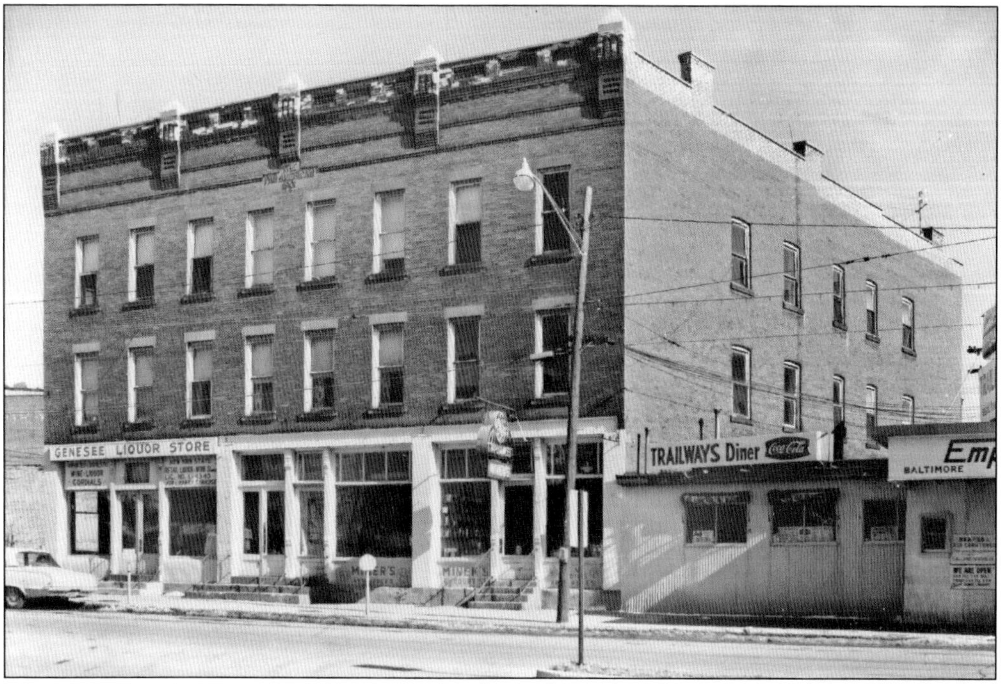

This is the Pan American Building erected at the beginning of the 20th century and located mid block on Court Street. Allegedly it was constructed with lumber that was salvaged from the 1901 Pan American Exposition held in Buffalo. Like most downtown buildings of the time, apartments were located on the upper floors. (Courtesy of LSGC.)

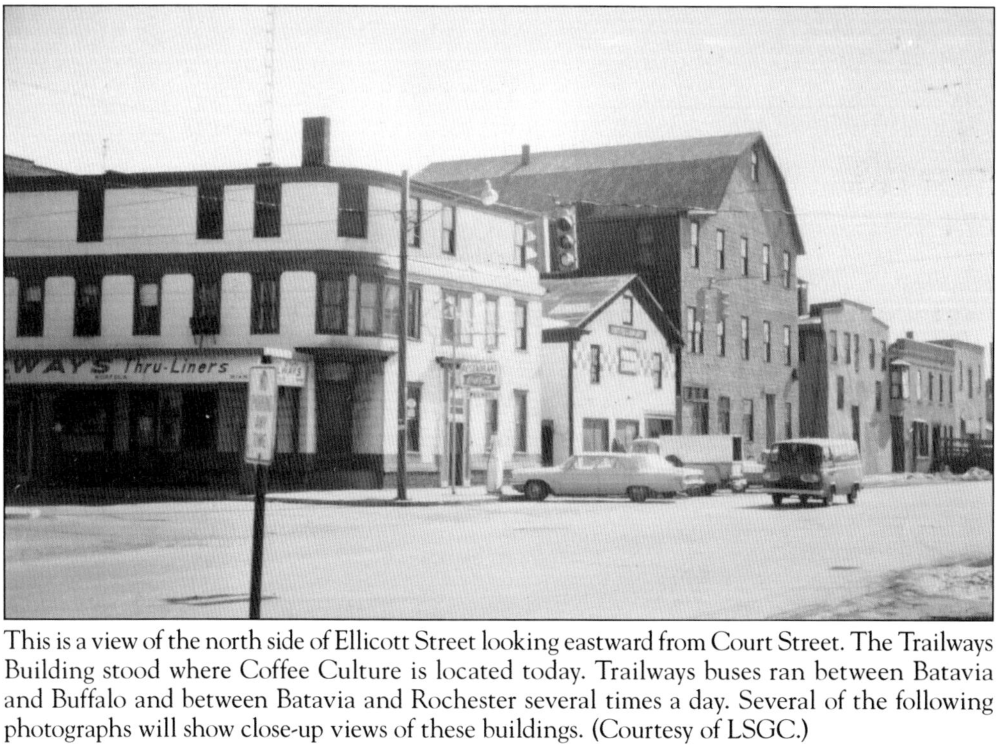

This is a view of the north side of Ellicott Street looking eastward from Court Street. The Trailways Building stood where Coffee Culture is located today. Trailways buses ran between Batavia and Buffalo and between Batavia and Rochester several times a day. Several of the following photographs will show close-up views of these buildings. (Courtesy of LSGC.)

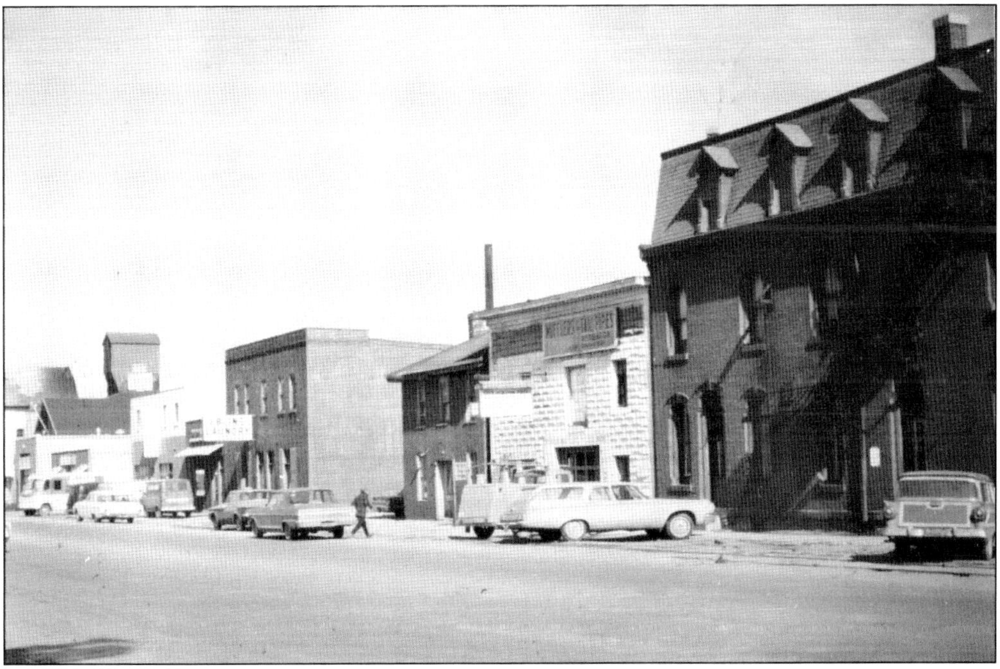

Above is another view along the north side of Ellicott Street, but facing westward from Jackson Street. The large building on the right is the Panzone Hotel, formerly known as the Ellicott House. Barely visible are the rails of a railroad spur that ran along Ellicott Street. (Courtesy of LSGC.)

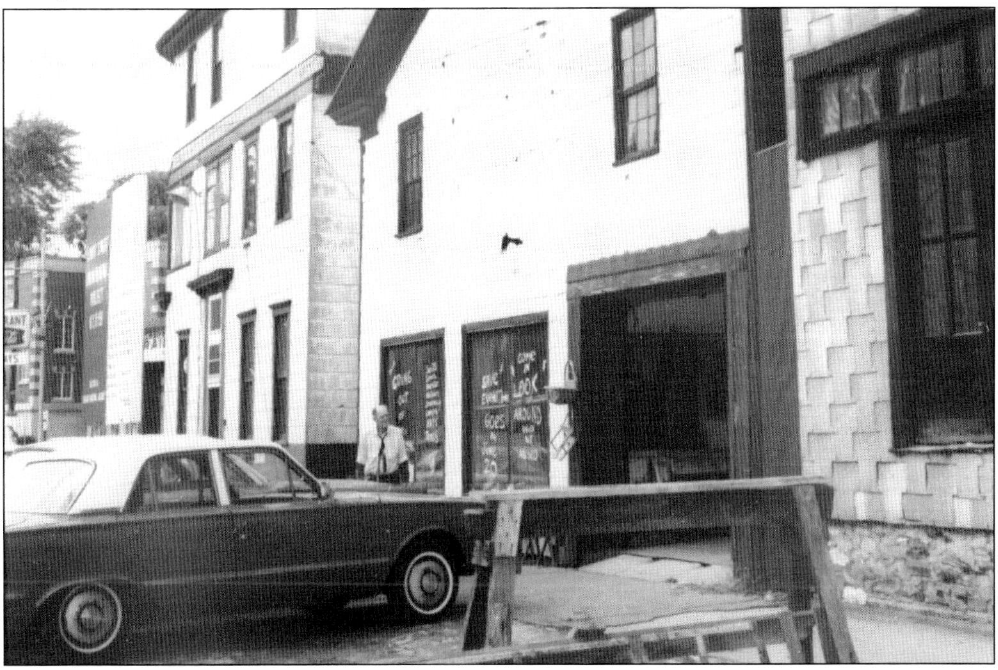

Back near Court Street, in the foreground and partially visible, is a close-up view of the Franklin Mills Building. Next door is the former Emens Feed and Farm Supply. Further up the street is the south end of the Trailways Building. The unidentified man appears to be taking advantage of a "going out of business" sale. (Photograph by Robert W. Emens, courtesy of RML.)

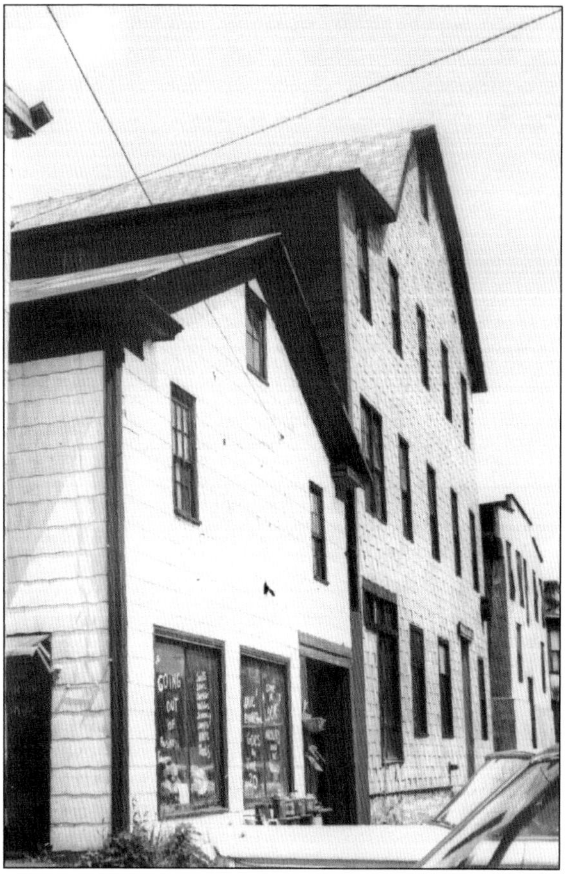

Looking east from the vicinity of the Trailways Building, the former Emens Feed and Farm Supply store is again visible. The advertising of a sale is still in the window, so it is likely this picture was taken on the same day as the preceding one. Next in line is the Franklin Mills Building. (Photograph by Robert W. Emens; courtesy of RML.)

Here is a photograph showing part of the R. A. Haitz Company complex, a business that specialized in roofing. The sign over the doorway identifies the building as a warehouse. The sign also points to the company's office across the Exchange Place intersection. When buildings in this area were taken down, the company relocated operations to Lewiston Road. (Courtesy of GCHD.)

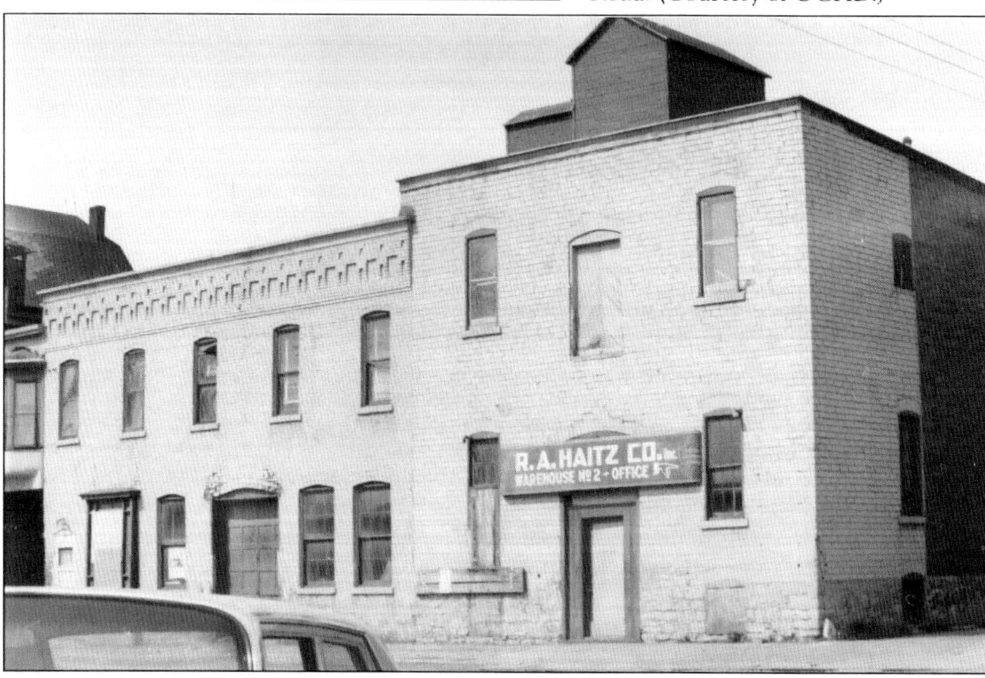

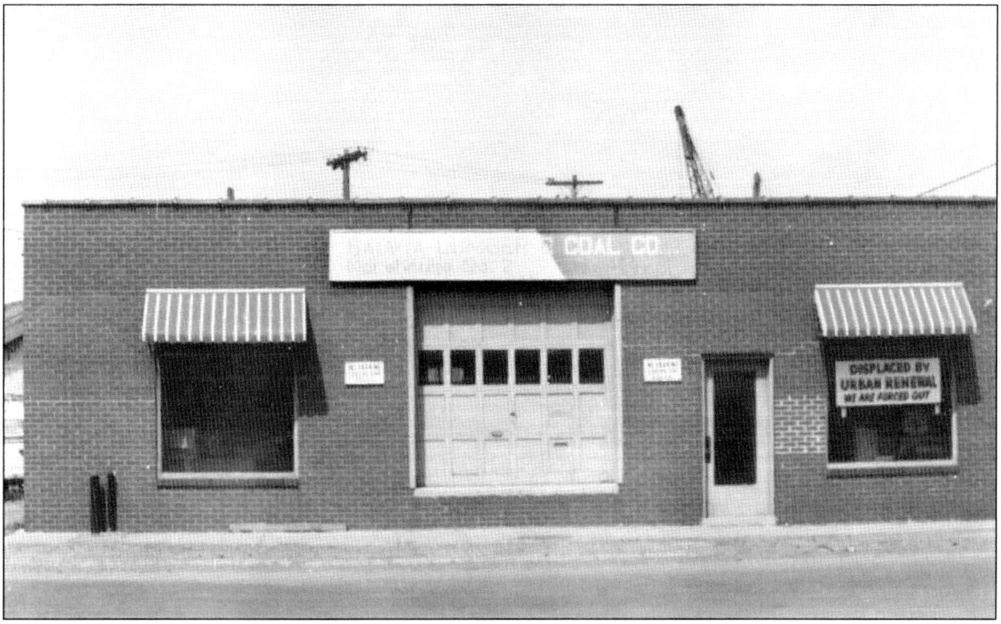

Continuing eastward, this close-up picture shows the building belonging to the Batavia Lumber and Coal Company. It looks modern and in good condition—not what one might expect as a candidate for a tear down. Apparently the owner felt the same way. In the window is a sign reading, "Displaced by Urban Renewal. We are forced out." (Courtesy of GCHD.)

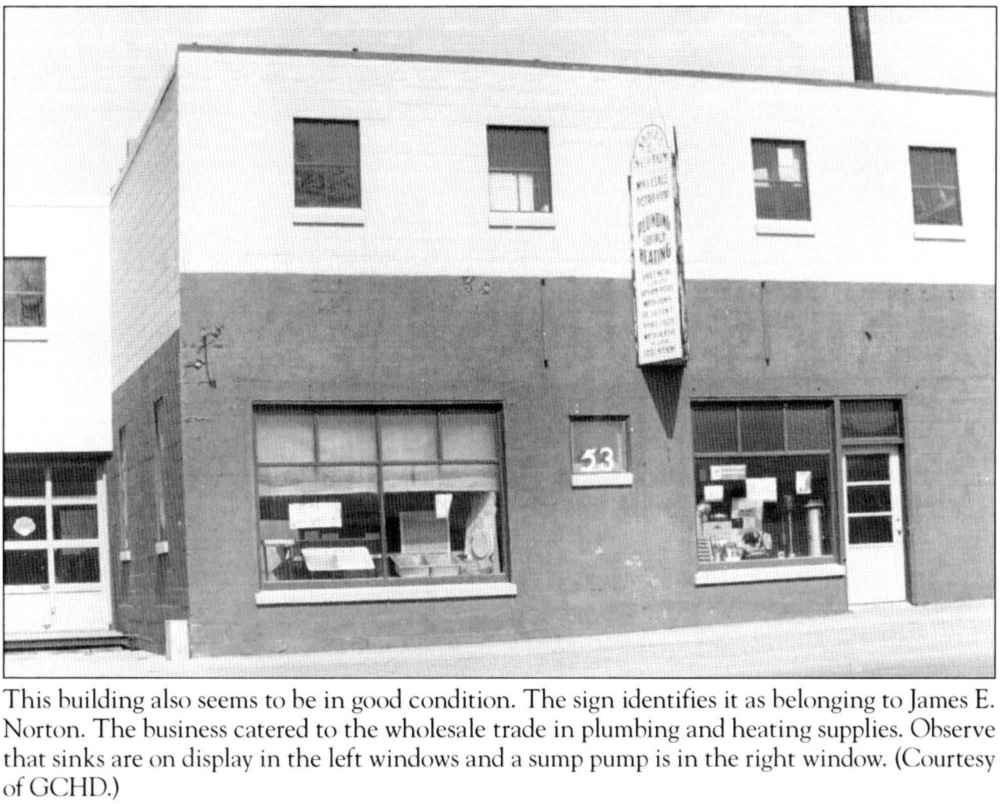

This building also seems to be in good condition. The sign identifies it as belonging to James E. Norton. The business catered to the wholesale trade in plumbing and heating supplies. Observe that sinks are on display in the left windows and a sump pump is in the right window. (Courtesy of GCHD.)

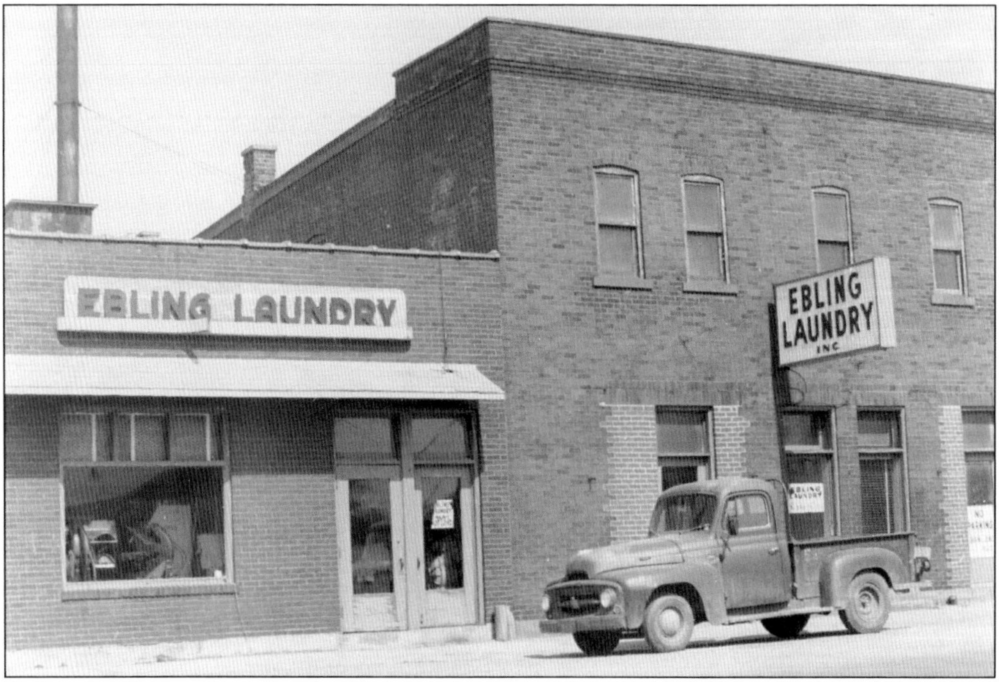

East of Norton's wholesale operation was this Ebling Laundry Building. When urban renewal took down businesses on this stretch of Ellicott Street, many of them moved to nearby locations. James Norton moved his to Evans Street. Ebling Laundry opened a new building on the south side of Ellicott Street less than a block east of Jackson Street. (Courtesy of GCHD.)

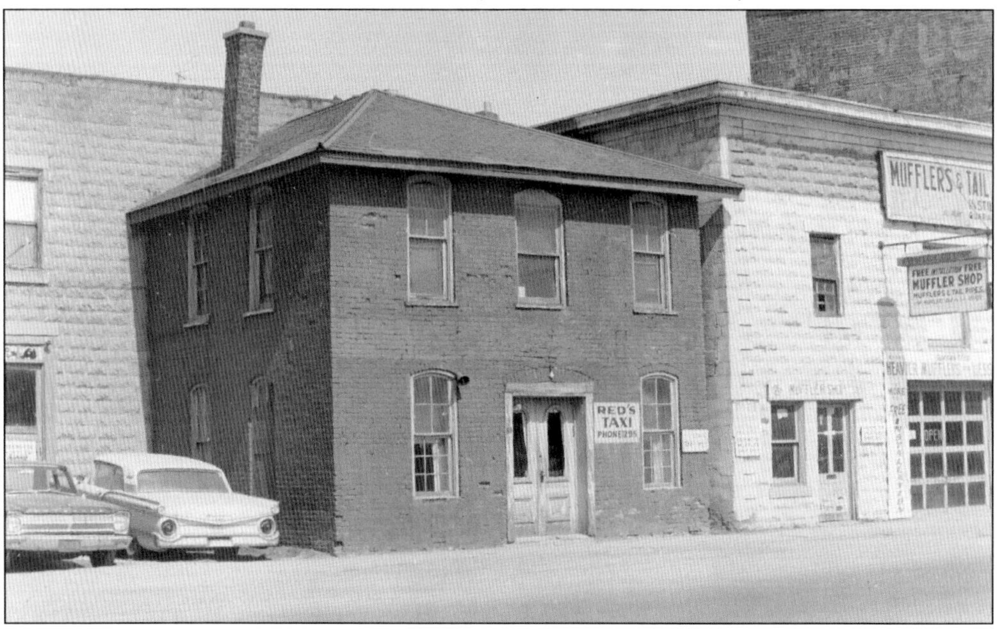

Red Goodenbury operated Red's Taxi next to the Muffler Shop. Red used the money he received from the urban renewal agency to purchase a two-way radio dispatching system, a step up from relying on telephone communication. His company employed several women over the years because he said they were good drivers and popular with the public. (Courtesy of GCHD.)

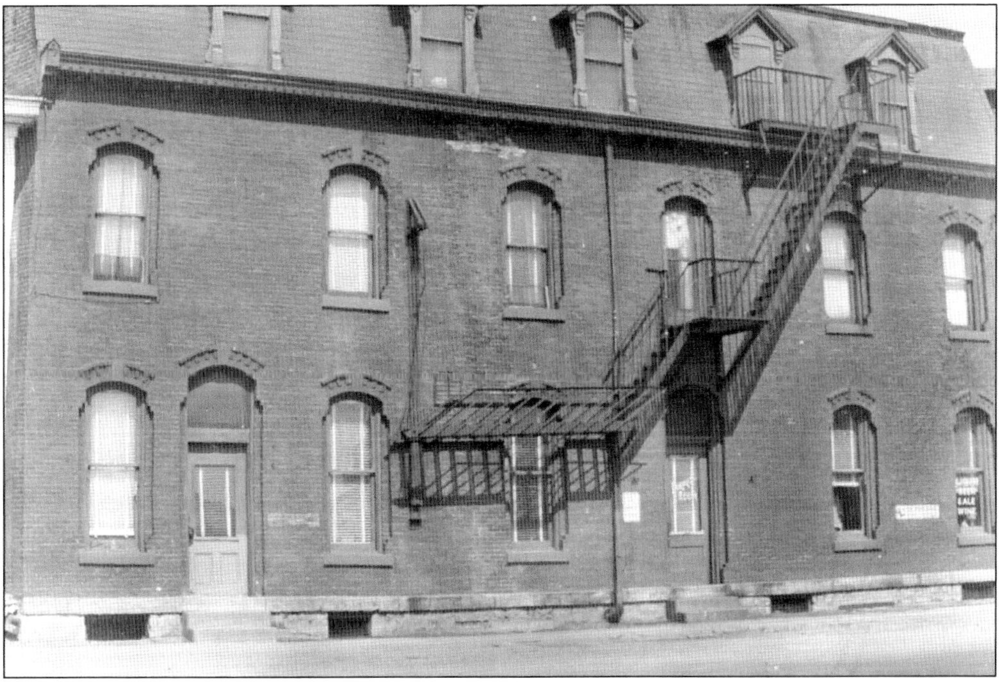

This building was popularly known as the Panzone Hotel, a name gained from its last operator, Thomas Panzone. For most of its existence, it was the Ellicott House. The above image shows the Ellicott Street side and the view at right shows the corner of the building at the intersection of Ellicott and Jackson Streets. The corner facade had a wrought iron balcony that local artists found particularly attractive; thus, the building was a popular subject for paintings. During the era of Prohibition, when the business was operated by the Callan family, the operators were too often caught selling liquor to special customers and the business was shut down. (Courtesy of GCHD.)

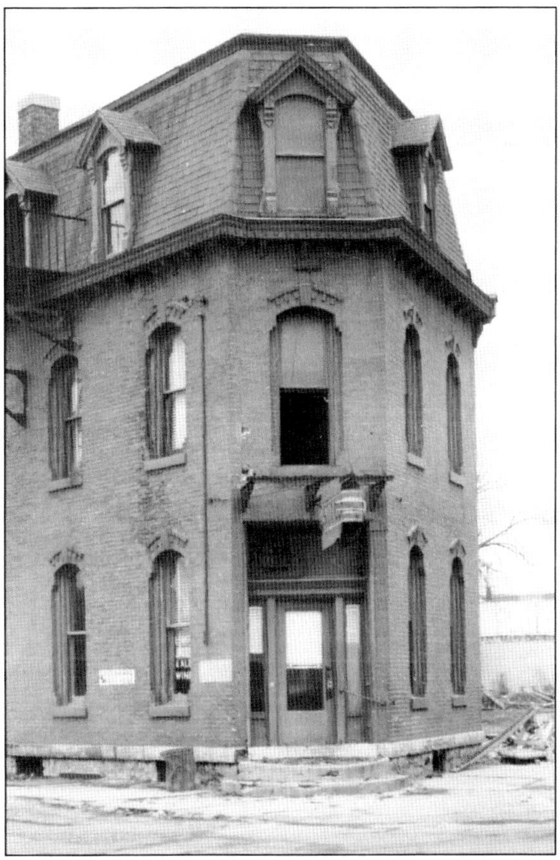

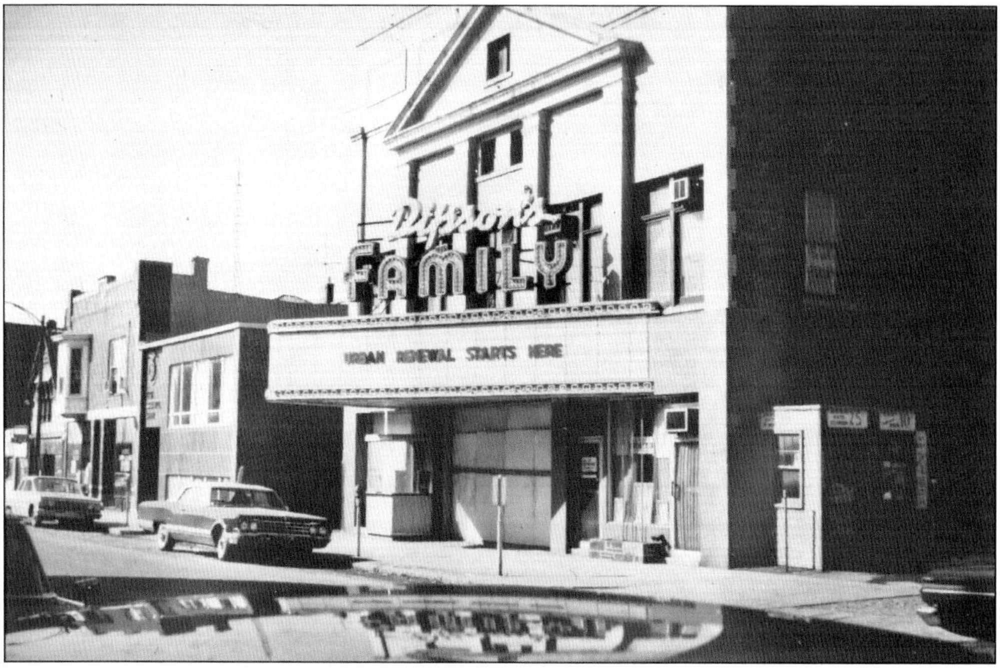

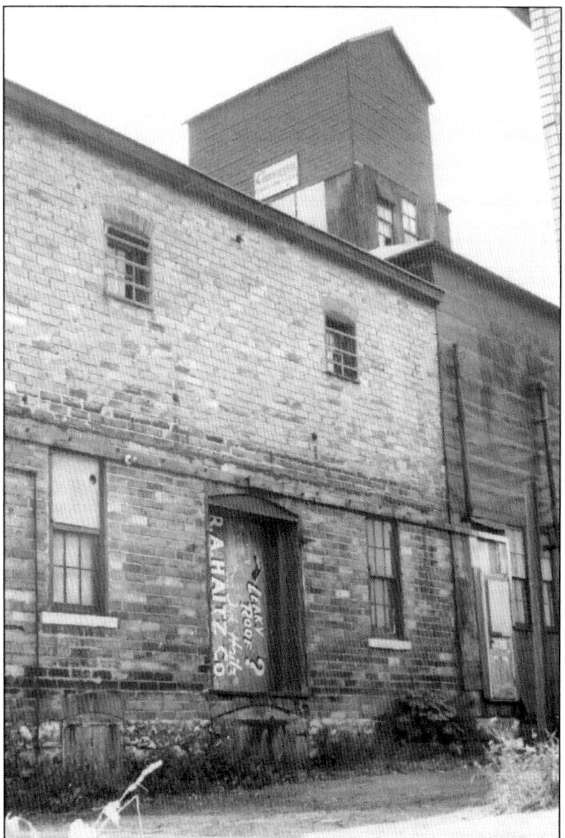

The Dipson Family Theatre, located on the west side of Jackson Street, got its name from Nikitas Dipson, a Batavian who operated a large number of movie houses in western New York. The first theater built at this location opened its doors in 1913. Note the words on the marquee, "Urban Renewal Starts Here." (Courtesy of GCHD.)

This and the next three pictures show scenes from the interior of the future Court Street Plaza. All were taken shortly before urban renewal began. In this picture, the rear of the R. A. Haitz property is visible. The company's business is reflected in a former sign used to seal off a doorway. It reads, "Leaky roof? R. A. Haitz Co." (Photograph by Robert W. Emens; courtesy of RML.)

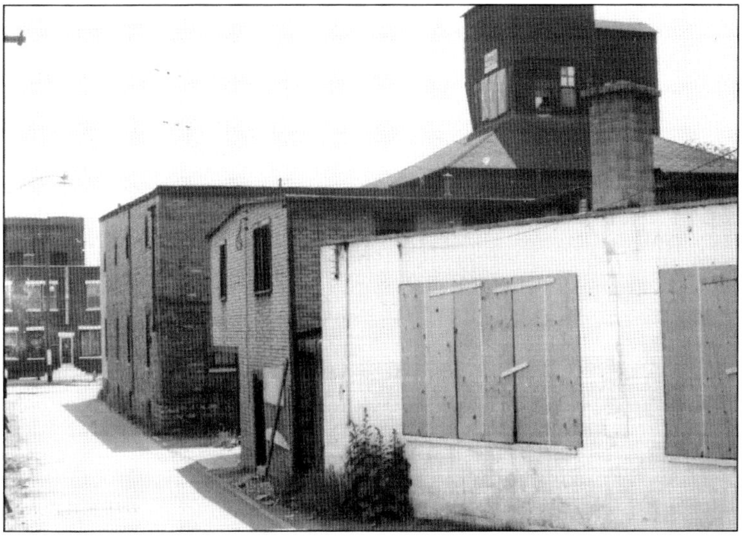

The view shown here is Exchange Place, looking south to Ellicott Street. The building on the right had been the Gerber bowling pin shop, and was later used by a sign painting business. Next is the former Raymond Hasselbeck auto garage, followed by the R. A. Haitz property. (Photograph by Robert W. Emens; courtesy of RML.)

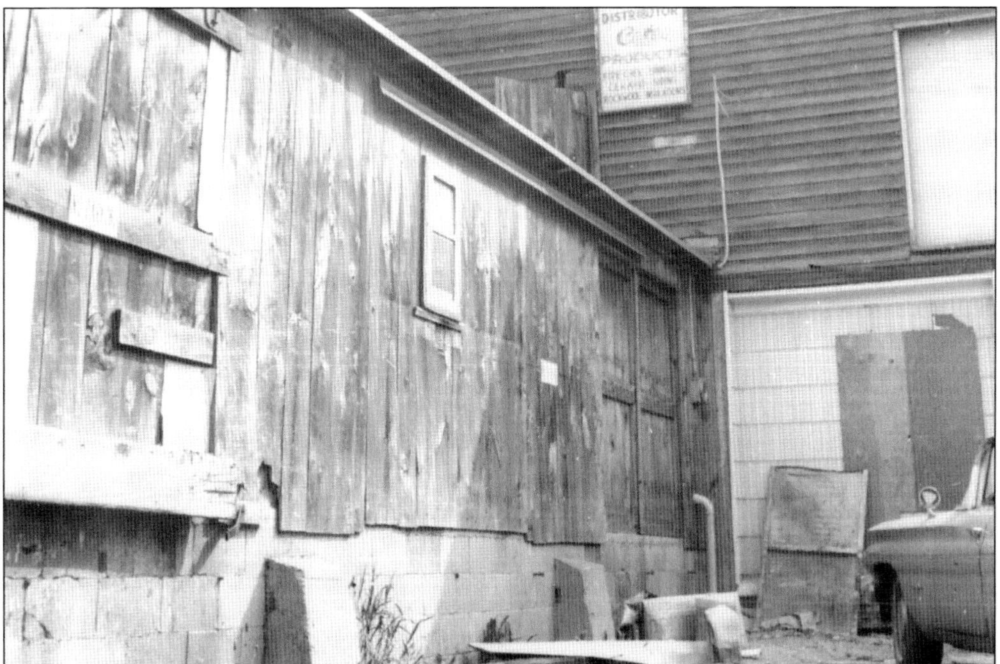

Shown here is the rear of an Ellicott Street Building belonging to the R. A. Haitz Company. According to notations on the back of the original print, this building had once been used as a church. As the structure was being torn down, some of its original church-related architecture and decorative features were visible. (Photograph by Robert W. Emens; courtesy of RML.)

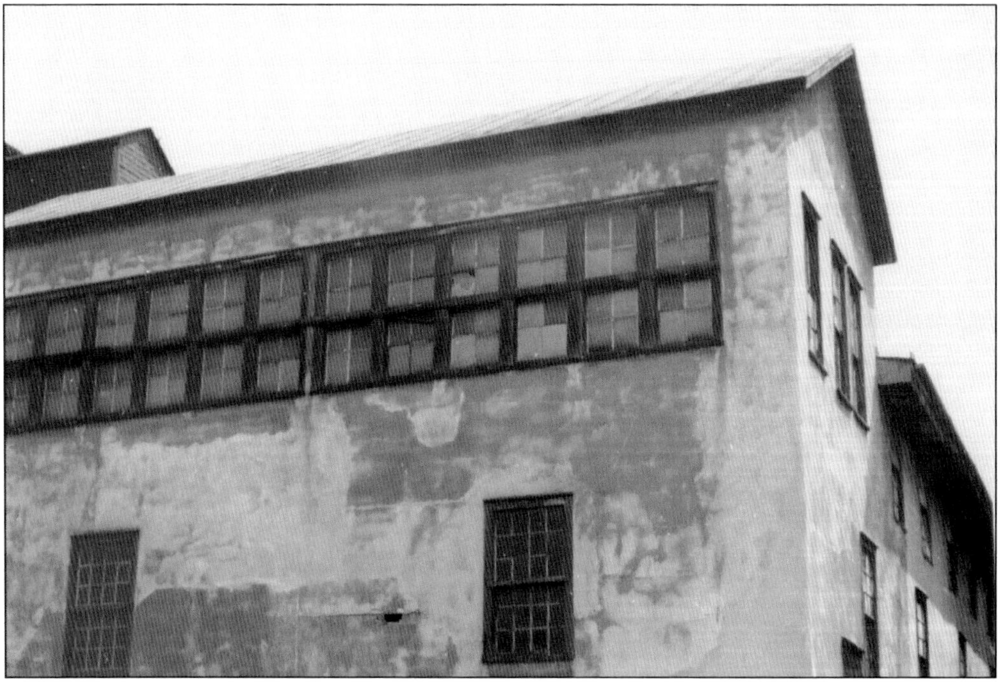

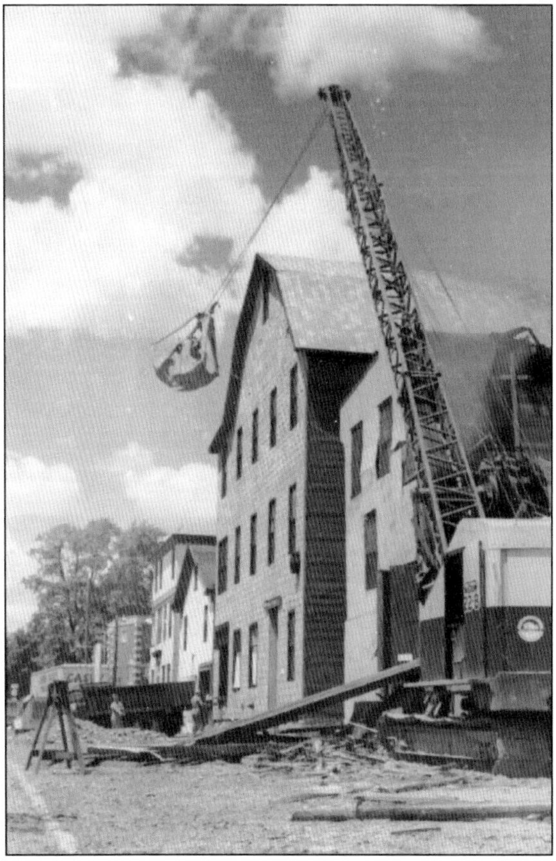

This final picture from within the future Court Street Plaza shows the rear of the Franklin Mills warehouse. The mill dated back at least to 1897 when it was the property of Robert Adams. The Franklin name originated with the Franklin Mills Company that moved from Lockport to this location in 1907. (Photograph by Robert W. Emens; courtesy of RML.)

As crews leveled the buildings in the first phase of the urban renewal work, a bucket is shown about to strike at the Franklin Mills Building. The former Emens Feed and Farm Supply store is just beyond. After that is the Trailways Building. County Building One can be seen across Court Street. (Photograph by Robert W. Emens; courtesy of RML.)

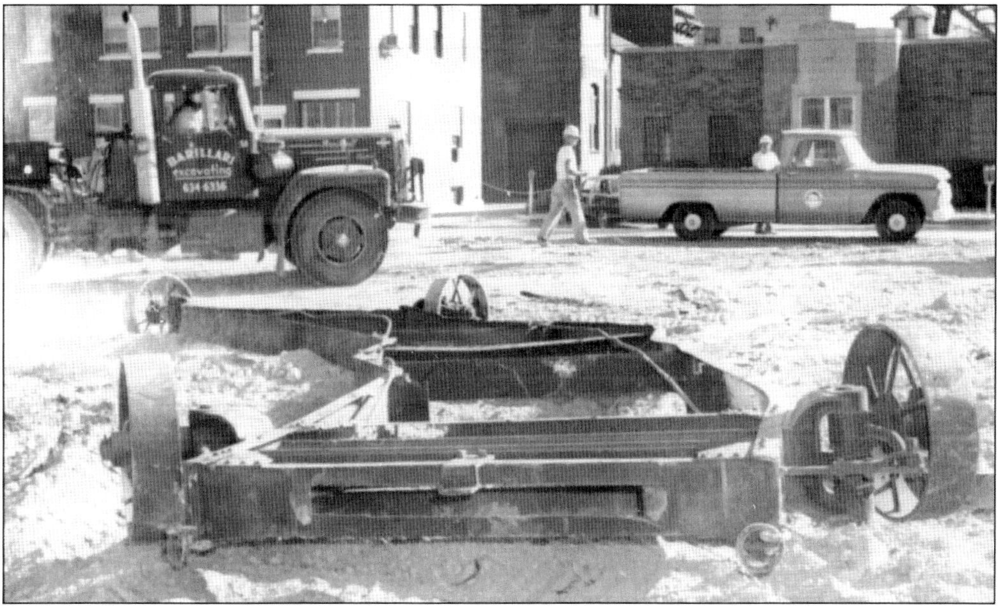

The twisted steel in the foreground is the chassis of the diner that had been on Court Street immediately north of the Trailways Building. In the background and on the left across Ellicott Street is a former Niagara Mohawk Power Company Building. To the right is the former Moose Lodge, now an office complex. (Photograph by Robert W. Emens; courtesy of RML.)

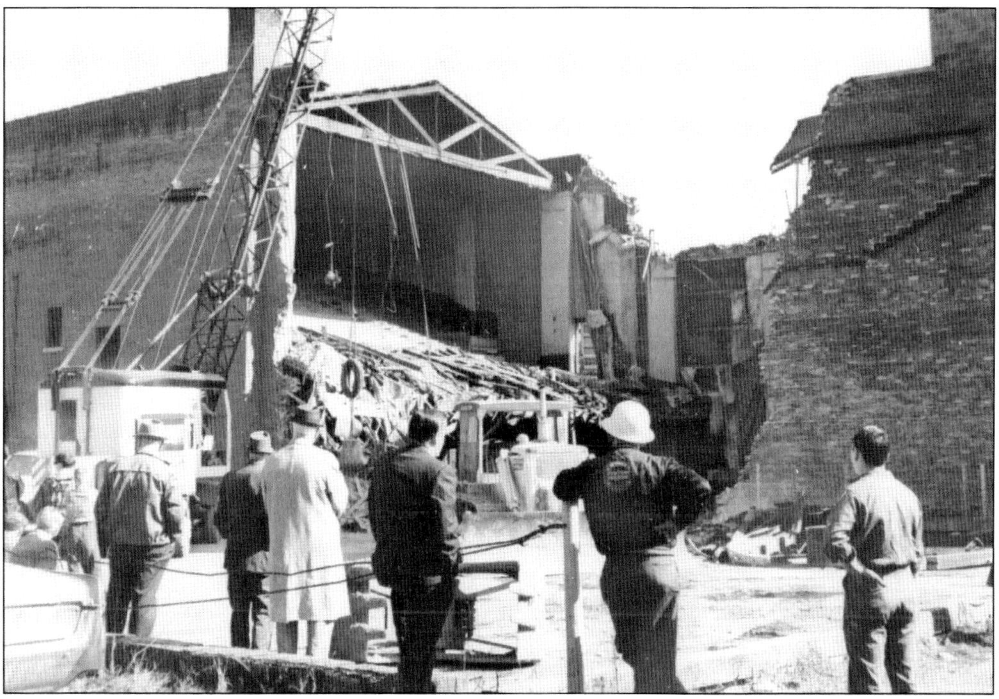

Above, a work crew member in a hard hat is accompanied by at least nine sidewalk superintendents surveying the day's work. This is the rear of the Dipson Family Theatre, located on the west side of Jackson Street. The theater stood on the original site of the First Baptist Church. (Photograph by Robert W. Emens; courtesy of RML.)

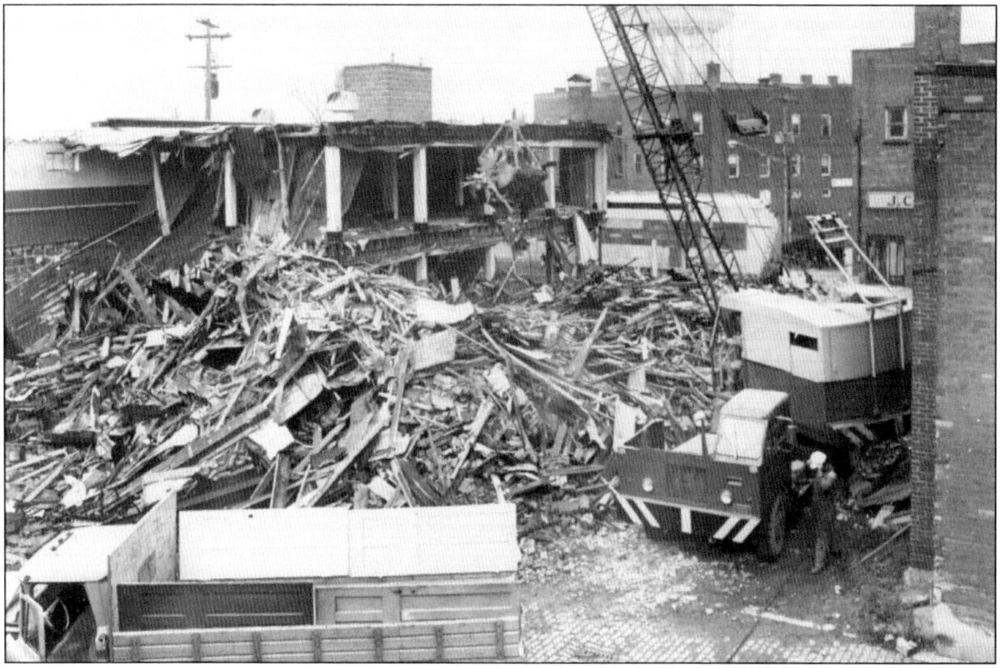

In this picture, debris is being loaded into the dump truck in the foreground. The area appears to be between Exchange Place and Court Street. Observe the sign at the far right denoting a rear entrance to the JC Penney store at 47–49 Main Street. (Photograph by Robert W. Emens; courtesy of RML.)

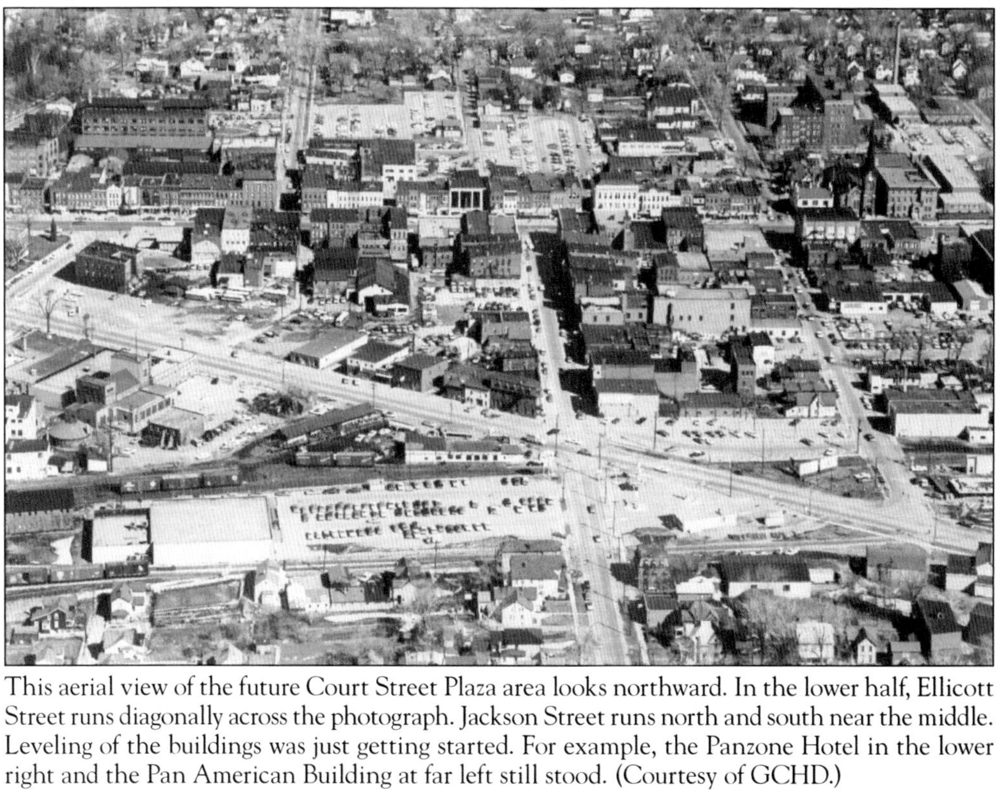

This aerial view of the future Court Street Plaza area looks northward. In the lower half, Ellicott Street runs diagonally across the photograph. Jackson Street runs north and south near the middle. Leveling of the buildings was just getting started. For example, the Panzone Hotel in the lower right and the Pan American Building at far left still stood. (Courtesy of GCHD.)

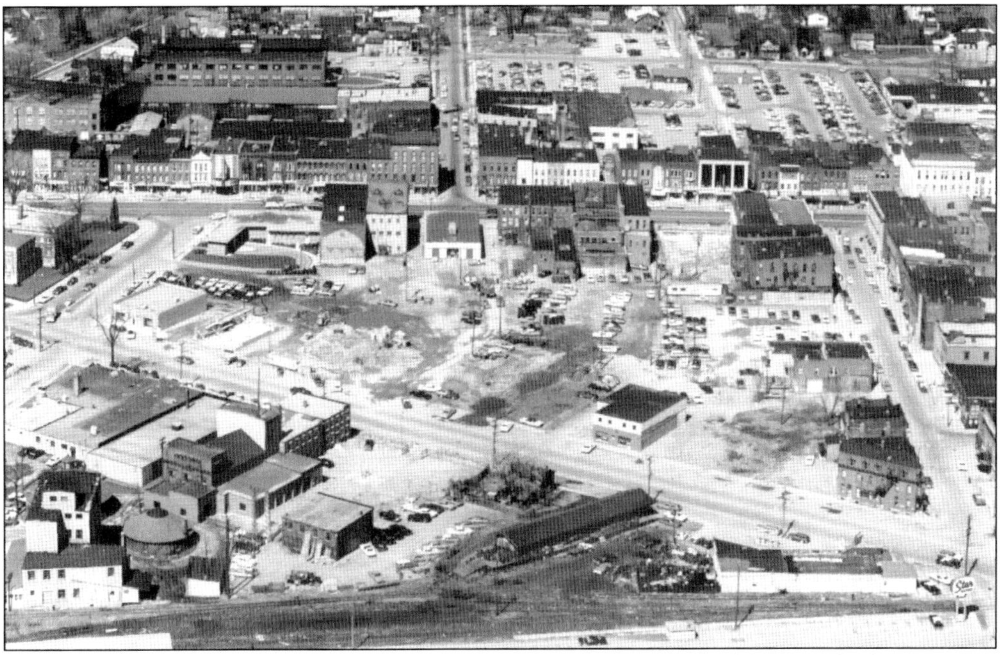

An aerial view documents further progress on the job of leveling the buildings in the future Court Street Plaza. The building occupied by the James E. Norton wholesale plumbing business appears to be the only surviving Ellicott Street structure. New construction has already started on the corner of Court and Ellicott Streets at the far left. (Courtesy of GCHD.)

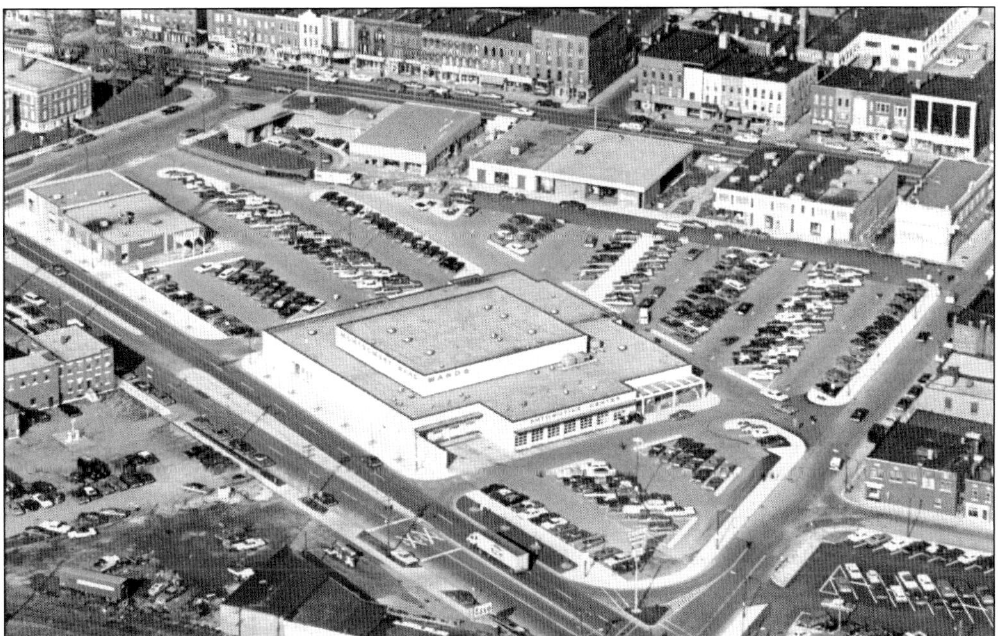

By 1968, the Court Street Plaza was finished with one exception. That was the building standing at the corner of Main and Jackson Streets, shown here in the upper right corner. It wasn't until 1973 that it was replaced by a new structure, one occupied briefly by Alexanders clothing store, which succumbed to financial problems brought on by the move. (Courtesy of GCHD.)

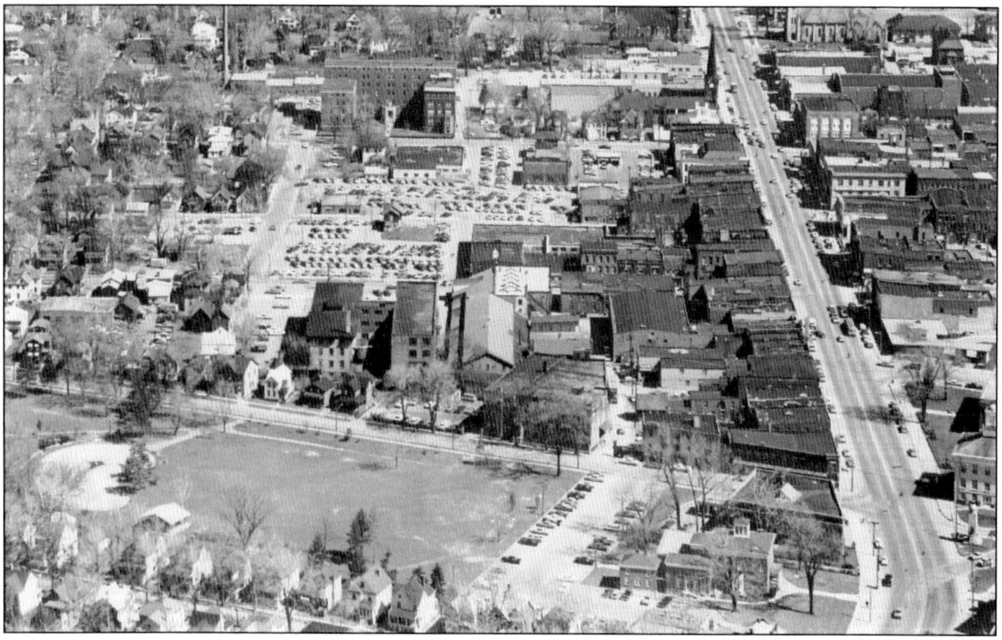

This aerial view facing east shows the area covered by the second phase of urban renewal. It extends up Main Street on the right, across Bank Street at the top, down Washington Avenue (partially in view on the left), and across Jefferson Avenue back to Main Street near the bottom. (Courtesy of GCHD.)

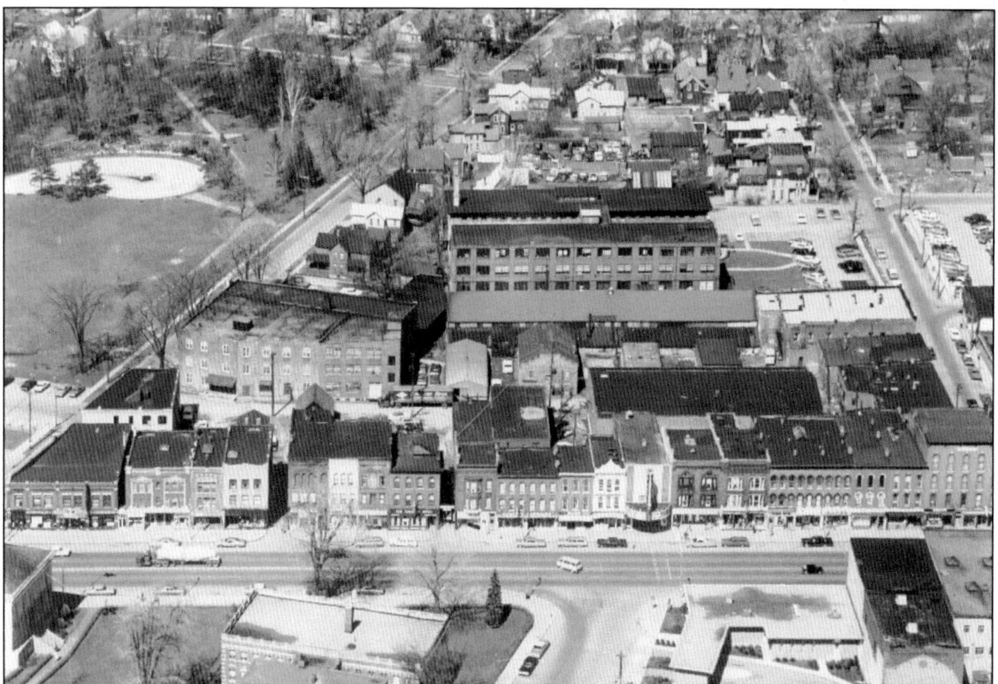

This photograph looking north shows the western portion of the second phase of urban renewal, from Jefferson Avenue on the left to State Street on the right. The white area in the upper left is a wading pool in Austin Park donated in 1929 by Arthur Brisbane, an internationally famous newspaper editor who worked for William Randolph Hearst. (Courtesy of GCHD.)

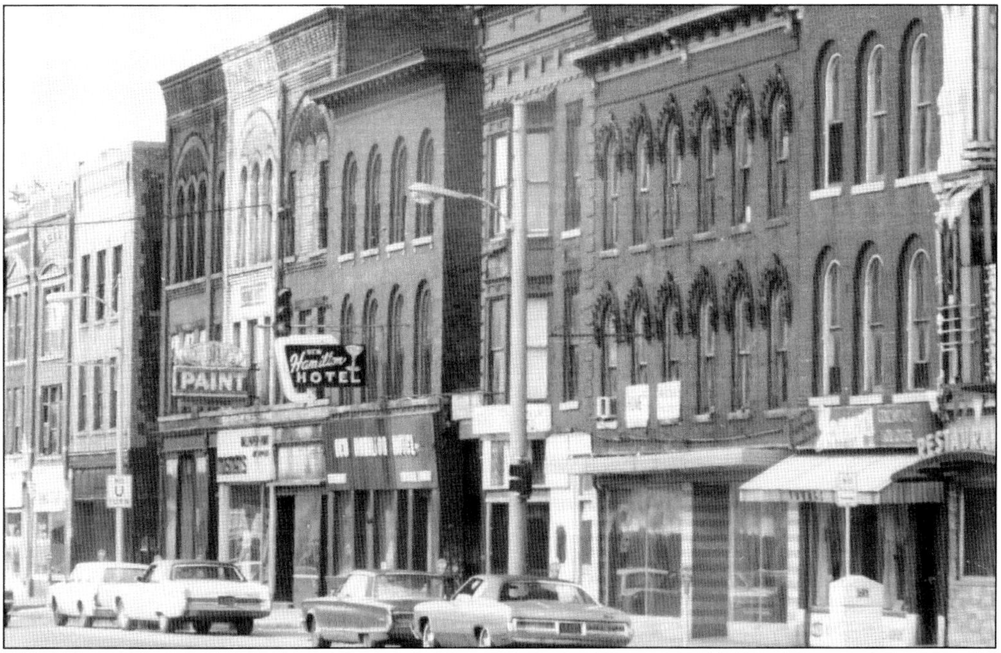

The second phase of urban renewal, referred to as the Jefferson Plaza phase, got underway in the very early 1970s. This and several of the following photographs illustrate how the north side of Main Street looked in the preceding decade. This view is looking westward from the Court Street intersection. (Courtesy of GCHD.)

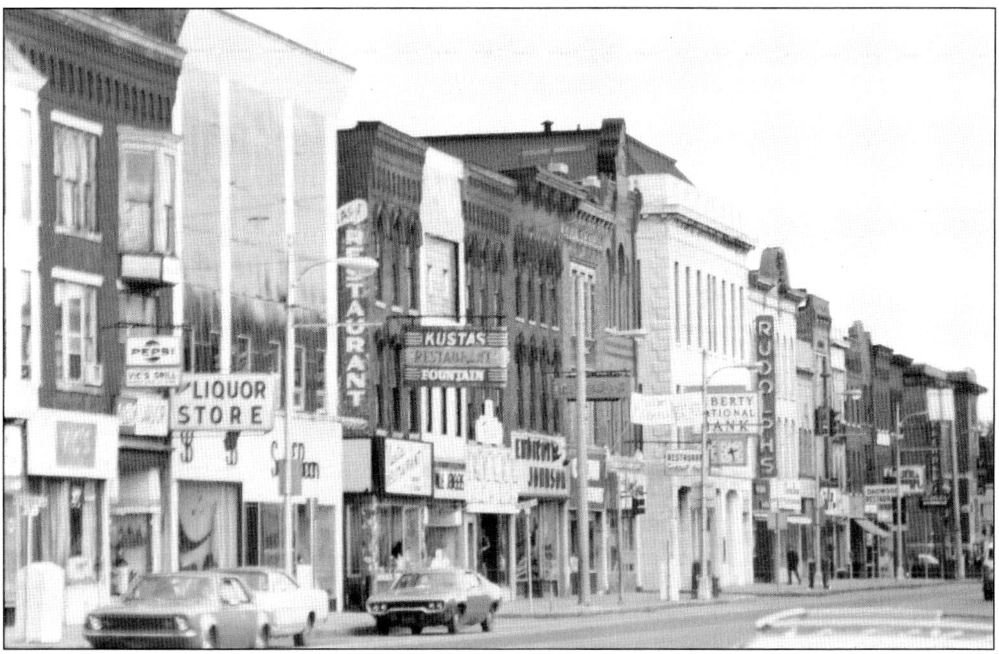

This picture shows the north side of Main Street from Russell Place eastward to Bank Street and slightly beyond. The facades of some older buildings had been remodeled, but most of the structures along Main Street retained the architecture from the time they had been constructed in the late 1800s or early 1900s. (Courtesy of GCHD.)

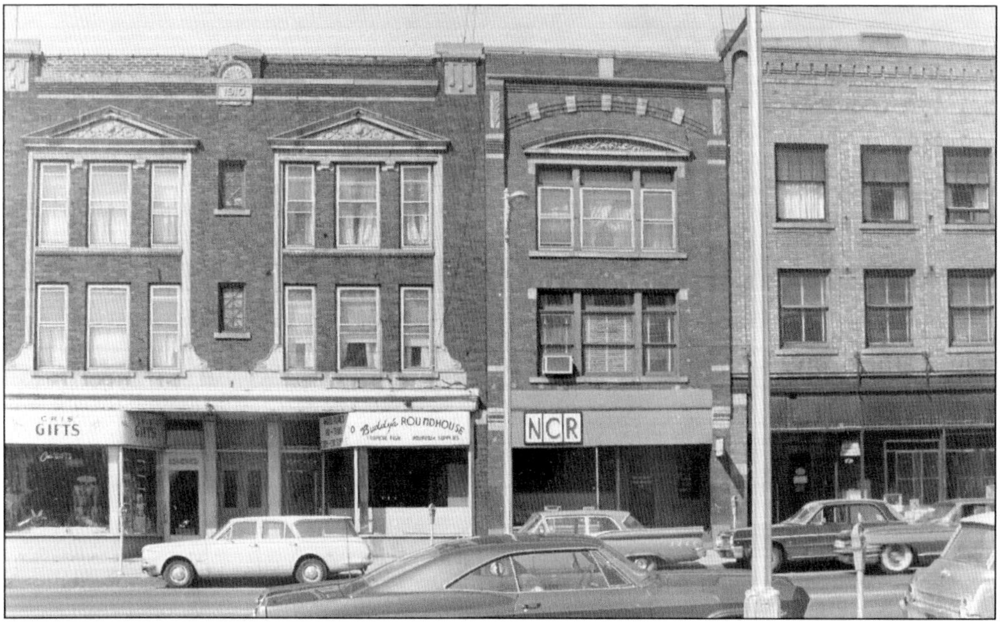

The building on the left, occupied by Chris Gifts and Buddy's Roundhouse, is the second structure from the corner of Main Street and Jefferson Avenue. Note the 1910 construction date displayed at the top center part of the building. The curtains in the upper windows suggest apartments, a feature common to the downtown buildings. (Courtesy of LSGC.)

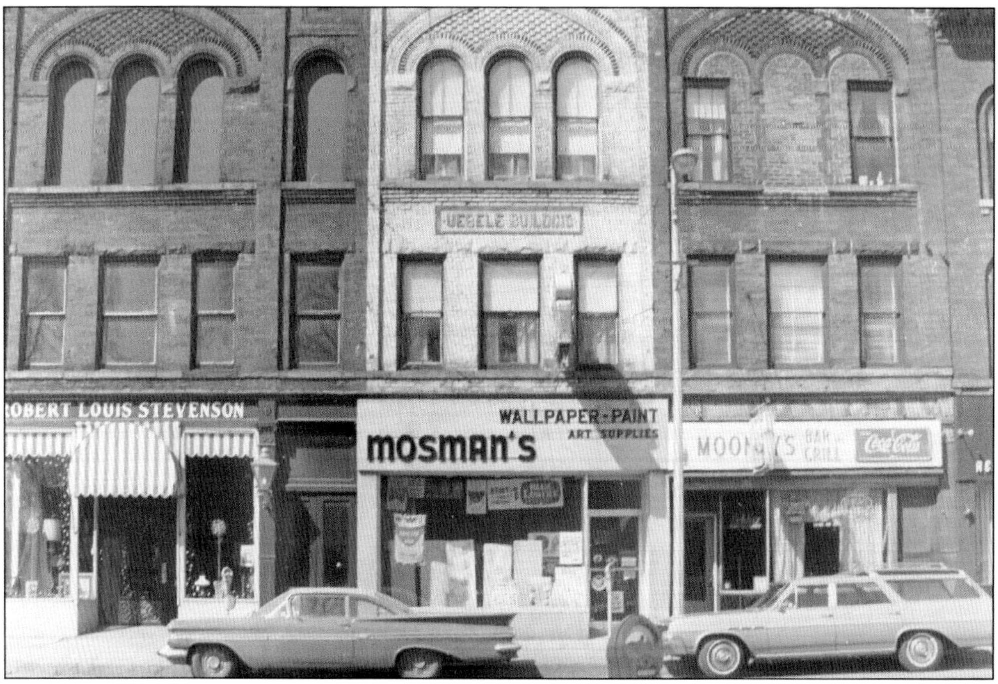

Moving eastward along Main Street, this photograph shows the Uebele Building. It extends across the entire picture and houses all three of the visible businesses: Robert Louis Stevenson, Mosman's, and Mooney's bar and grill. The structure once housed a bakery owned by the German-American family that erected the building. (Courtesy of LSGC.)

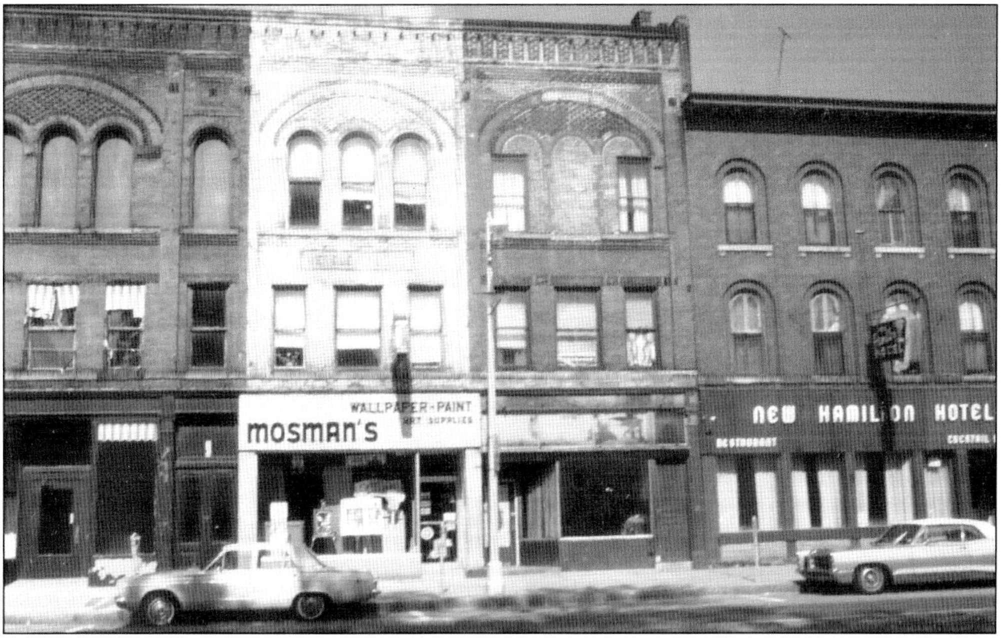

This picture shows the Uebele Building and part of the New Hamilton Hotel. It appears to be at a later date than the preceding picture, as Stevenson's and Mooney's businesses are no longer in evidence. As buildings emptied out, the urban renewal agency often made the space temporarily available to nonprofit groups at no charge. (Courtesy of LSGC.)

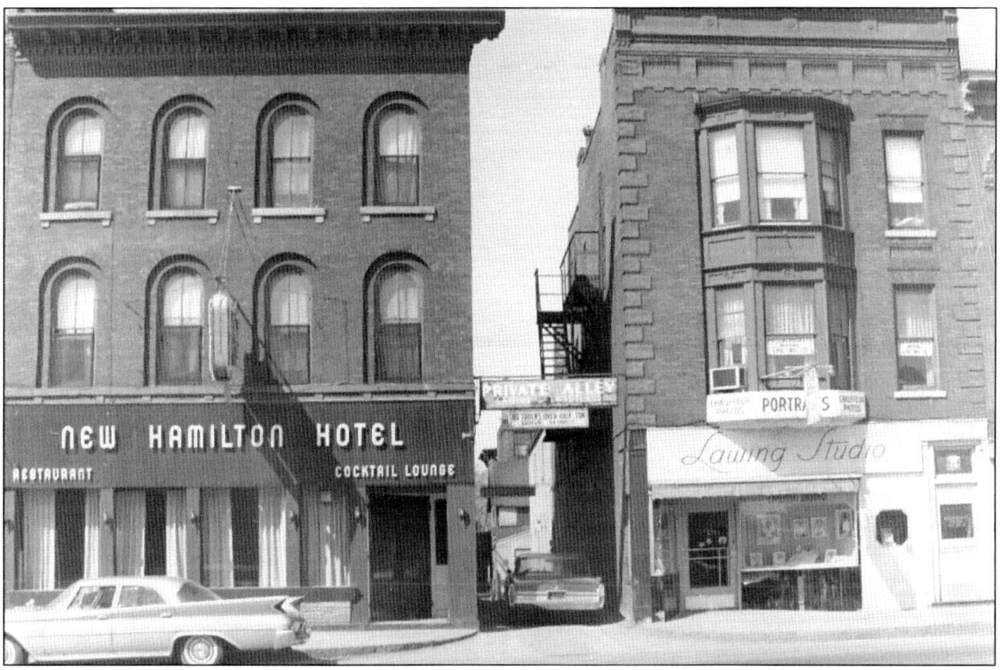

The New Hamilton Hotel replaced a place called The Berry Patch, which, in turn, was preceded by the original Hamilton Hotel. The earlier Hamilton Hotel reportedly had an excellent menu and tables set with fine linen. Note the private alley shared by the New Hamilton and the Lawing Studio next door. (Courtesy of LSGC.)

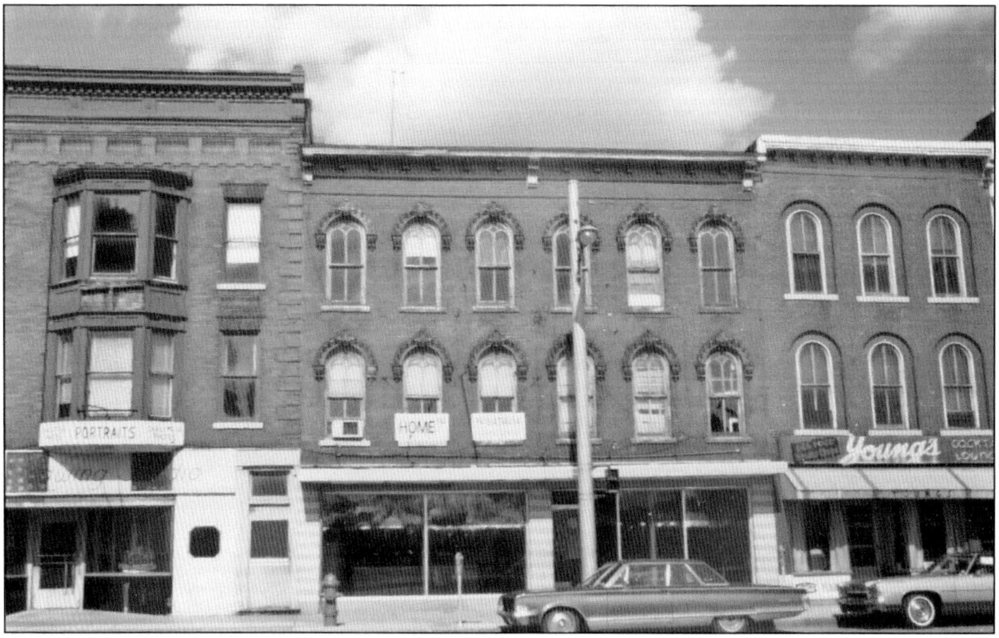

In this photograph is the Lawing Studio with vacant space previously occupied by Genesee Hardware. Farther east is Young's restaurant. Genesee Hardware moved to a new building on Ellicott Street. The "HOME" sign designates an early location of the Batavia Youth Center. The center later moved to a new building on Bank Street. (Courtesy of LSGC.)

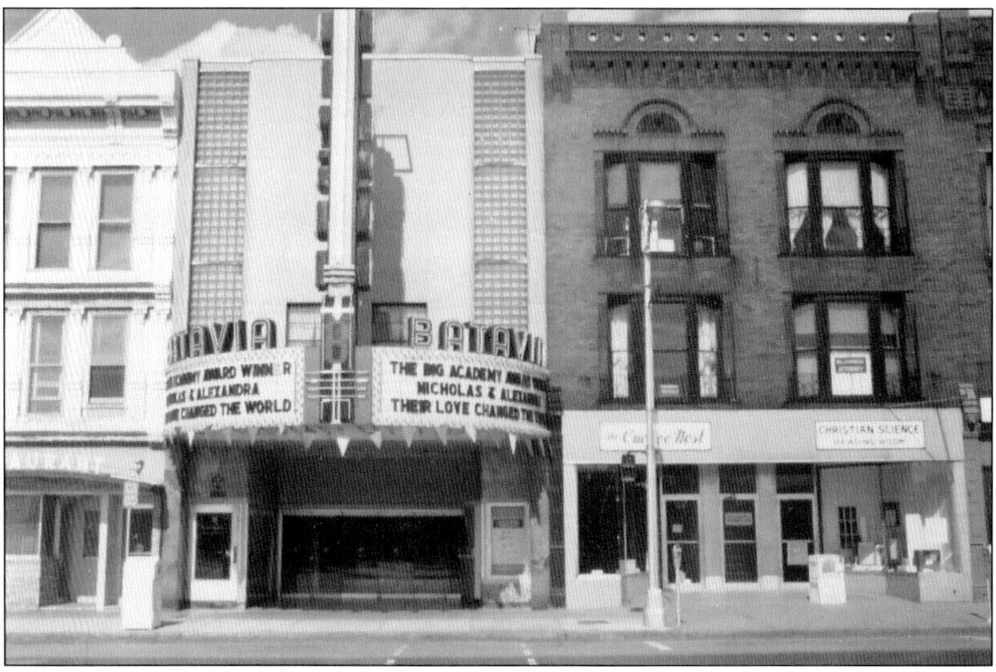

Above is the Batavia Dipson Theatre. The entrance was at 36 Main Street, but the auditorium was at a right angle behind storefronts located at 40 Main Street and eastward. The entrance corridor was 107 feet long. The lobby was decorated by a mural depicting scenes from early Genesee County history. (Courtesy of LSGC.)

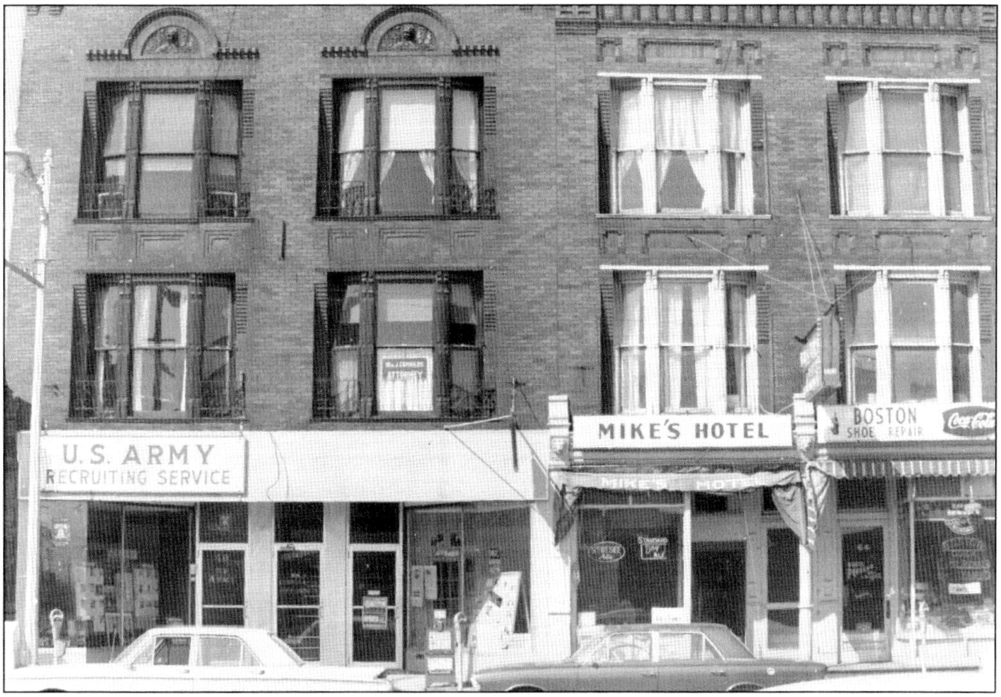

The building at 40 and 42 Main Street is again in view, but the Cuckoo's Nest and Christian Science Reading Room are both gone. The U.S. Army Recruiting Service may have been taking advantage of the opportunity for nonprofit organizations to temporarily use vacated space. Upper floors in downtown buildings sometimes housed offices, as is the case here. (Courtesy of LSGC.)

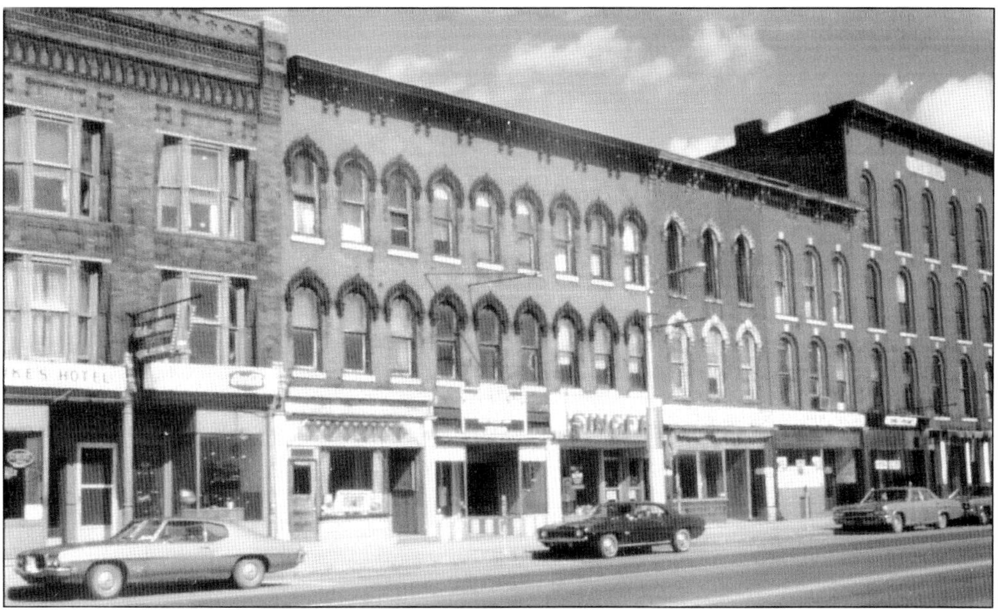

This photograph shows the architectural detail displayed in the downtown buildings that were leveled during urban renewal. Many voices were raised against the loss of these structures because of their architectural and historical significance. Newspaper accounts from the period carried complaints about the "apparent indifference" of urban renewal officials. (Courtesy of LSGC.)

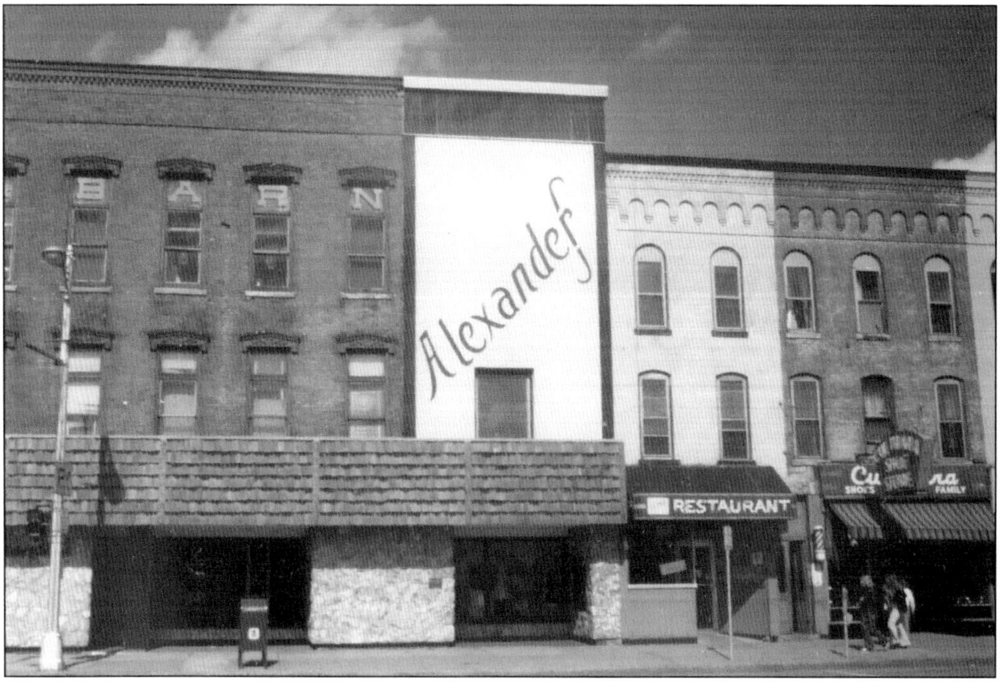

The previous picture showed buildings eastward to State Street. This image begins with the first building east of State Street. Alexanders clothing store, shown here on the north side of Main Street, fell victim to the costs associated with relocating to a new location. The Main Barber Shop, next to Cultrara Shoe Store, was on an upper floor. (Courtesy of LSGC.)

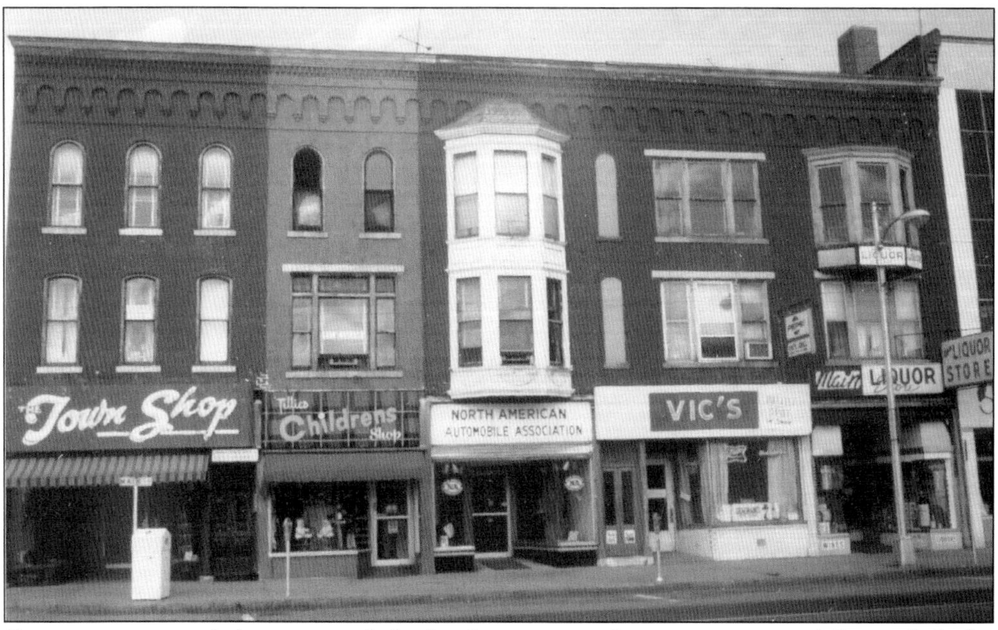

Continuing eastward, the image includes four businesses no longer in operation. They include the Town Shop, Tillies Childrens Shop, Vic's Tavern for those who wanted to drink on the premises, and Main Liquor Store for those who didn't. Note the presence of bay windows, a common feature of buildings in the downtown area. (Courtesy of LSGC.)

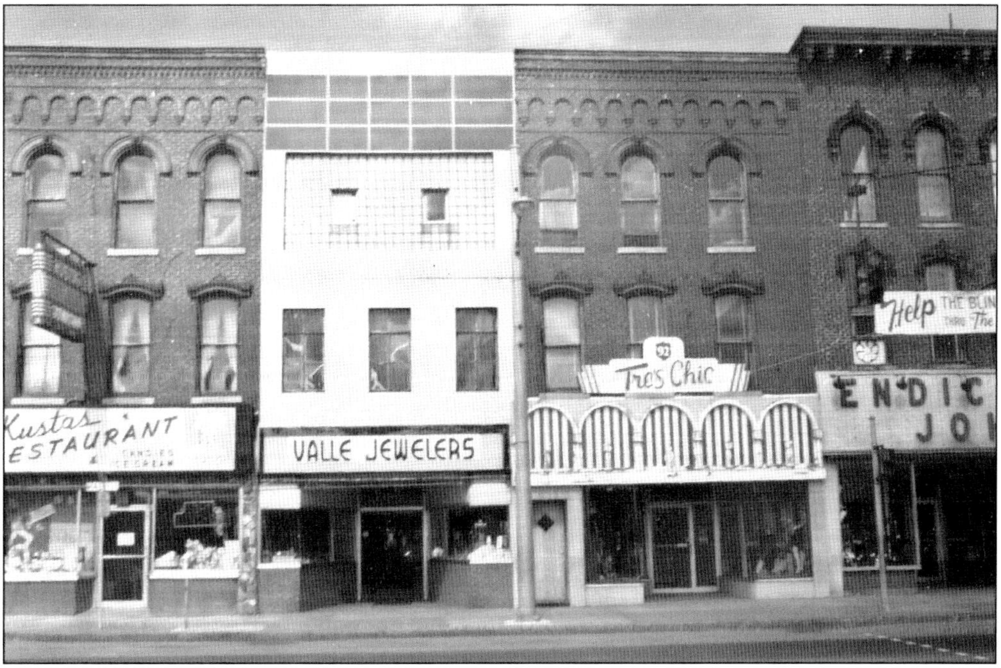

Even before urban renewal, many downtown merchants moved along Main Street from one location to another. Tres Chic, here, and Valle Jewelers, next door, were two examples. After urban renewal, Valle Jewelers continued to move. For many years, it was in the Genesee Country Mall. Today it is located on Jackson Street. (Courtesy of LSGC.)

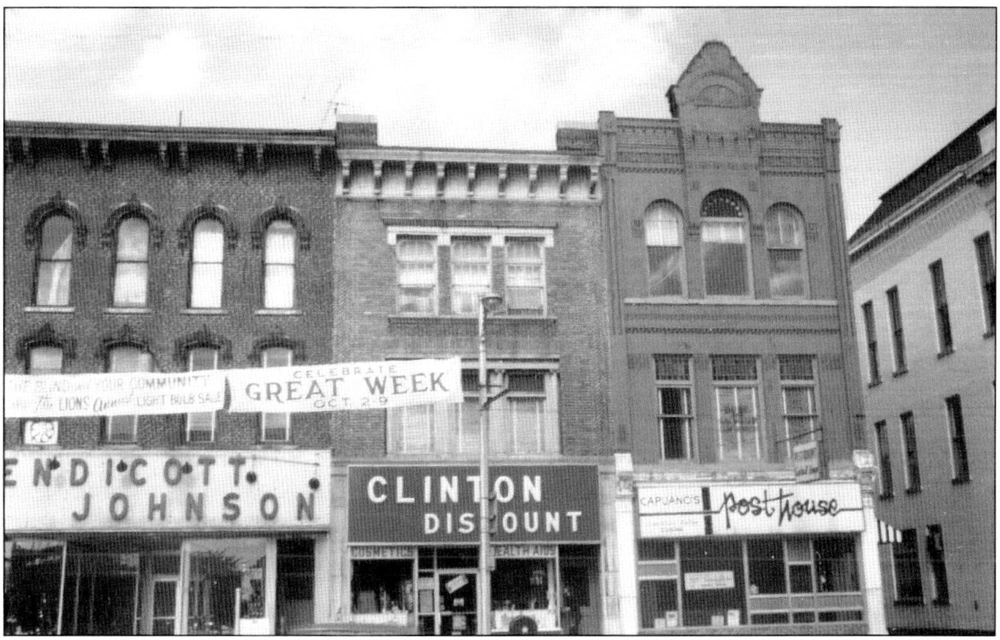

The Post House stood just west of Park Place. The offices of well-known Batavia attorneys John D. LeSeur and Theodore A. Buhl were located above the restaurant. The Post House opened in 1949 with a name chosen in recognition of the recent opening of Batavia Downs. In 1961, the main entrance was moved around the corner. (Courtesy of LSGC.)

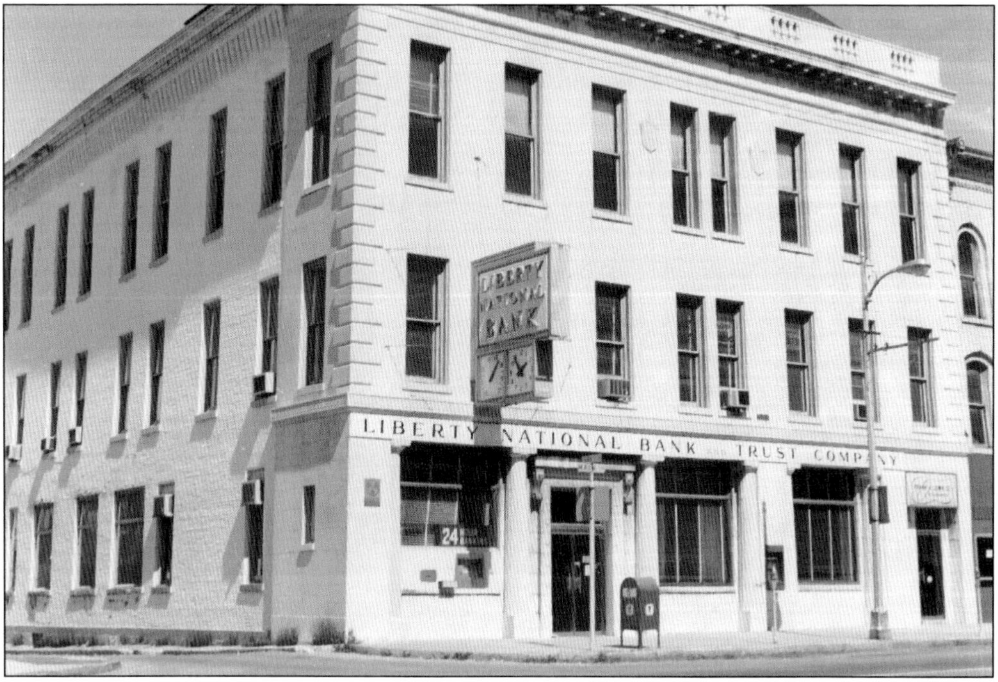

Liberty National Bank originated from the second oldest bank in Batavia, the First National Bank, established in 1864. It moved to this location in 1924. The bank doubled its floor space in 1961 by taking the space next door that had been occupied by the Stroh Florist Shop. The Bank of America now at Bank and Main Streets is its successor. (Courtesy of LSGC.)

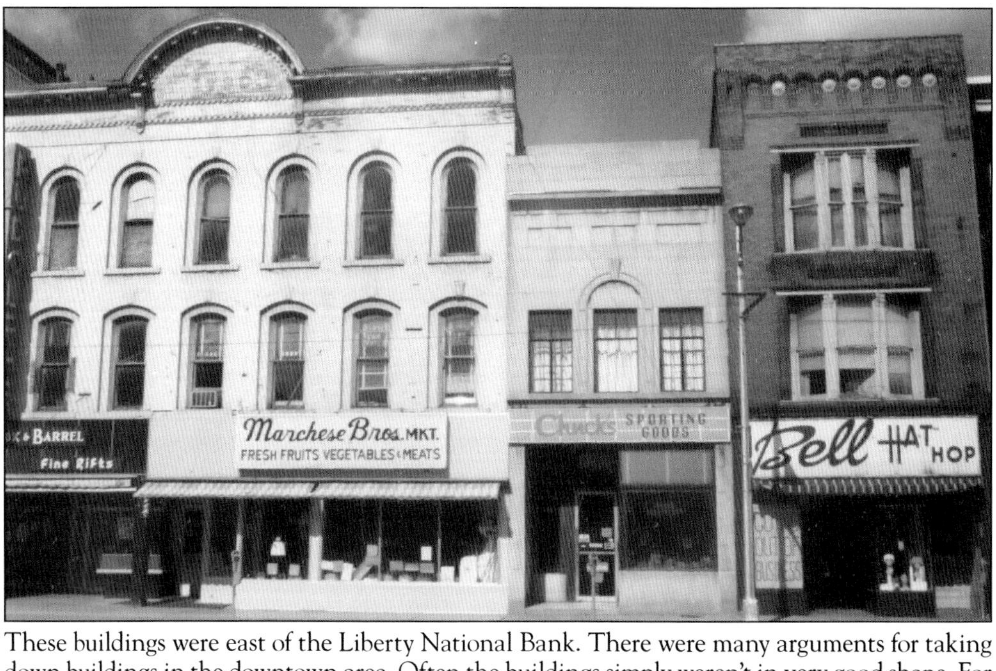

These buildings were east of the Liberty National Bank. There were many arguments for taking down buildings in the downtown area. Often the buildings simply weren't in very good shape. For example, plywood has been nailed into the window openings on the third floor of the building on the left. (Courtesy of LSGC.)

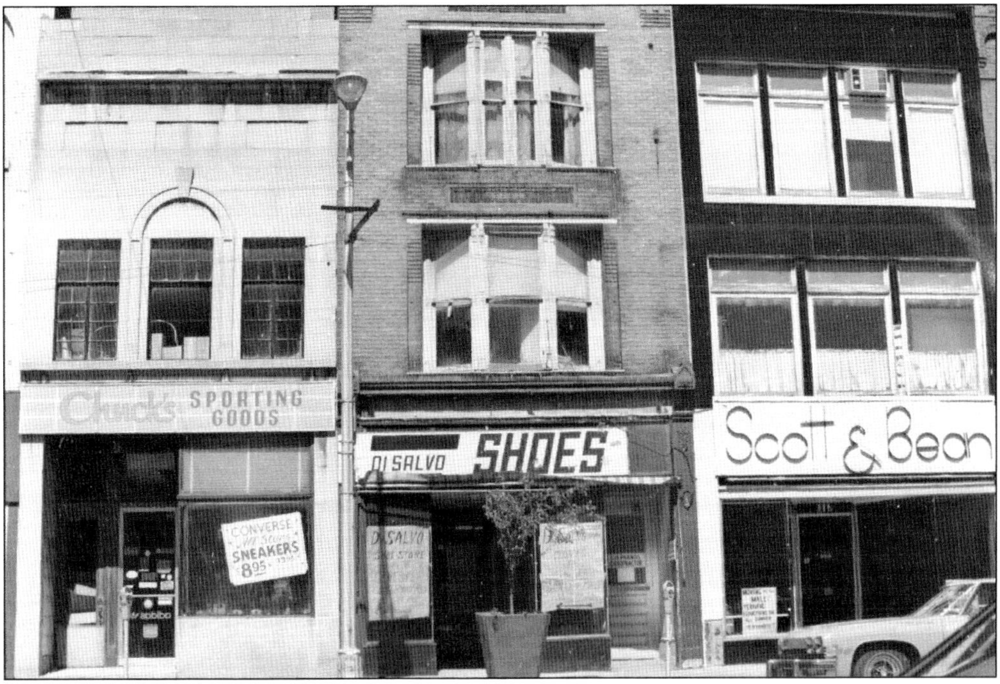

The condition of wiring and plumbing was an issue. Virtually none of the upper floors of the downtown buildings were handicapped accessible. Upgrading structures such as those in this picture would have been a very expensive proposition. Furthermore, funds were available for leveling the old buildings and starting over, but generally not for renovation or restoration. (Courtesy of LSGC.)

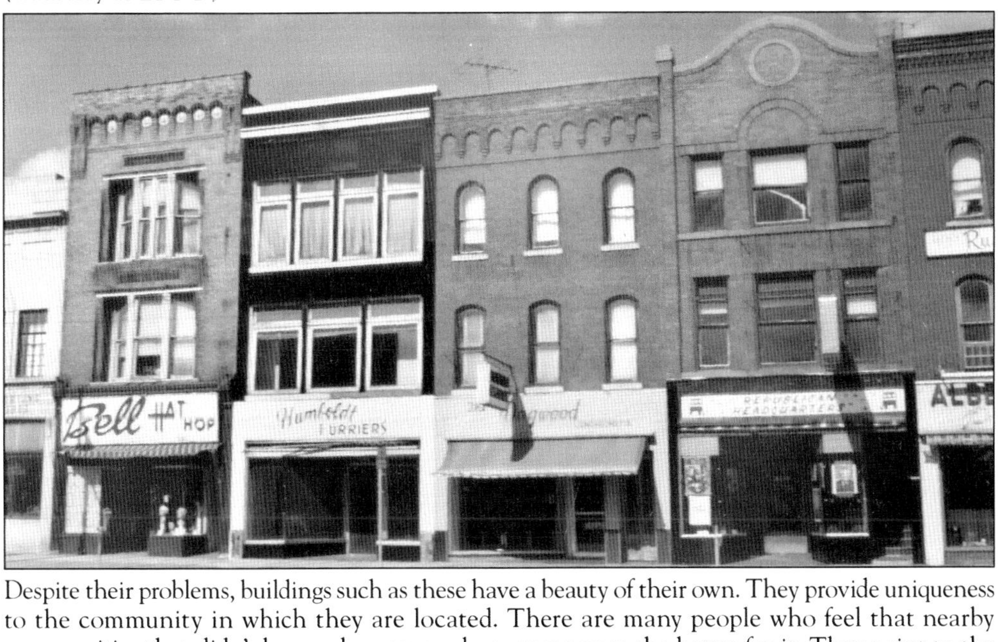

Despite their problems, buildings such as these have a beauty of their own. They provide uniqueness to the community in which they are located. There are many people who feel that nearby communities that didn't have urban renewal programs were the better for it. They point to the downtowns of LeRoy, Brockport, Albion, and Medina as examples, communities that are now capitalizing on their century-old architecture. (Courtesy of LSGC.)

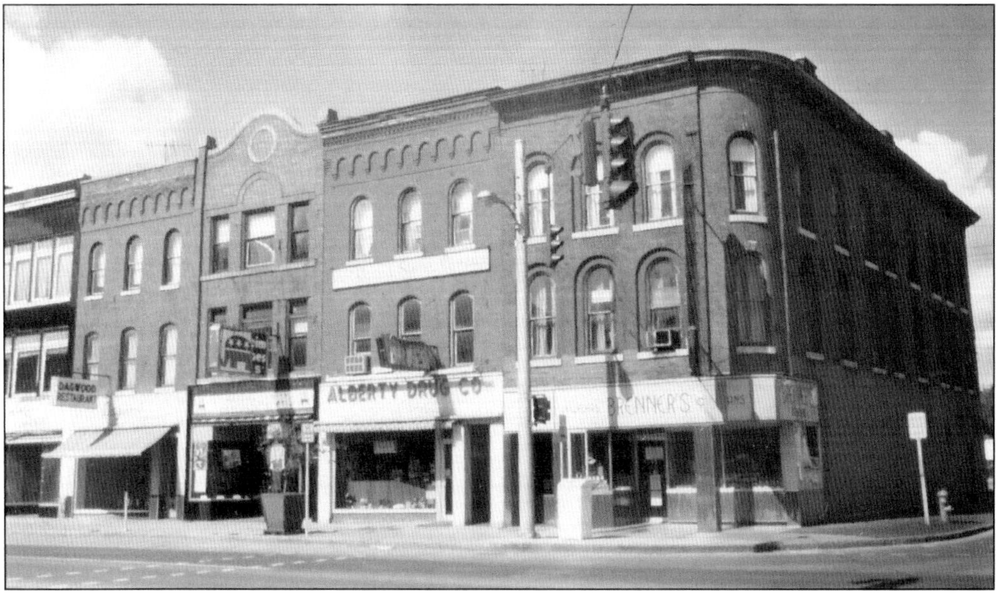

The series of pictures along Main Street ends here. The building on the corner, the intersection of Bank and Main Streets, housed Brenner's jewelry store. Batavians who have lived in the city for several decades will recall the store's slogan, "It's always okay to owe Herb Brenner." It was a time before credit cards and easy money. (Courtesy of LSGC.)

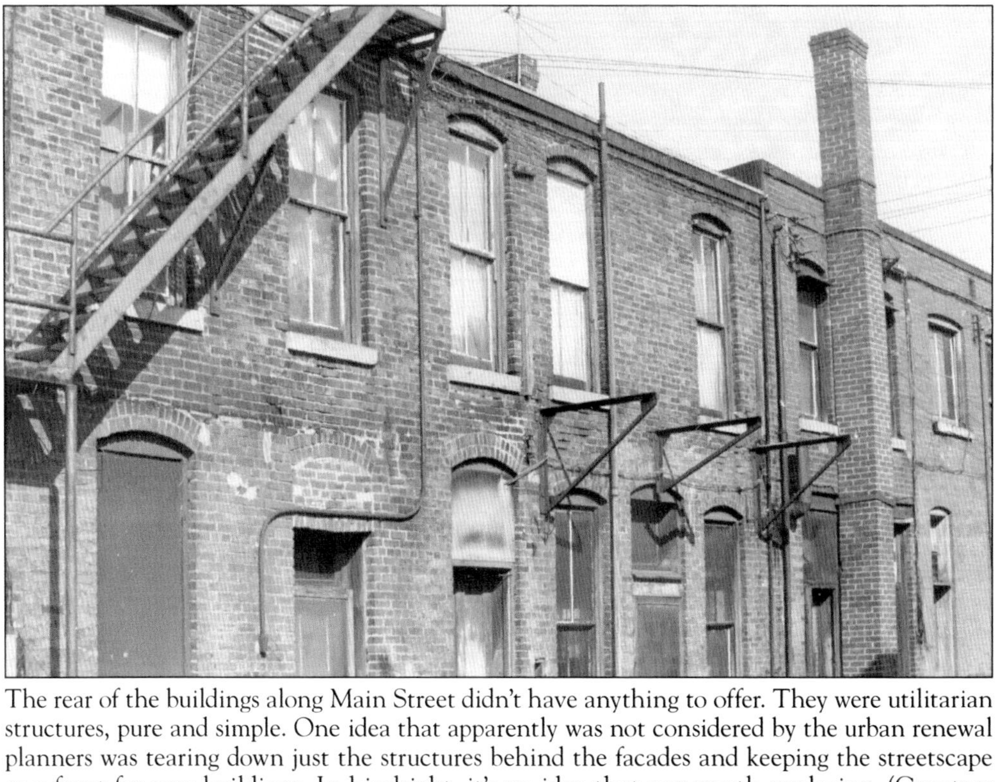

The rear of the buildings along Main Street didn't have anything to offer. They were utilitarian structures, pure and simple. One idea that apparently was not considered by the urban renewal planners was tearing down just the structures behind the facades and keeping the streetscape as a front for new buildings. In hindsight, it's an idea that was worth exploring. (Courtesy of LSGC.)

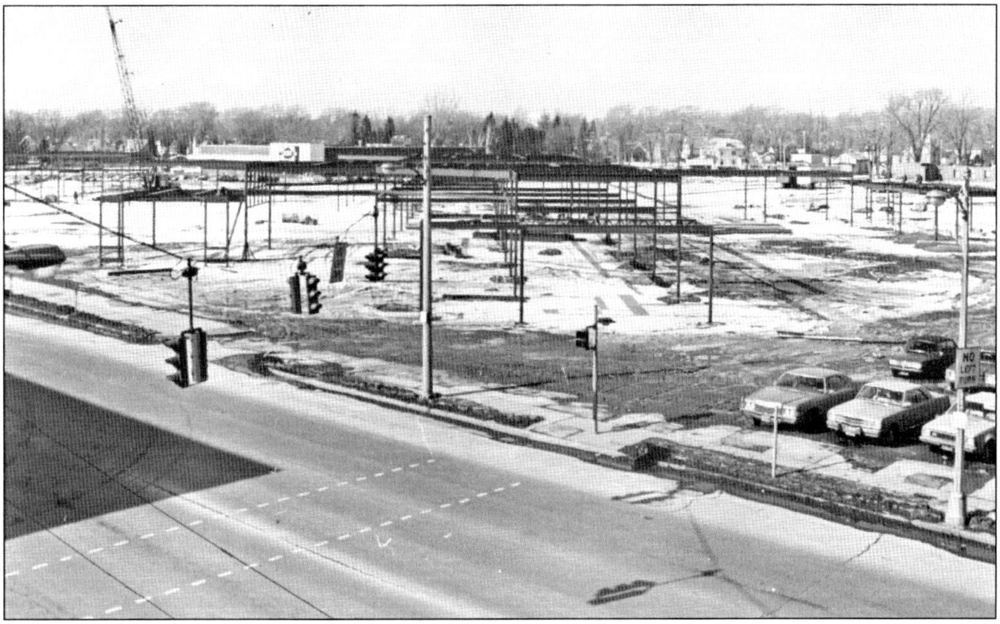

The original plan for the area north of Main Street called for individual, freestanding buildings. It was not until after the fourth director of urban renewal assumed office that a decision was made to construct a single enclosed mall to house all the relocating merchants. Construction began in the mid-1970s. (Courtesy of GCHD.)

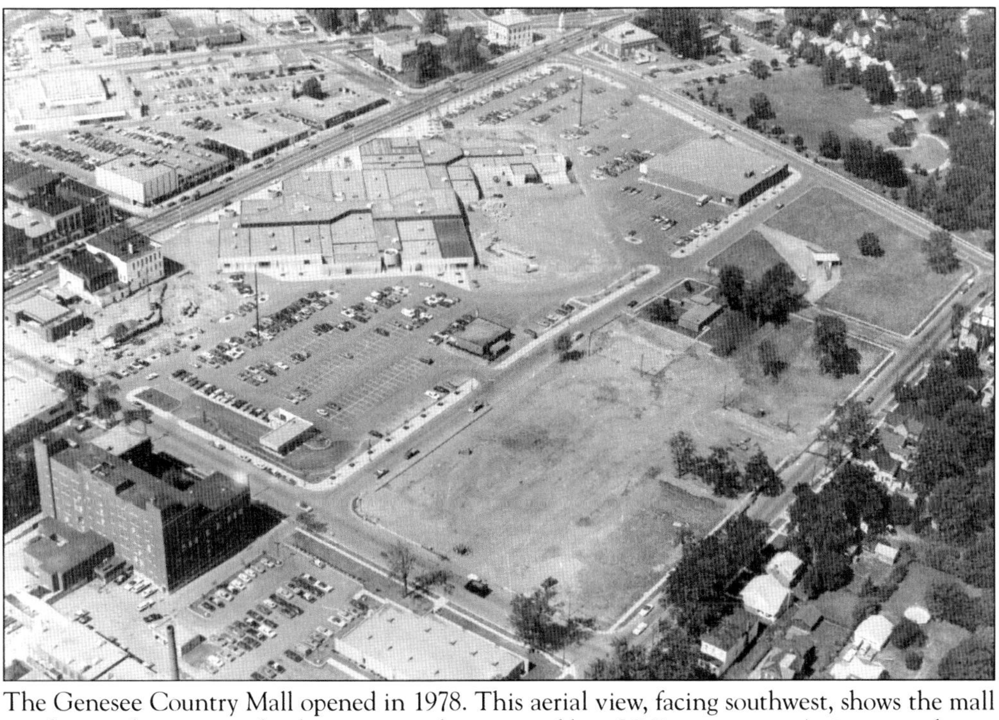

The Genesee Country Mall opened in 1978. This aerial view, facing southwest, shows the mall nearly complete, except for the section to be occupied by a JC Penney store. A time capsule was buried at the southwest corner, but when the new city hall was added a few years ago, the capsule was dug up and placed in a storage room. (Courtesy of GCHD.)

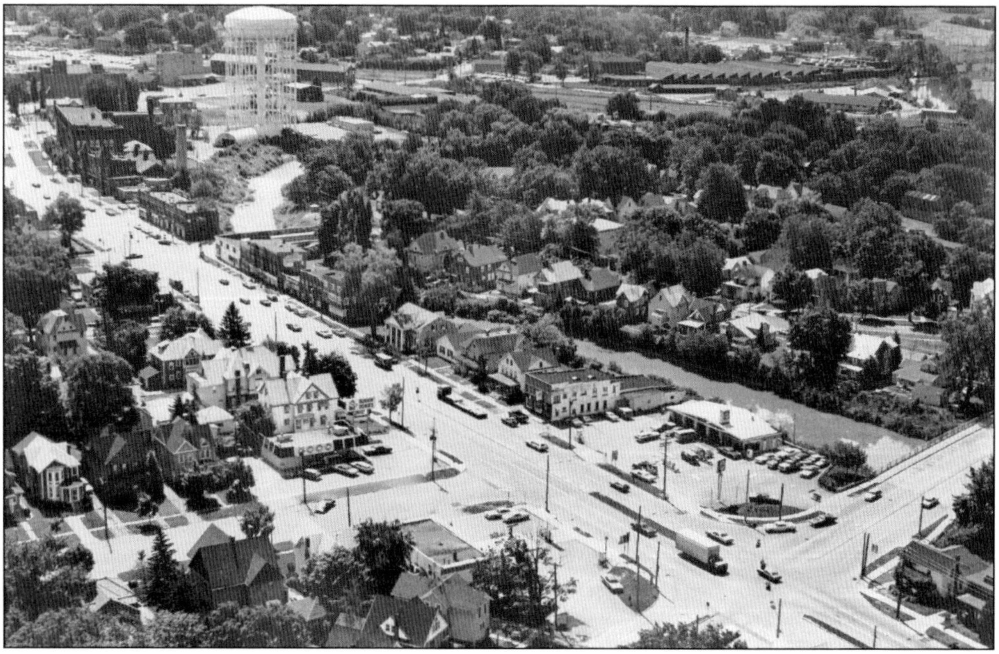

In the mid to late 1970s, city leaders decided to expand the scope of the second phase of the urban renewal work. The area shown here along Tonawanda Creek from Oak Street east to a little beyond the Ellicott Street intersection was chosen. Eventually, most of these buildings were removed to create a green space. (Courtesy of GCHD.)

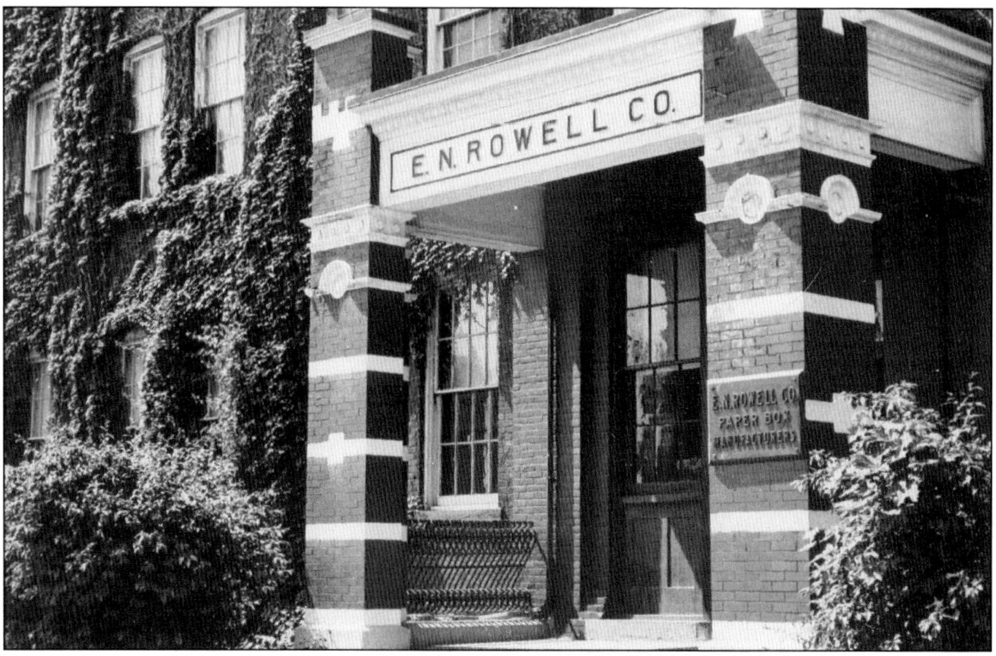

The E. N. Rowell Factory Building no. 1 stood at Ellicott and West Main Streets. The building was erected in 1895. A fourth floor was added in 1912. In the late 1970s, a debate arose over a proposal to convert the building into housing for the elderly. Eventually the proponents of this adaptive reuse lost out and the building was razed. (Courtesy of GCHD.)

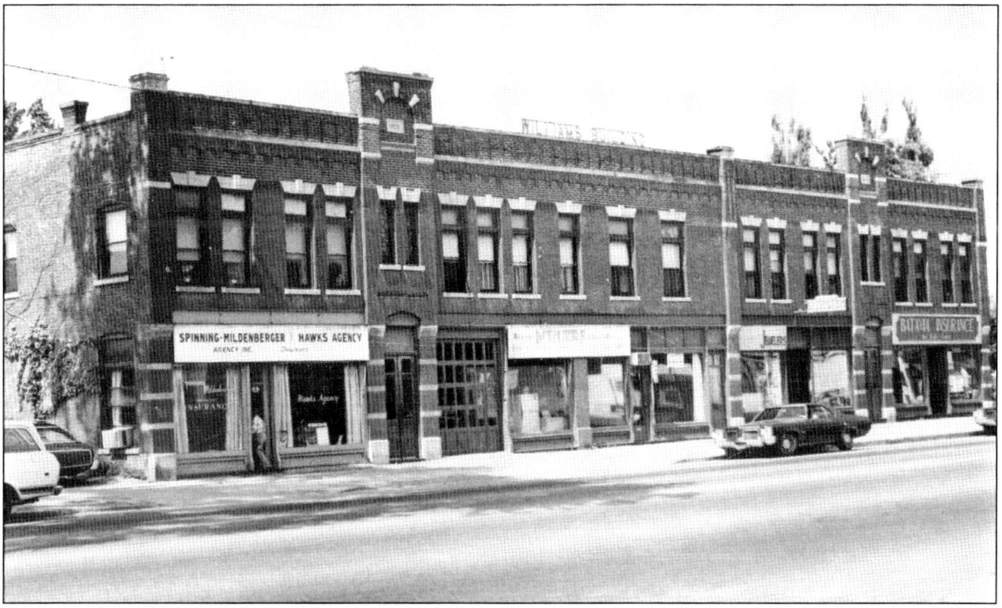

The Williams Building stood just east of the former Walnut Street intersection. (By then the Walnut Street Bridge had been closed.) The above picture shows the street side and the below picture shows the backside along Tonawanda Creek. The building, owned by the Williams family for over 70 years, was erected in 1909. Before its construction, a barn had existed on the property, also belonging to the Williams family. The barn was used for an early automobile repair shop that went by the name of Midway Garage. Before the building shown in the picture was constructed, the barn was moved to a location on Lewiston Road. When the expanded urban renewal program proposed to level the 1909 structure, co-owner Ralph "Bud" Williams and others raised strenuous objections, but to no avail. Bud was a printer at the *Daily News* who was well known for his outspoken views on a variety of topics. (Courtesy of GCHD.)

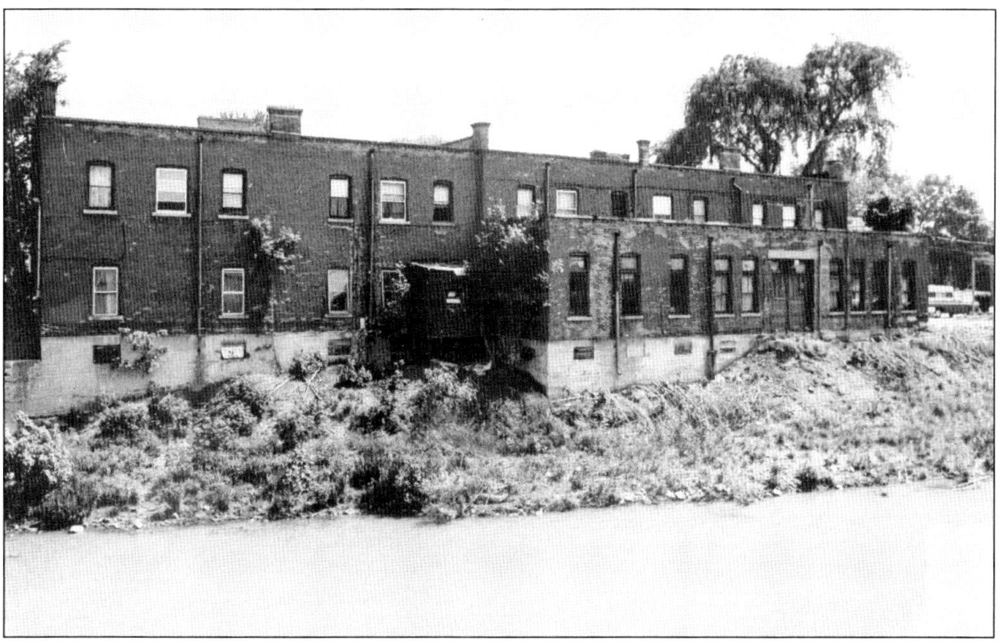

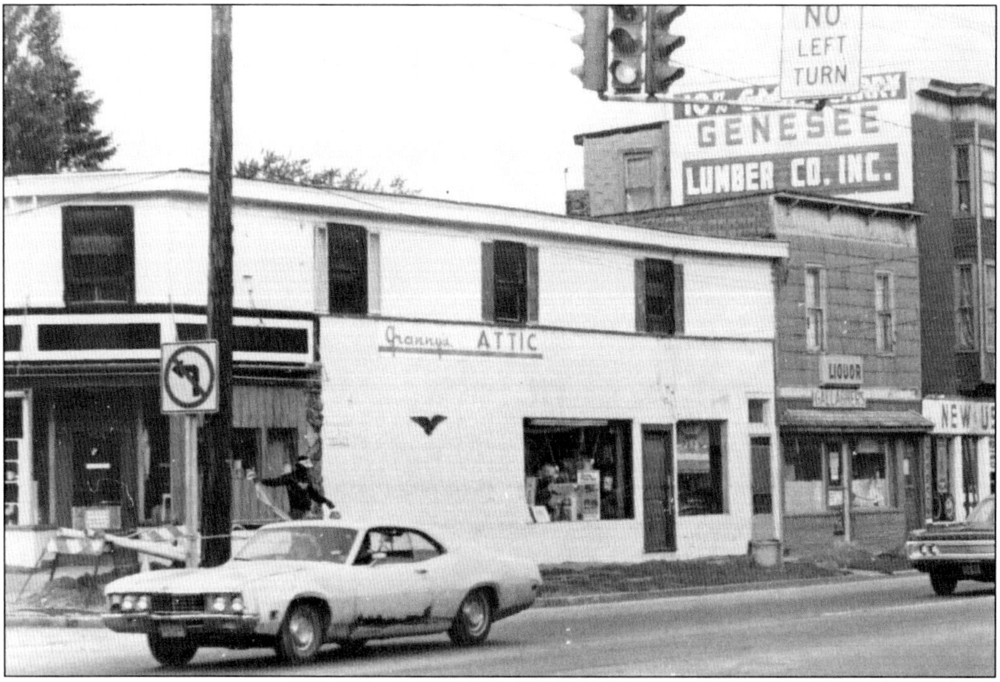

This picture shows buildings from the former Walnut Street intersection westward. Granny's attic was a store selling a wide variety of novelty and other items. One story that periodically circulates is that a Batavia trolley car was discovered when the site was excavated, but the author has found no evidence supporting this claim and suspects it is just an urban myth. (Courtesy of GCHD.)

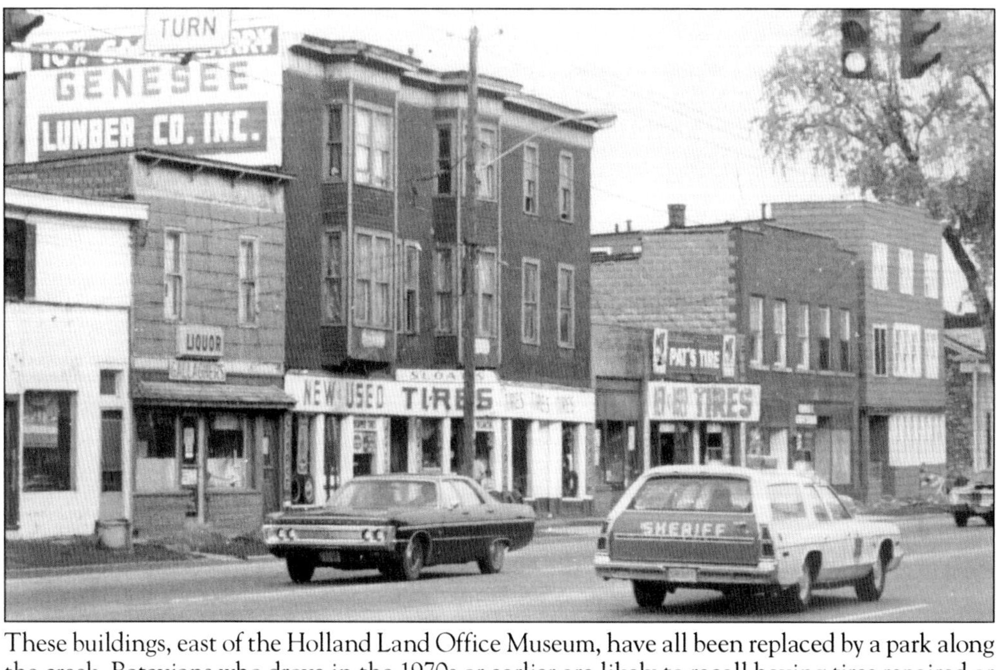

These buildings, east of the Holland Land Office Museum, have all been replaced by a park along the creek. Batavians who drove in the 1970s or earlier are likely to recall having tires repaired or replaced at Sloats. Vehicles were serviced at curbside in the street, a practice that would probably be disallowed today. (Courtesy of GCHD.)

Five

LANDMARK PRESERVATION

Batavia's Main Street, particularly East Main, was once a thoroughfare with many mansions and imposing homes. A good number, such as those belonging to Heman Redfield, Joseph Ellicott, Trumbull Cary, Dean Richmond, and Kate Fisher McCool, are now gone. The first few to disappear, including the Ellicott Mansion, seem to have slipped away without opposition. In more recent times, the actions that led to the destruction of notable buildings such as the Richmond Mansion and the Fisher McCool home were resisted both by individuals and organized groups like the Landmark Society of Genesee County, Inc.

The Landmark Society was formed in the 1960s by a group of local citizens. It continues to be active today. The society's creation was initially spurred by two concerns in particular. One was the perceived threat to historically significant architecture posed by urban renewal. The other was the desire to save the Richmond Mansion, probably the most notable piece of historic architecture in the city of Batavia.

The Landmark Society's efforts to save the Richmond Mansion were unsuccessful, and some might say the same in regard to mitigating the threat of urban renewal. However, the society has succeeded in other instances. Most notably, it purchased and restored the St. James Rectory on Ellicott Street. And in 1984, it arranged and paid for a replacement cupola on the former Brisbane Mansion, also known as the old city hall. The Landmark Society has also published a compendium of historic buildings, *The Architectural Heritage of Genesee County, N.Y.* Also each year, owners who have restored and maintained historic property are given public recognition.

More recently, city government has also begun to assume a role in saving Batavia's landmarks. In 1995, the Historic Preservation Commission was created to promote preservation of historic structures. This was followed in 2000 by the creation of a historic overlay district in the downtown area. The commission has designated over 40 landmarks in the community.

This chapter focuses on the successful efforts of private individuals, organizations, and the city government to preserve the historic landmarks that enrich the community.

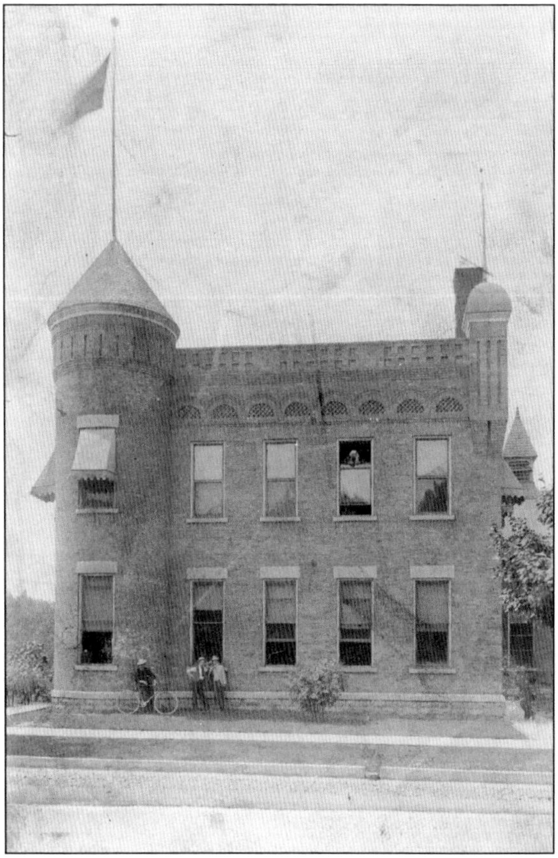

Photographed here is the municipal building at 3 West Main Street. Over the years, it was expanded or modified many times, but the original architectural style was always maintained. The building began in the mid-1880s as a small, two-room pump station designed by Henry Homelius for the city's water system. A few years later, he was hired to enlarge the building. The result is shown here. (Courtesy of GCHD.)

Over the course of time, the village aldermen voted to light the village streets with municipal power. The equipment was installed in the municipal building. A chamber for meetings of the aldermen, offices, and committee rooms were added. It's not clear at what point these various developments occurred, but Homelius was always the builder hired to do the job. As further time passed, the municipal building assumed this appearance. (Courtesy of GCHD.)

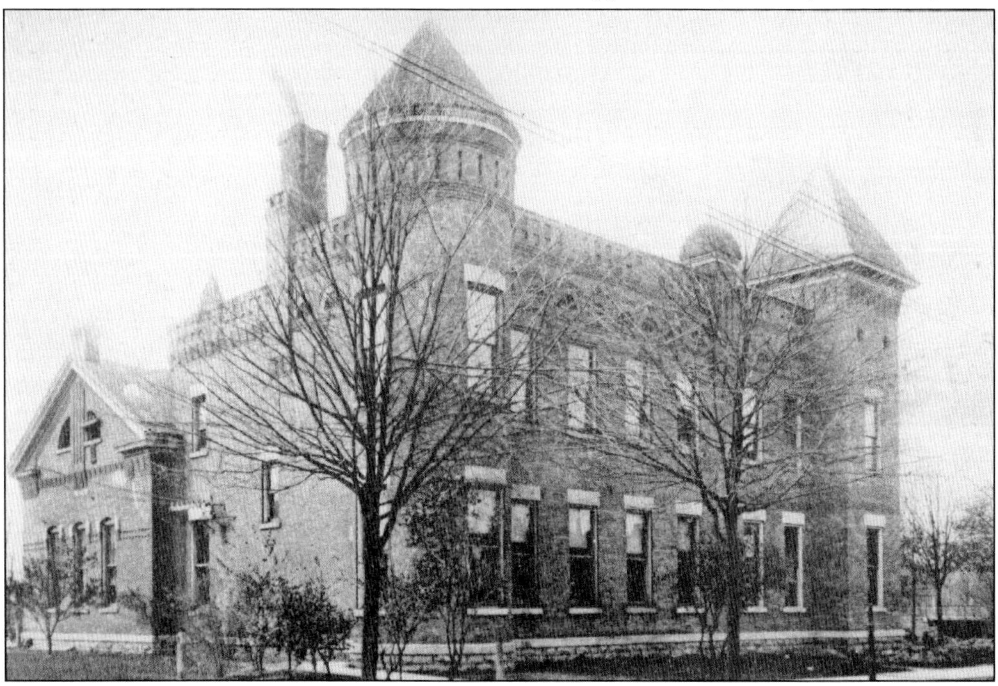

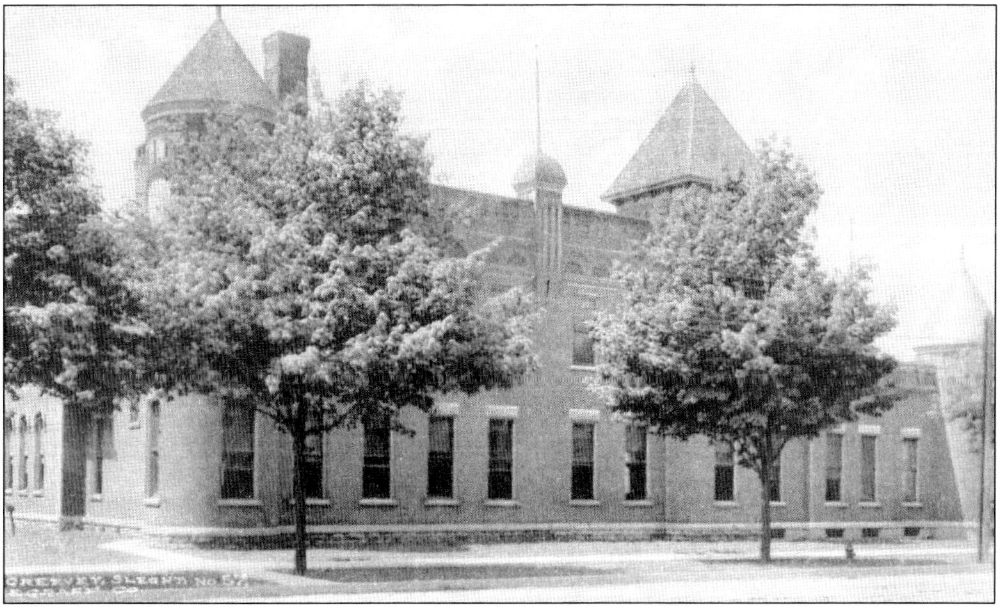

Eventually the municipal building served not only as a pumping station for village water, but it also had a large sewage collection tank in a basement area. Sewage was pumped from there to a treatment facility on Hillcrest Avenue. The author believes the right end of the building, as seen in the picture above, was the location of the sewage pump. (Courtesy of GCHD.)

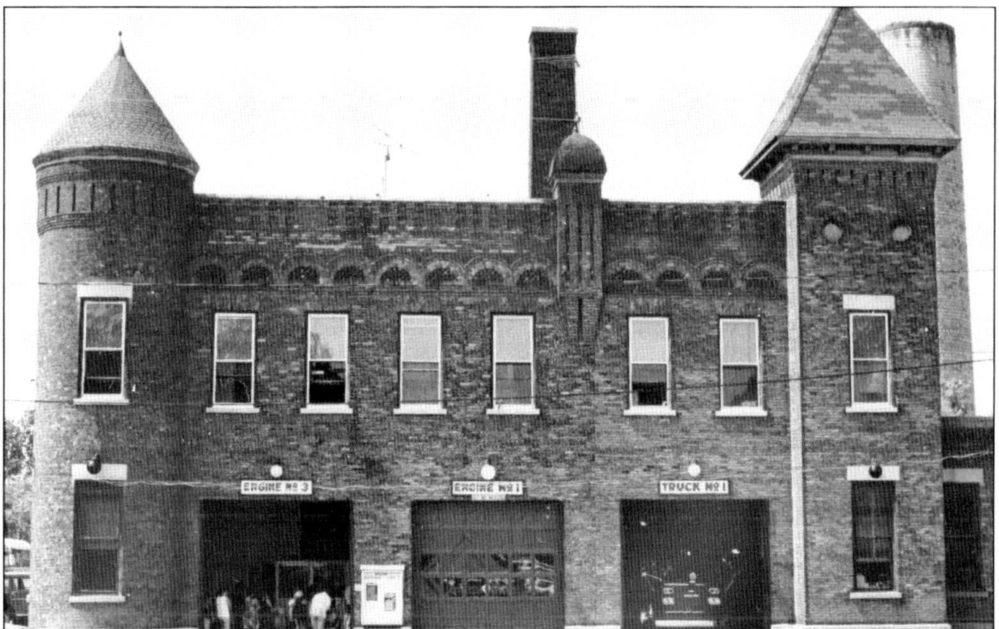

In 1915, an explosion blew apart the far right end of the building. An employee died in the blast, the cause of which was never clearly established. That end of the building wasn't rebuilt and an alternative structure for pumping sewage was constructed. About the same time, a new water plant was built upstream. Three decades later, the municipal building became the fire station seen here. (Courtesy of GCHD.)

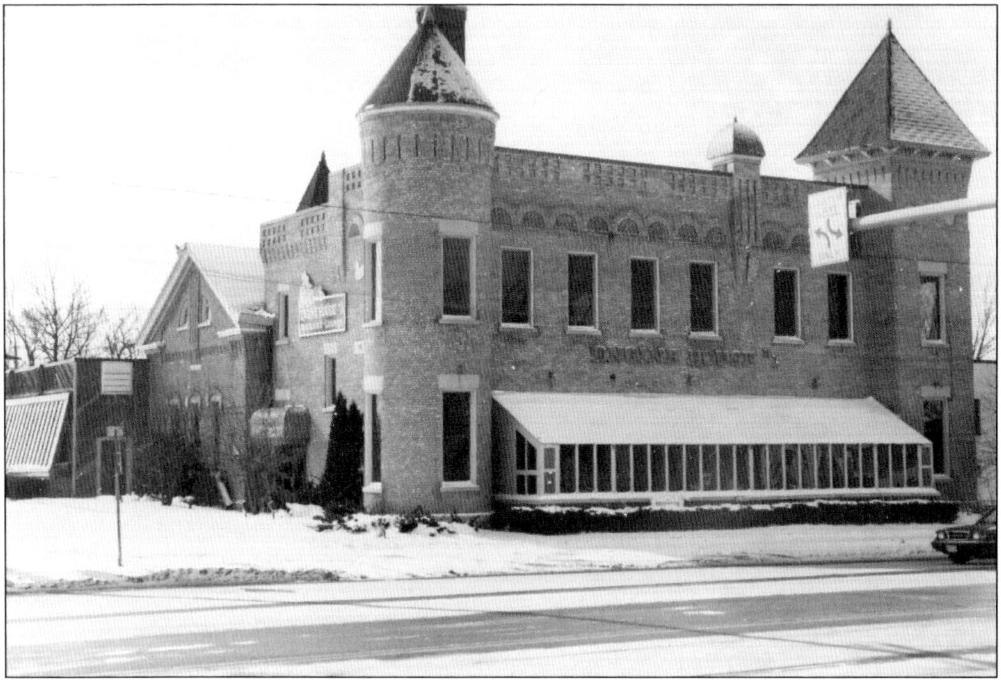

In the late 1970s, the fire department moved into new quarters on Evans Street and the building at 3 West Main Street was sold to private investors. A restaurant named the Engine House opened for business. It utilized a motif consistent with the building's previous use as a fire station. (Courtesy of GCHD.)

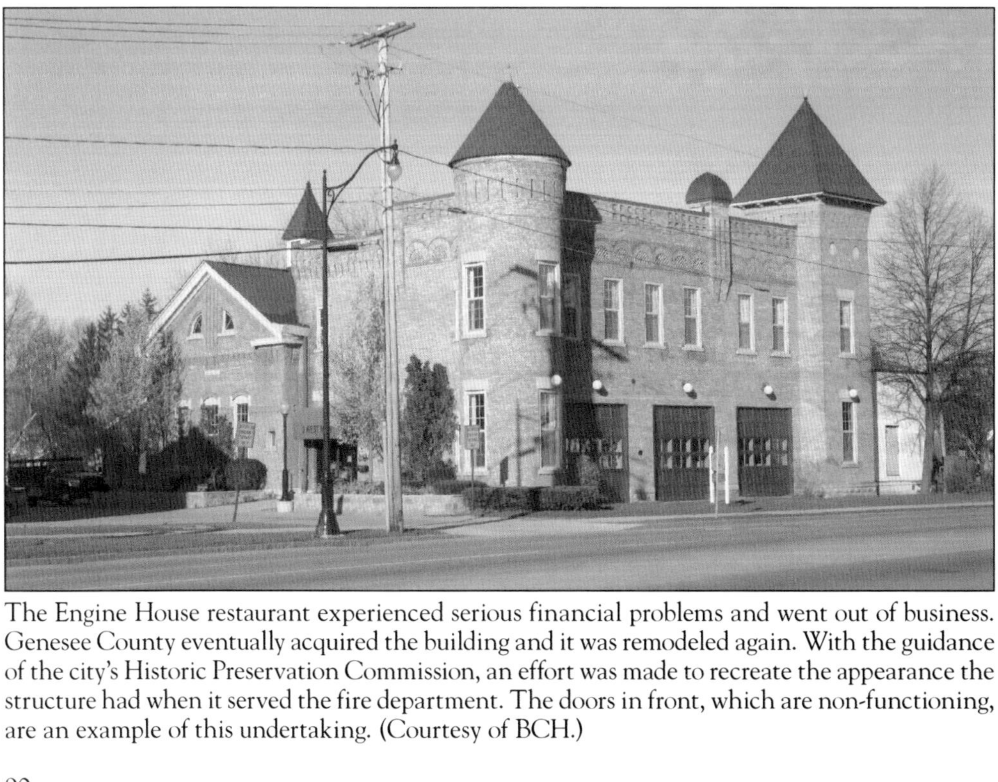

The Engine House restaurant experienced serious financial problems and went out of business. Genesee County eventually acquired the building and it was remodeled again. With the guidance of the city's Historic Preservation Commission, an effort was made to recreate the appearance the structure had when it served the fire department. The doors in front, which are non-functioning, are an example of this undertaking. (Courtesy of BCH.)

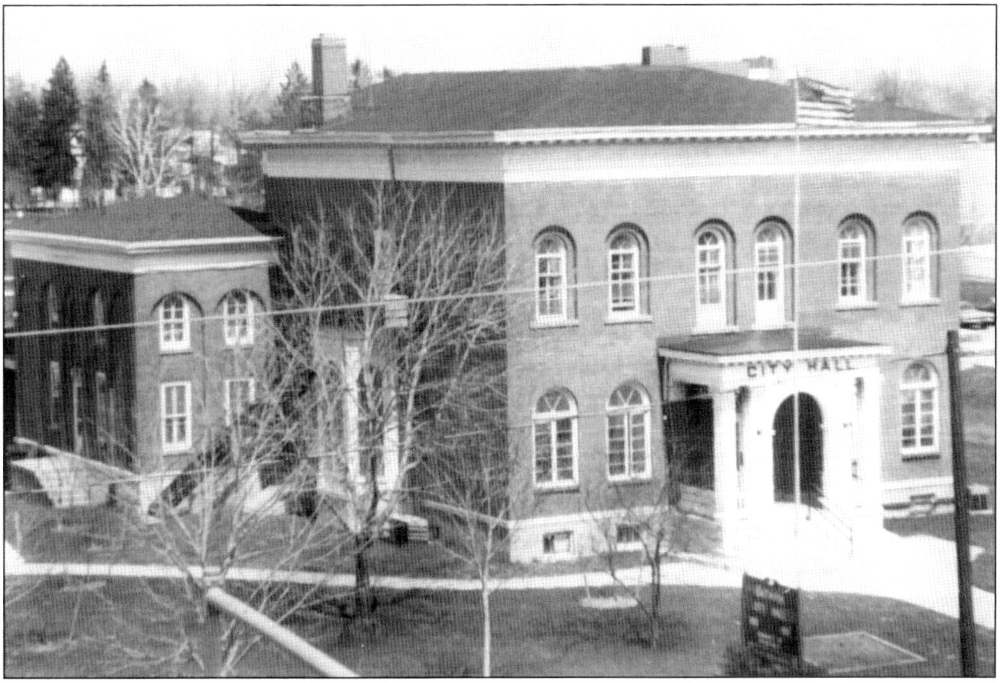

In late 1917, the city purchased the former Brisbane Mansion from James Brisbane, son of its builder, George Brisbane. In 1918, it became city hall. The structure originally had a cupola that provided light down to the ground floor. When the cupola needed maintenance in the 1960s, a decision was made to tear it off rather than carry out repairs. (Courtesy of GCHD.)

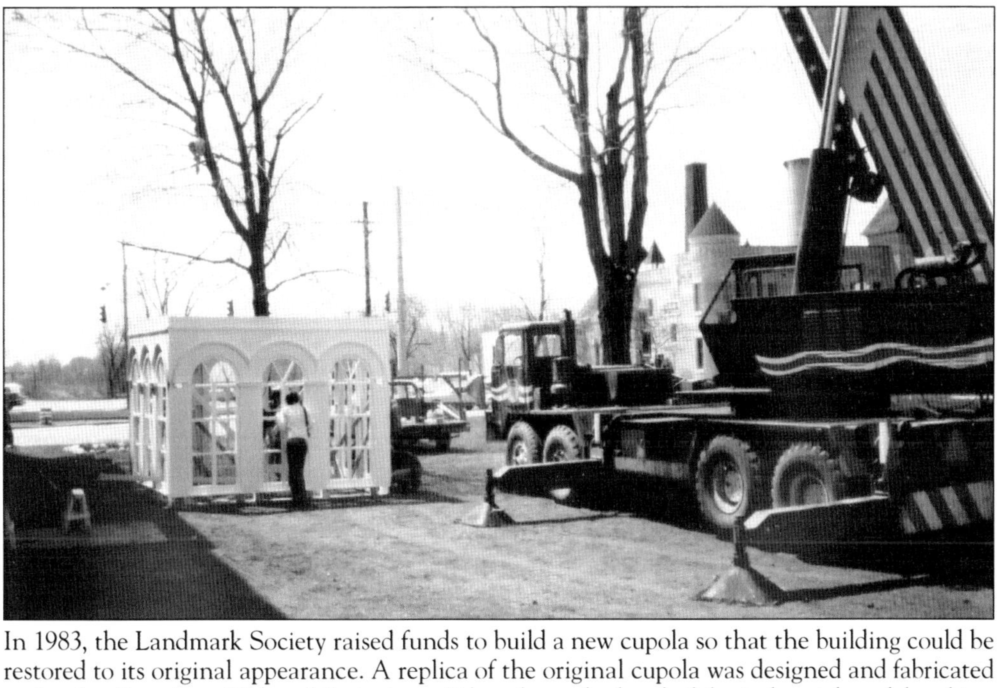

In 1983, the Landmark Society raised funds to build a new cupola so that the building could be restored to its original appearance. A replica of the original cupola was designed and fabricated under the direction of Edward Stringham. Edward was the head of the industrial model making program at Genesee Community College. (Courtesy of LSGC.)

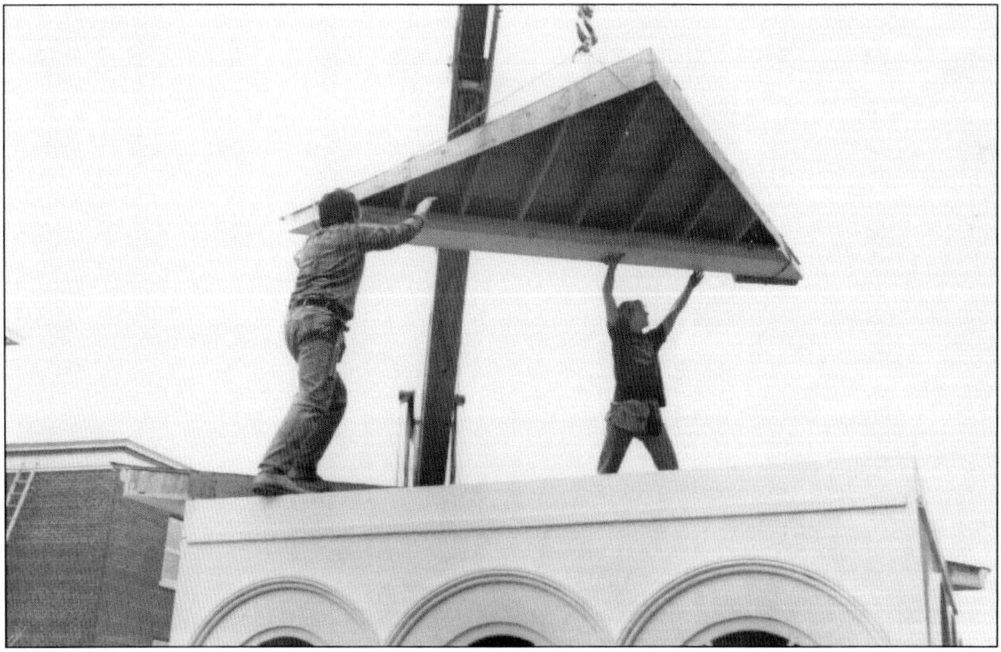

The pieces of the new cupola were constructed in the industrial model making shop on the Genesee Community College campus. Then these pieces were trucked the three miles to downtown Batavia where they were assembled with the help of a crane. Edward Stringham, left, and an unidentified student are shown guiding a section of the cupola into place. (Courtesy of LSGC.)

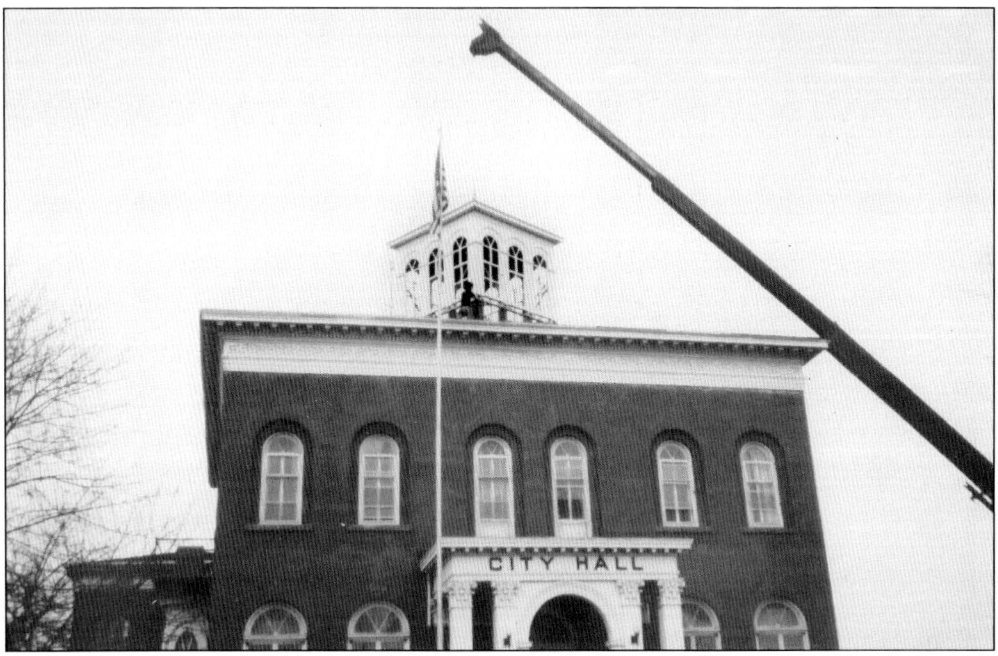

The crane was used to raise the assembled cupola to the roof. In order to keep costs to a reasonable level, large sheets of Plexiglas were used for glazing in place of the original glass panes. Liberal use of plywood was substituted for the solid wood panels employed when George Brisbane built the mansion in 1853. (Courtesy of LSGC.)

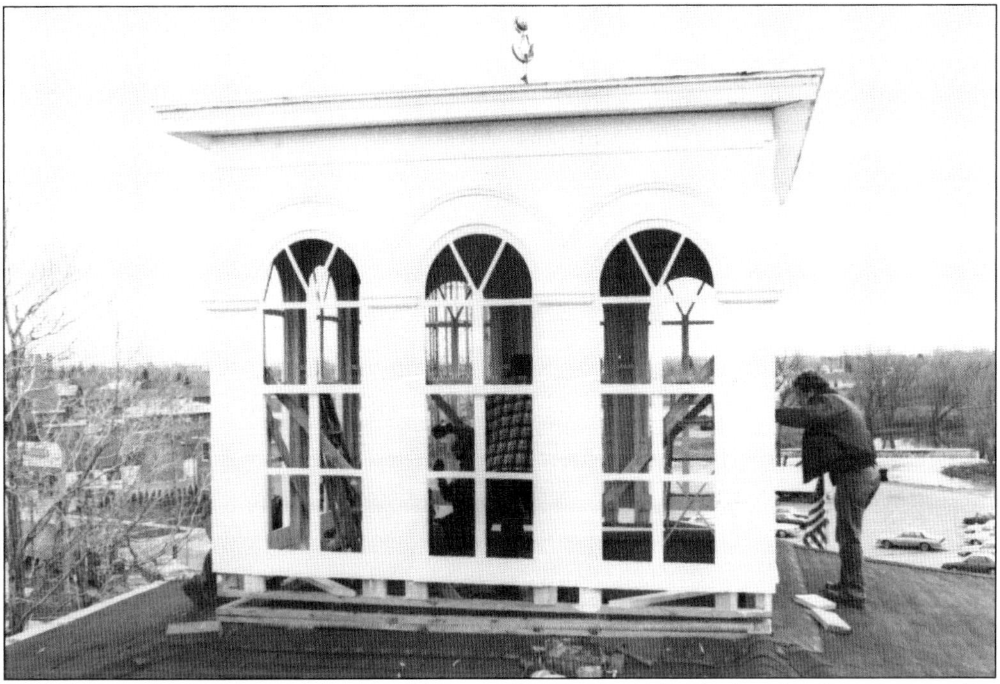

Seen here, the work crew is fitting the new cupola on a base that had earlier been prepared to receive the structure. Edward Stringham is on the right. While the original cupola stood above an open area that allowed light down to the ground floor, the floor was sealed off long ago and light no longer passes through. (Courtesy of LSGC.)

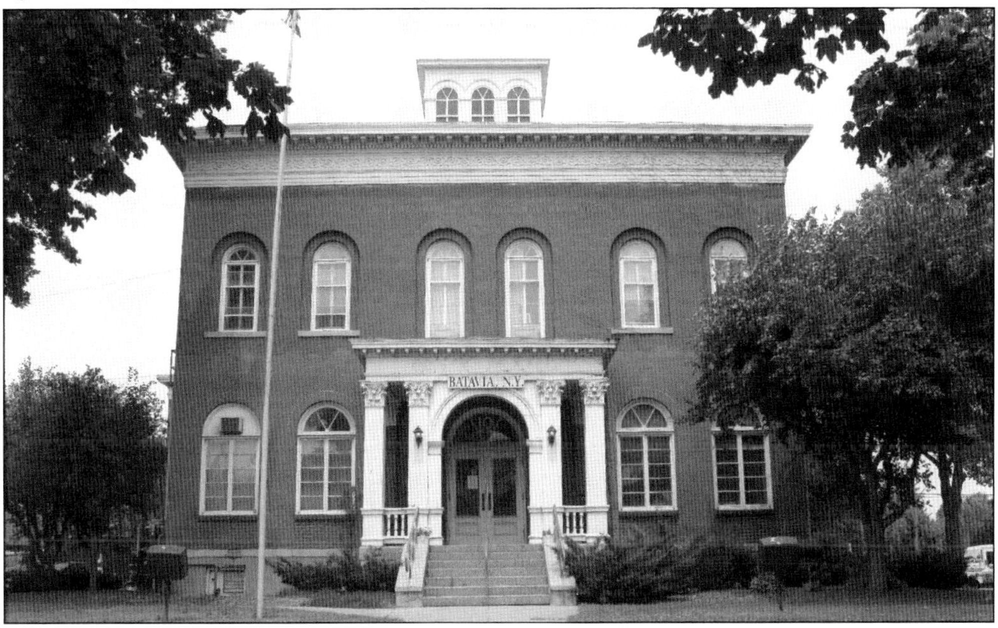

Several years ago, a new city hall was constructed. The primary occupant of the former Brisbane Mansion now is the city police department. An assessment of the building indicates that the whole structure will need significant work in the next few years if Batavia doesn't want to lose one of its most important buildings. (Courtesy of LSGC.)

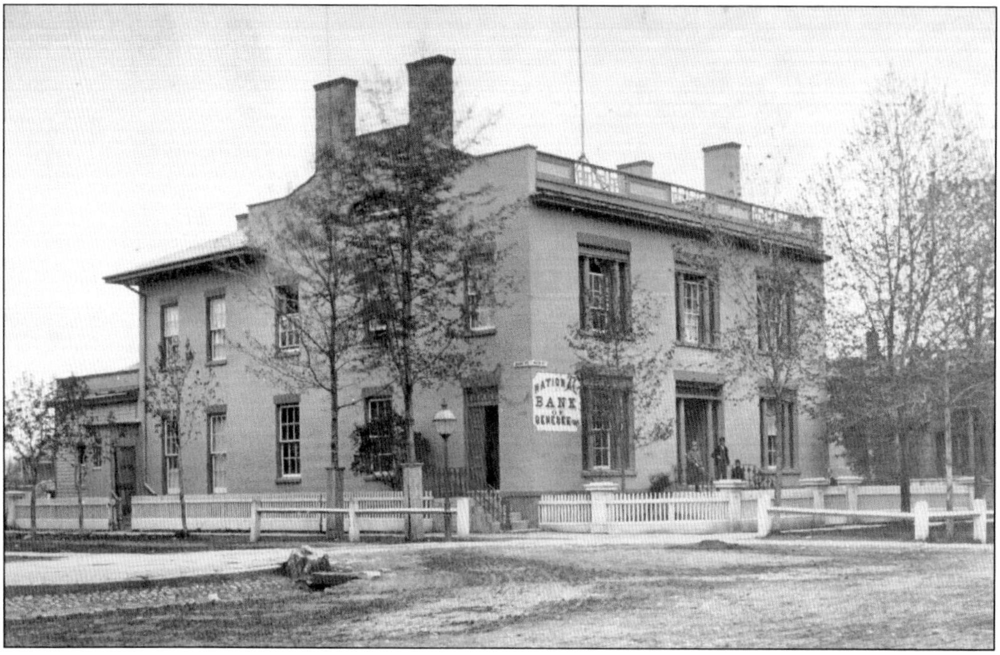

The Bank of Genesee was established in 1829 by Trumbull Cary and others. It was the first bank west of the Genesee River. This building was occupied beginning in 1831. The above picture shows the sides of the building best known to the public. Note the wood fence defining the edges of the property. The photograph below is a rare view of the building taken from the northeast. It may have been made when the neighboring Methodist church was about to be built in the late 1860s. Banking business was conducted on the ground floor, while the bank manager and his family resided on the second floor. (Courtesy of GCHD.)

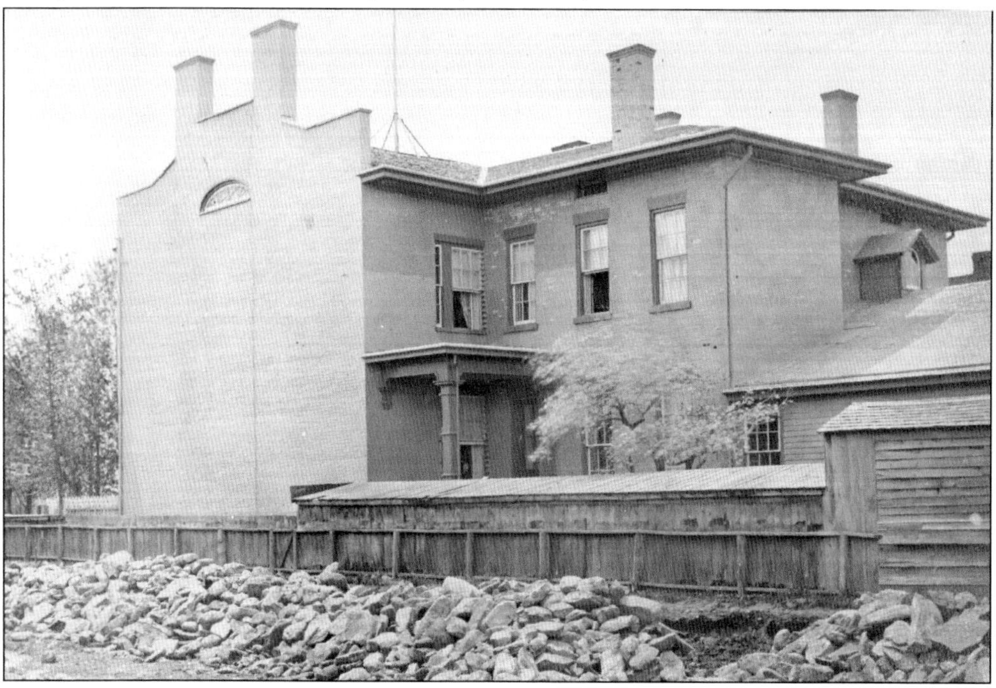

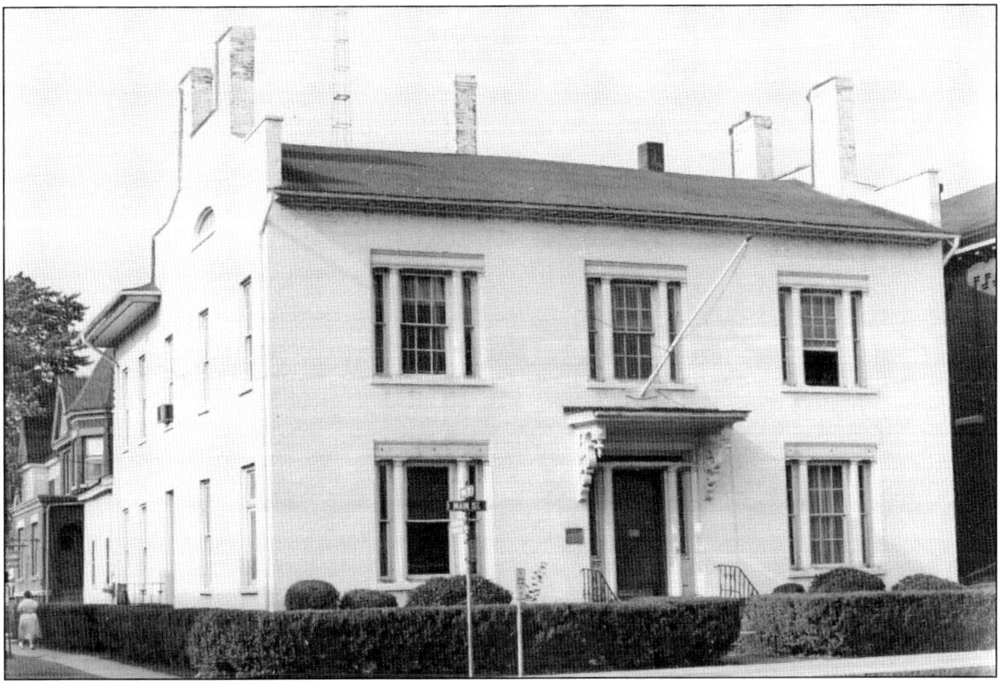

In the 1880s, the Bank of Genesee moved to a new location. In this same period, the newly formed Batavia Club leased and then outright purchased the former bank building. In this image is the building during the club's ownership around 1960. The Batavia Club prospered throughout the last century, but a dwindling membership led to its demise before the current century was a decade old. The building was then acquired by the Genesee-Orleans Regional Arts Council and restored close to its early appearance, as seen in the picture below. The building is now known as Seymour Place, in recognition of the many community contributions of Richard and Kathryn Seymour. (Above, courtesy of Elizabeth Rowsick; below, courtesy of BCH.)

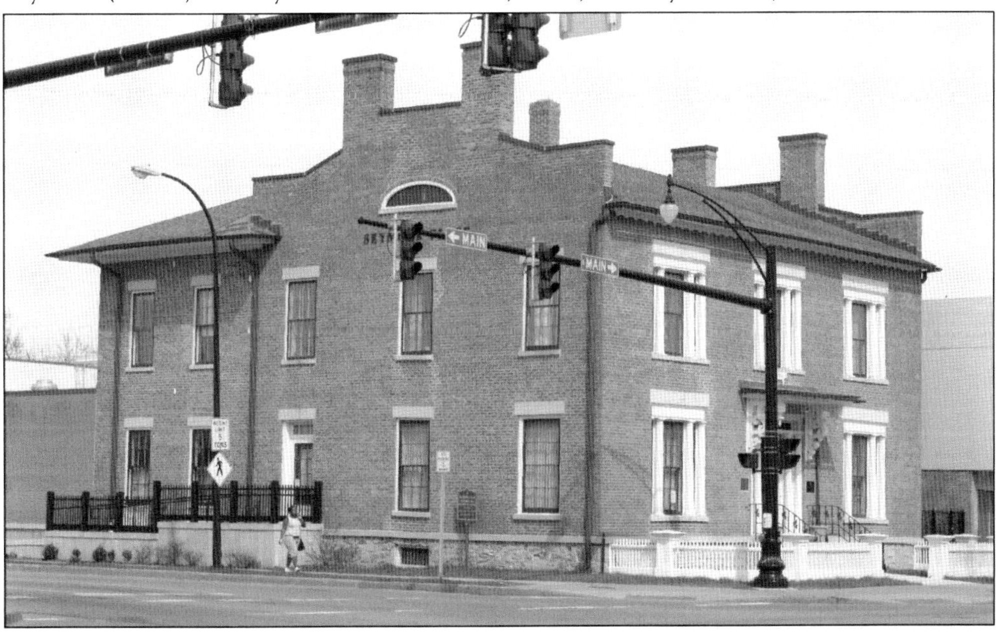

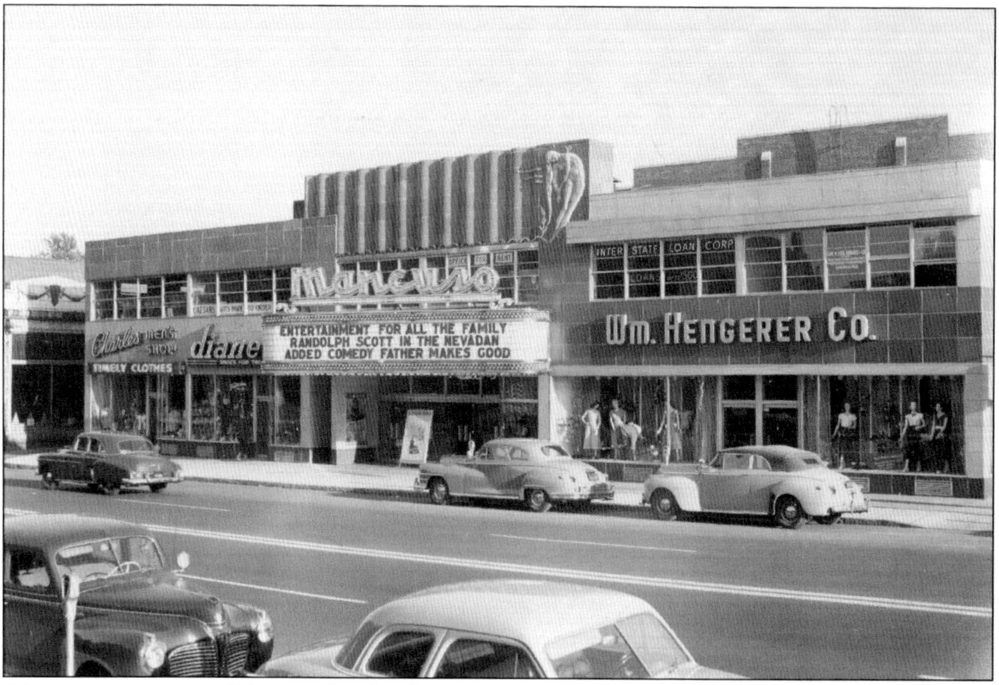

Above is the Mancuso Theatre shortly after its opening in 1948. It featured an electrically powered revolving stage and could seat 1,600 persons. The theater was used for operatic productions, band and orchestra concerts, and high school graduations in addition to movies. The walls were decorated by flat-sculptured figures depicting mythological characters. In 1973, the theater was divided into two mini-cinemas. More recently, the City Church has occupied the building. The congregation rebuilt the interior in a manner keeping with its needs as a church. The exterior, however, has been preserved as Genesee County's only example of Art Moderne design. (Above, courtesy of GCHD; below, courtesy of BCH.)

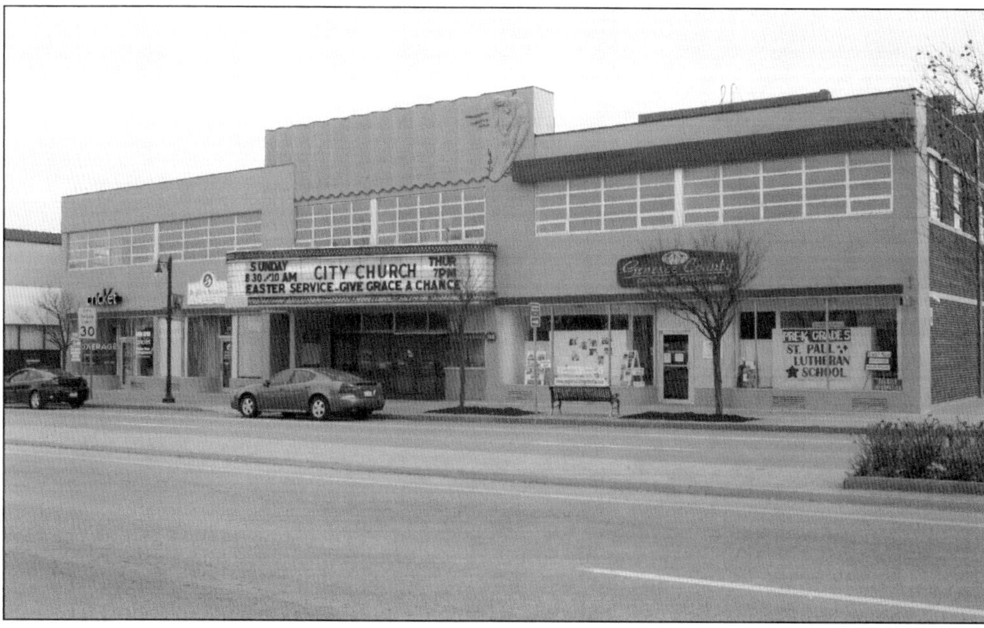

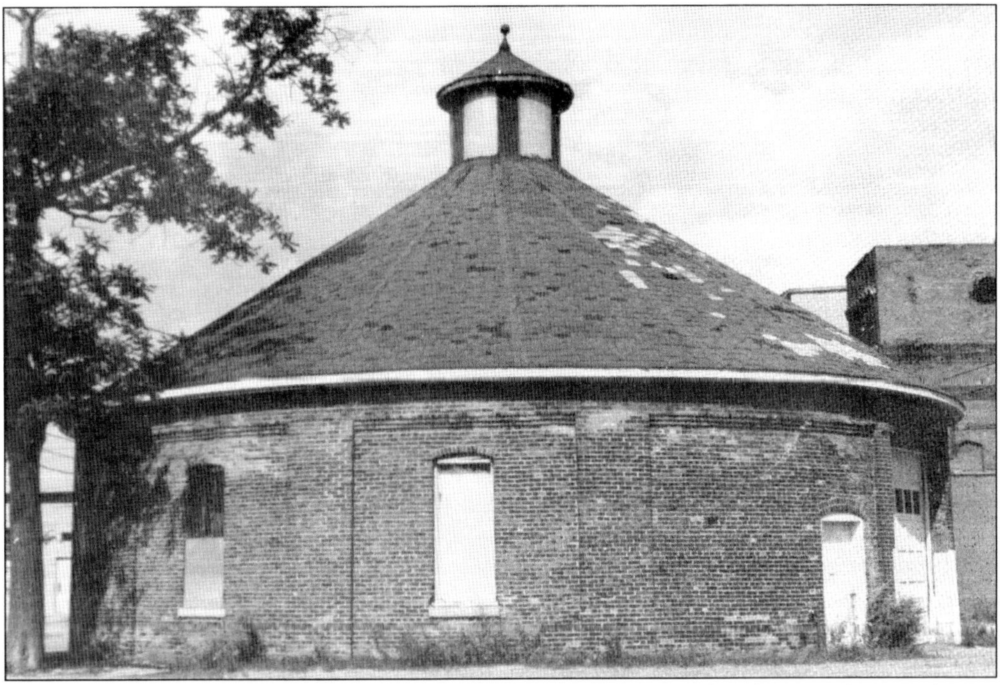

The streets of Batavia and some homes were illuminated by gaslights from 1855 to 1885. Two structures, such as the one shown here, were used to store gas manufactured from crude oil by the Batavia Gas Light Company. This gasholder, the larger of the two, was built in 1878 and had a storage capacity of 35,000 cubic feet. The picture above was taken in 1986 after the building had been used for many years as a warehouse facility. In an excellent example of adaptive reuse, the Evans Street structure now serves as a medical office for Dr. Anna Lamb. (Above, photograph by James Dusen, courtesy of LSGC; below, courtesy of BCH.)

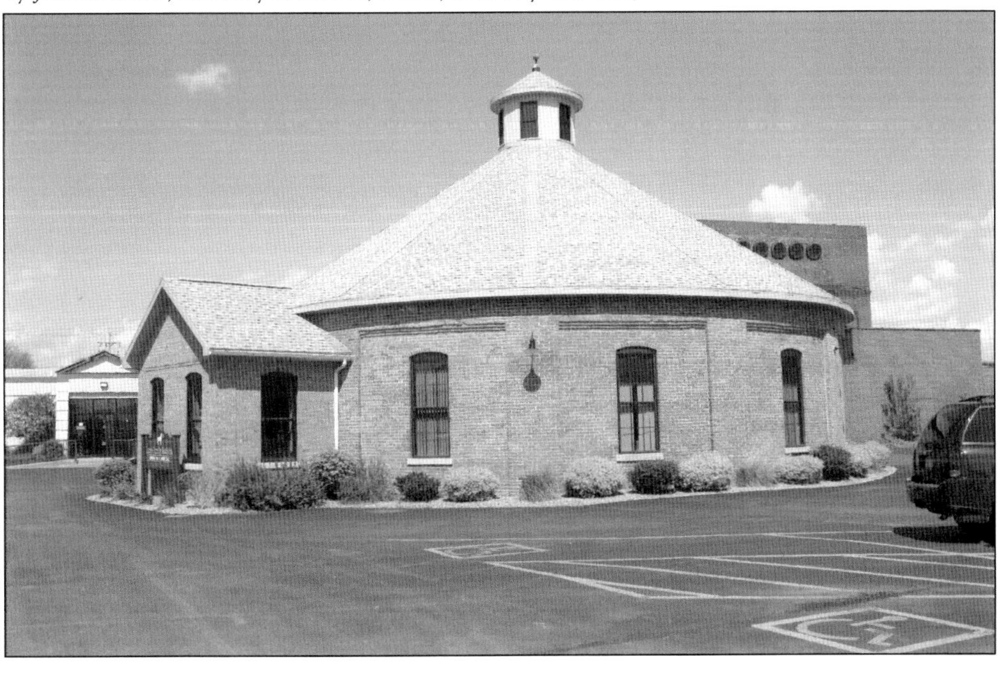

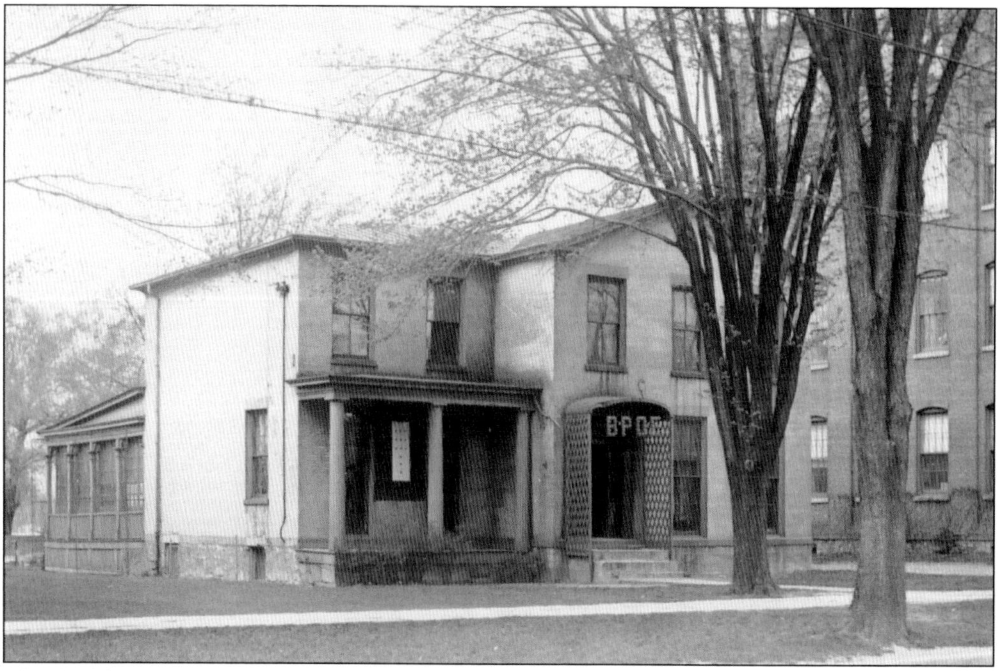

This building, located on Ellicott Street just east of the new Genesee County Courthouse, was constructed in 1836. Built from bricks salvaged from the first Episcopal church, it served as a rectory for the second Episcopal church. When the Episcopalians built a third church on East Main Street in 1909, this building was sold to the Elks. (Courtesy of GCHD.)

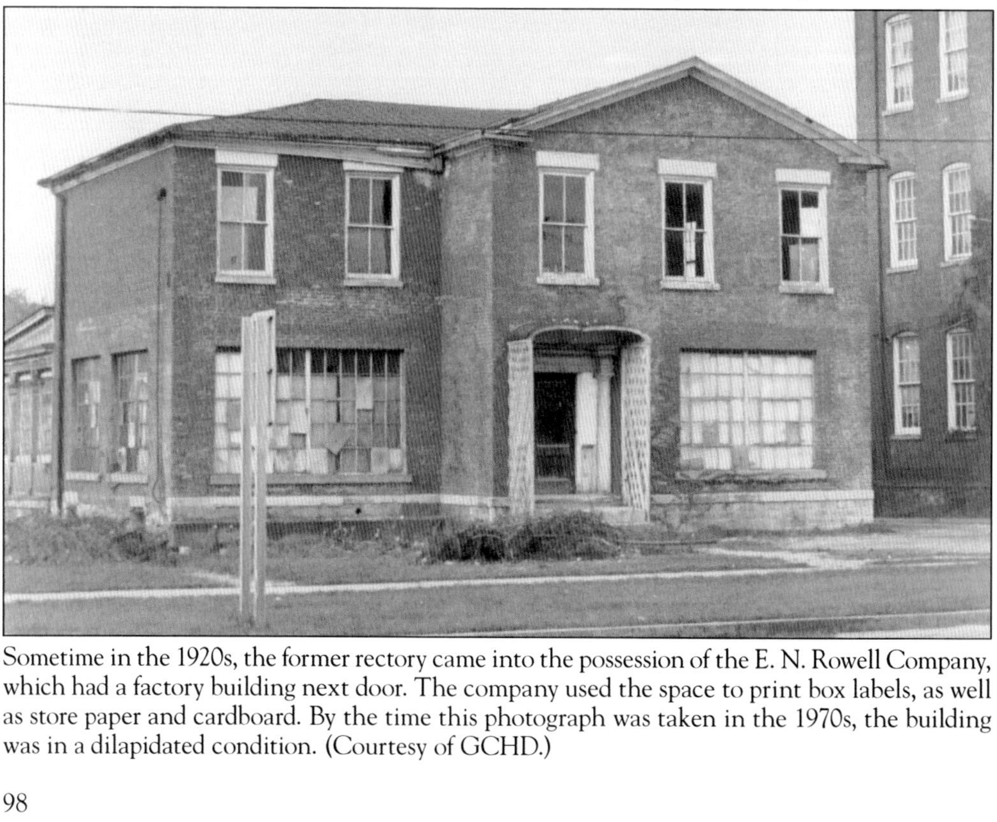

Sometime in the 1920s, the former rectory came into the possession of the E. N. Rowell Company, which had a factory building next door. The company used the space to print box labels, as well as store paper and cardboard. By the time this photograph was taken in the 1970s, the building was in a dilapidated condition. (Courtesy of GCHD.)

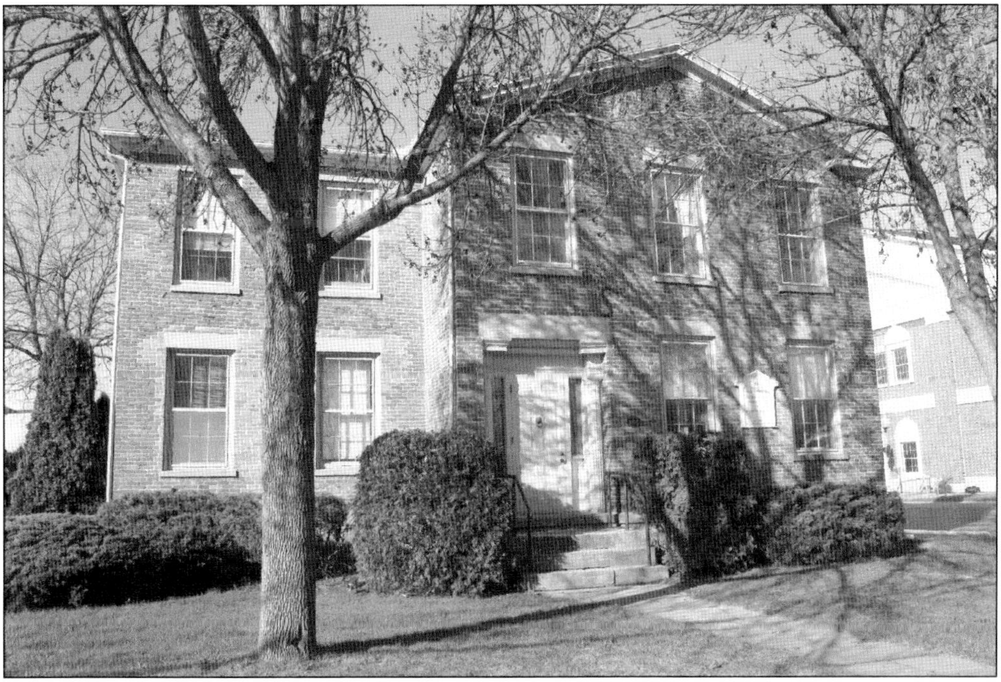

In 1979, the Landmark Society of Genesee County purchased the former rectory to save it from demolition. The Landmark Society then restored the building to its original appearance as much as possible. The structure was subsequently sold to local attorneys for use as office space. More recently, William Kistner, who has been investing his personal funds in further restoration, has owned it. (Courtesy of BCH.)

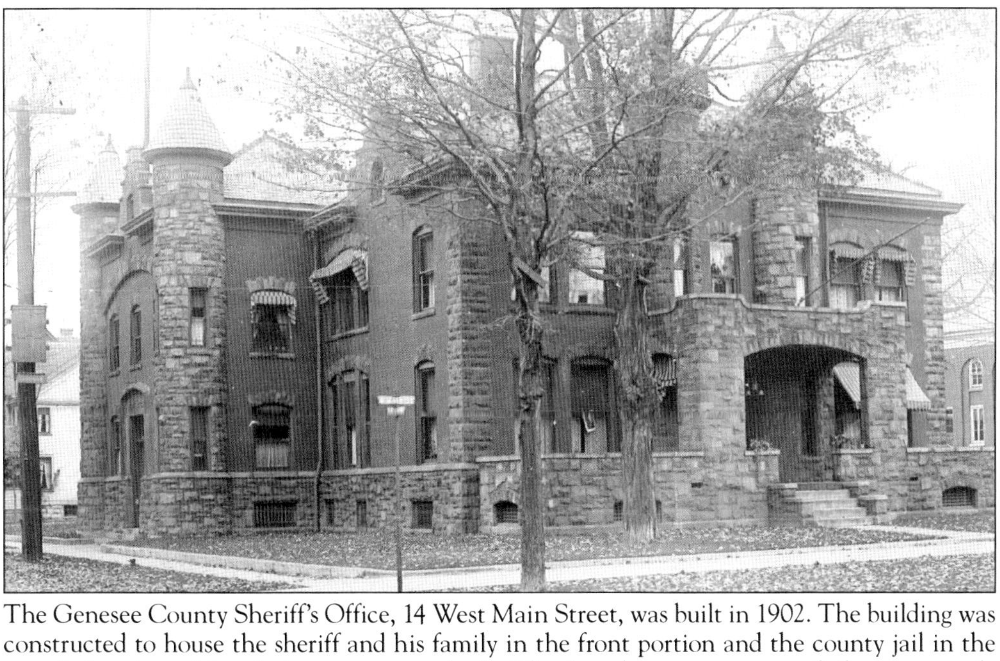

The Genesee County Sheriff's Office, 14 West Main Street, was built in 1902. The building was constructed to house the sheriff and his family in the front portion and the county jail in the rear. In keeping with a desire to preserve the building's early appearance, roof tile was recently replaced with a synthetic product indistinguishable from real tile. (Courtesy of GCHD.)

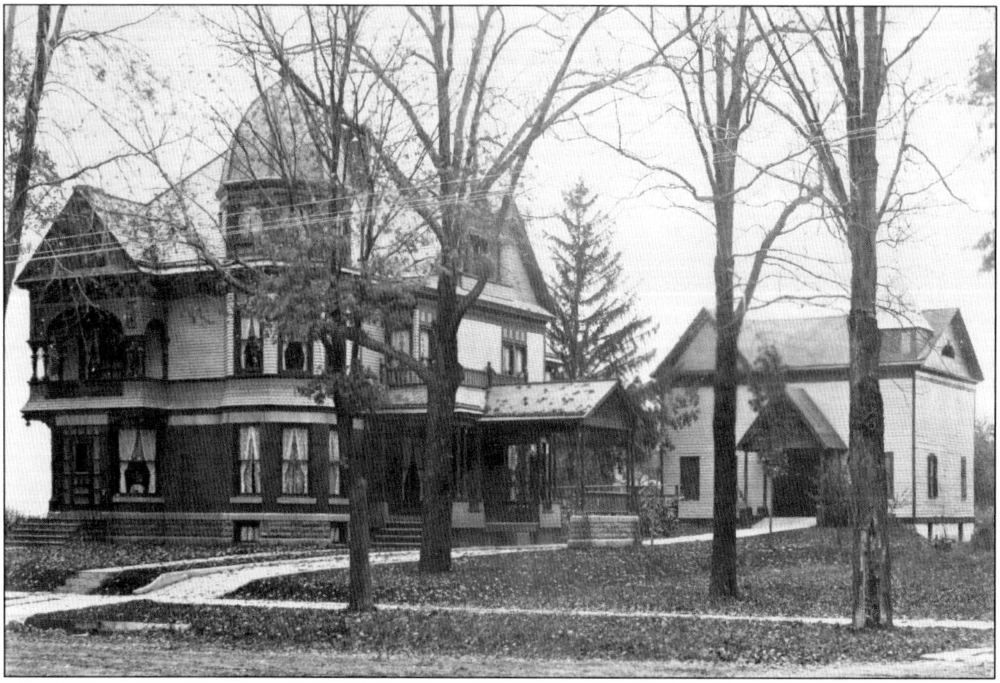

This house at 130 West Main was built in 1889 by George Weaver, a retired lumber dealer from Troy, New York. The building at the rear is believed to have been moved from the front of the property, where it had been the home of Judge Horace Soper. The current owner was recognized by the Landmark Society for his preservation efforts. (Courtesy of GCHD.)

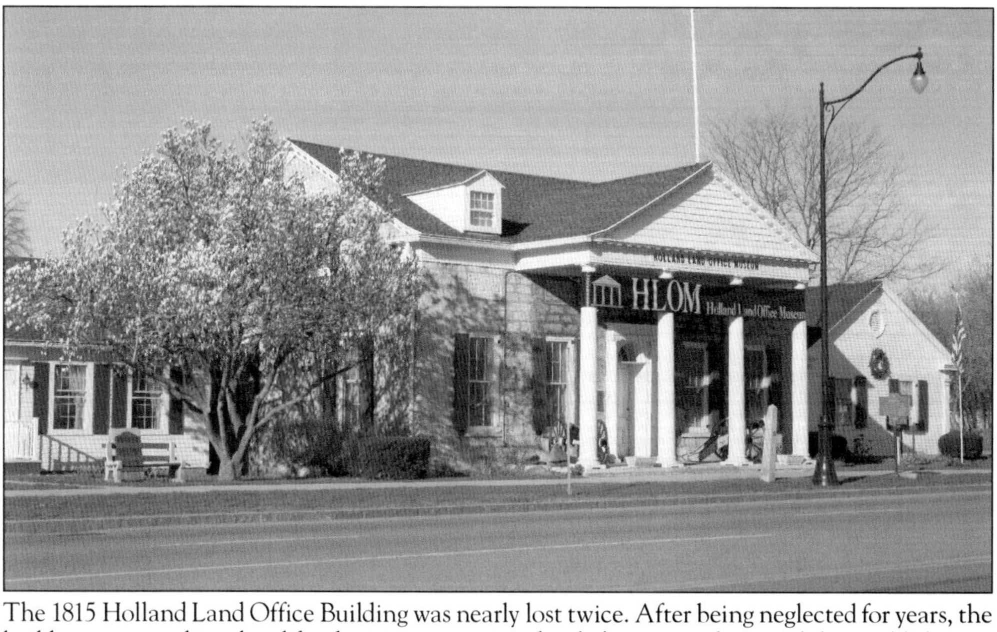

The 1815 Holland Land Office Building was nearly lost twice. After being neglected for years, the building was saved in a local fund-raising campaign that led to its purchase and the establishment of a museum in the 1890s. However, by the 1940s, the museum was essentially out of business. Fortunately Genesee County assumed ownership in 1948 and the museum was reopened in 1950. (Courtesy of HCB.)

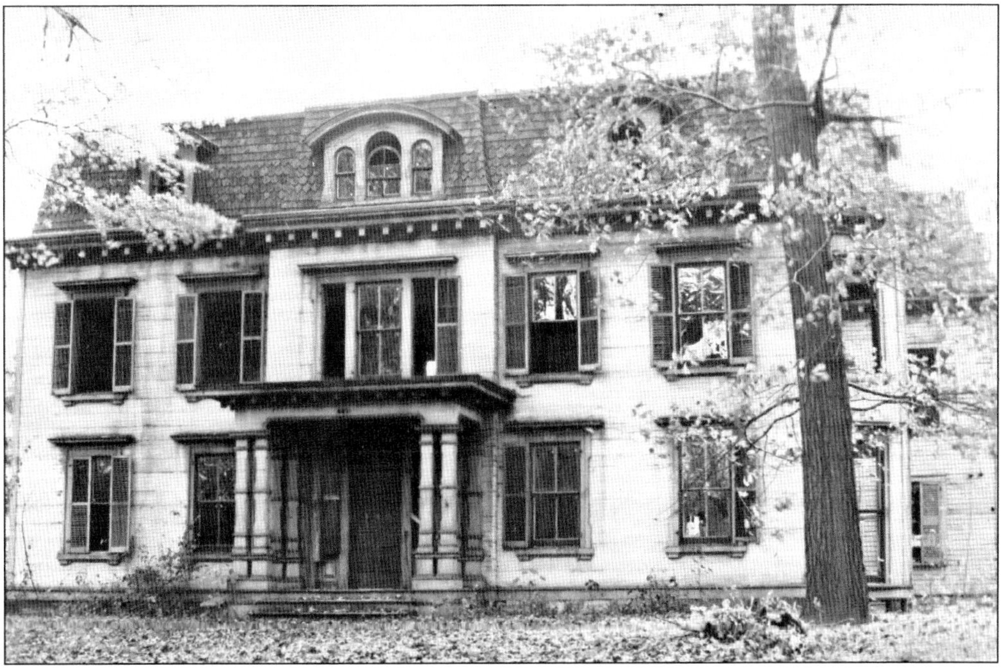

The Lay Mansion, located at 420 East Main Street, was constructed in 1820. Its original owner was George Washington Lay, a member of congress and also charge d'affairs to the courts of Norway and Sweden. The mansion was remodeled into its present appearance by Lay's son in 1874. The image above shows the building at its low point in the mid-1940s. When efforts to tear it down were frustrated by a 6-foot wide foundation and heavy beams, the owner of the building, the Farm Bureau, moved to rehabilitate the structure. The success of later efforts to return the building to its former glory is documented below. (Above, courtesy of GCHD; below, courtesy of BCH.)

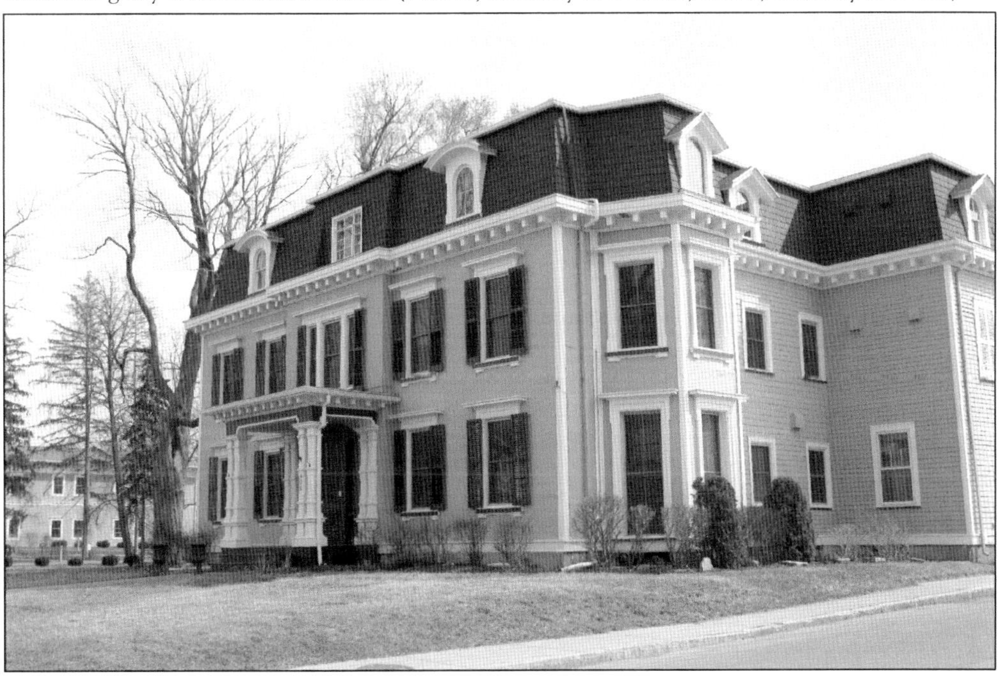

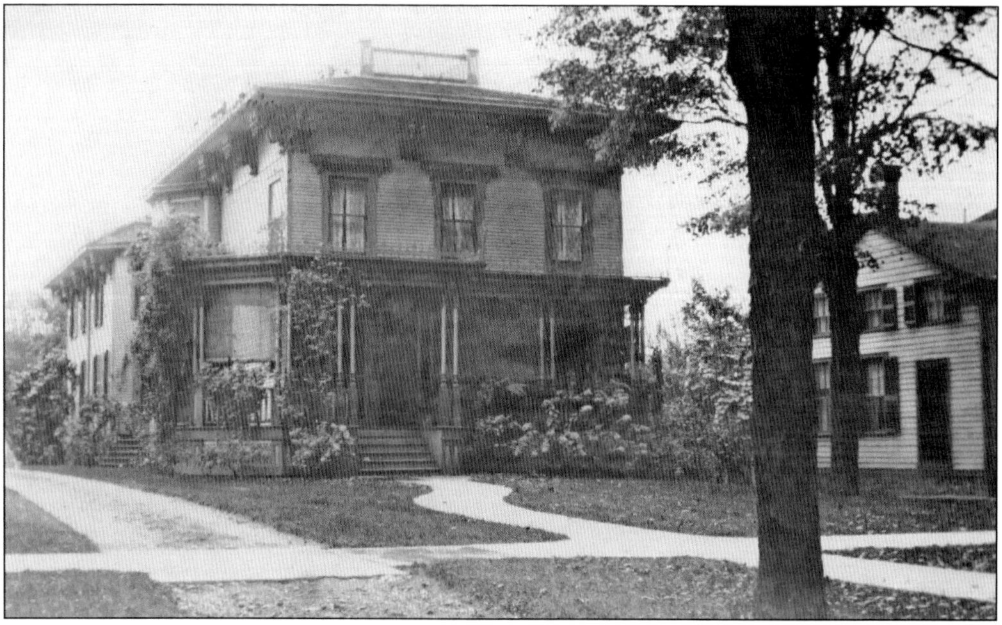

This home at 430 East Main Street was the residence of Judge Edward Washburn. Judge Washburn presided over the county court for three terms. He was also president of the First National Bank beginning in 1928. Edward and his wife, Frances, were the parents of Roweena Atwater, who lived just down the street at 424 East Main Street. The Washburns and Atwaters were among Batavia's most prominent residents at that time. Above is the Washburn house in about 1910. The Genesee/Orleans Council on Alcoholism and Substance Abuse eventually acquired both the Washburn and Atwater properties for adaptive reuse. The success of the organization's efforts with the Washburn residence can been seen below. (Above, courtesy of GCHD; below, courtesy of BCH.)

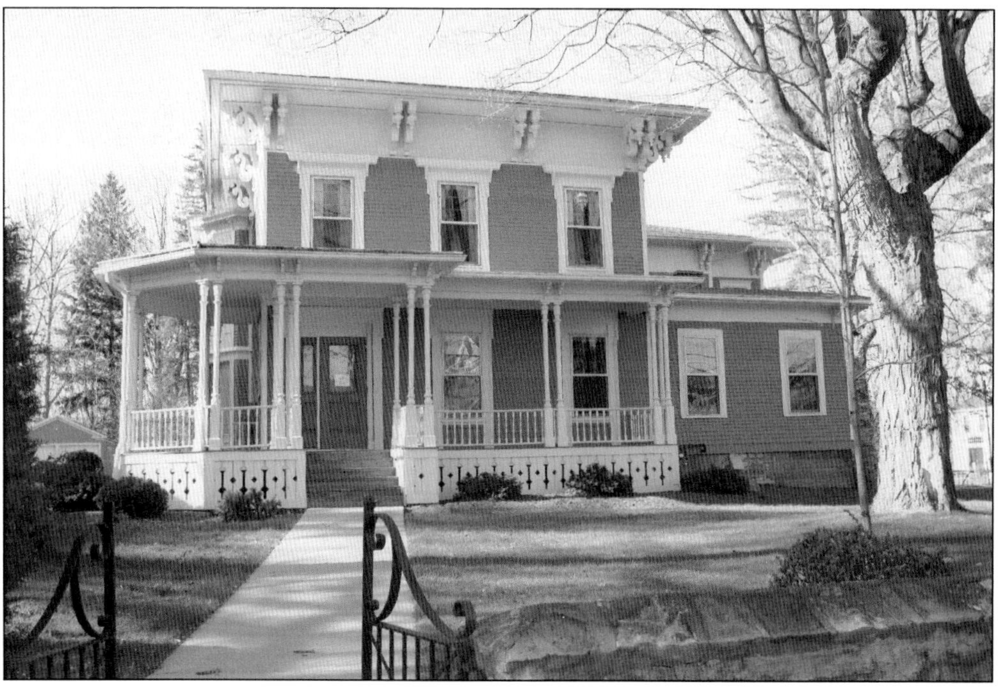

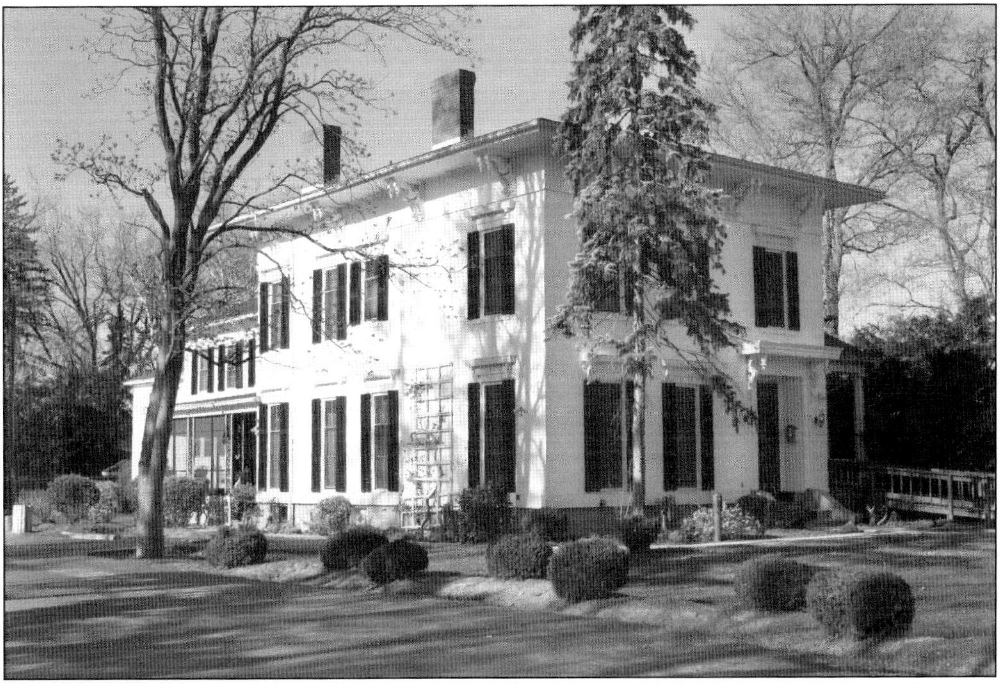

Above is the former Atwater house at 424 East Main Street. The house was probably built in two stages beginning with a west wing about 1830, eventually followed by the addition of the other sections. Before its acquisition by the Genesee/Orleans Council on Alcoholism and Substance Abuse, it had been the residence of Edward and Roweena Atwater. Edward succeeded his father-in-law, Edward Washburn, as president of the First National Bank. (Courtesy of BCH.)

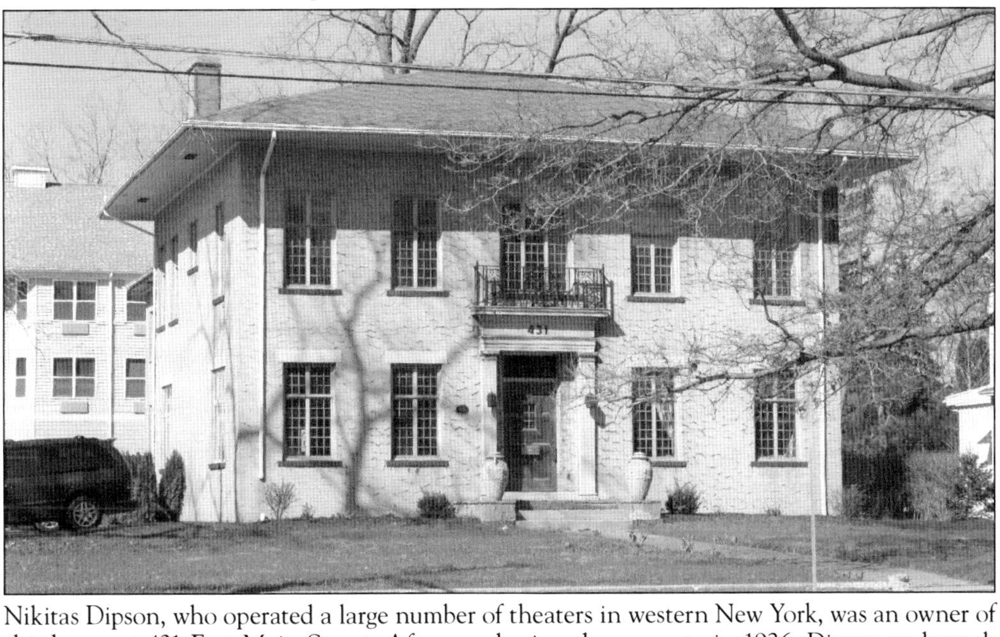

Nikitas Dipson, who operated a large number of theaters in western New York, was an owner of this house at 431 East Main Street. After purchasing the property in 1926, Dipson undertook alterations that dramatically changed its appearance. For example, he added the stucco walls and tile roof. The building is protected as a designated landmark. (Courtesy of HCB.)

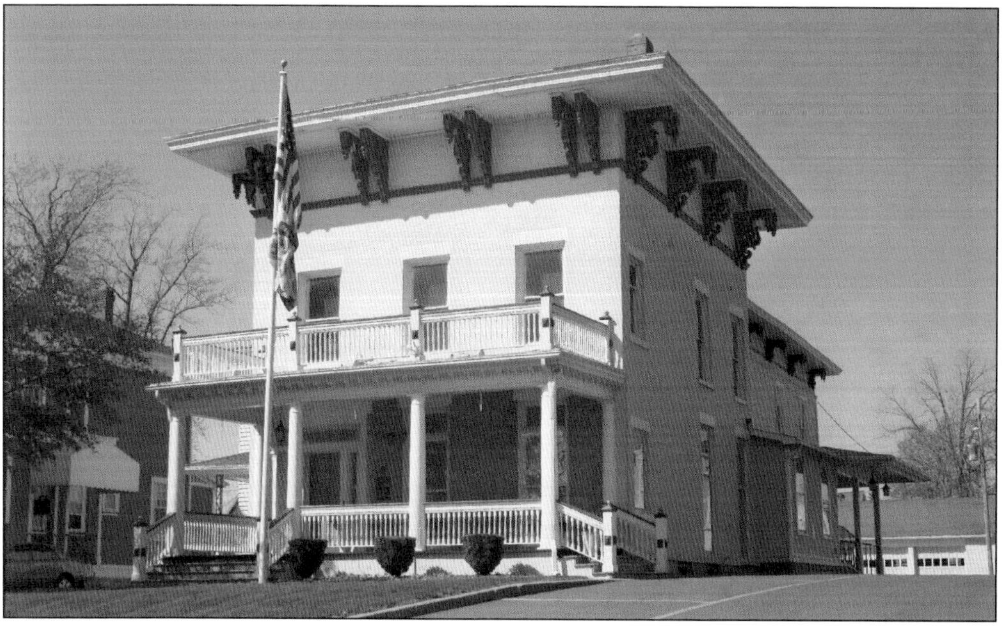

This building at 403 East Main Street was erected in the 1850s. About 1935, it was purchased by Harry Turner who previously had been using the former Cary Mansion for his mortuary business. The structure has lost its cupola, but otherwise the Turner mortuary owners have successfully retained the building's Italianate features. (Courtesy of BCH.)

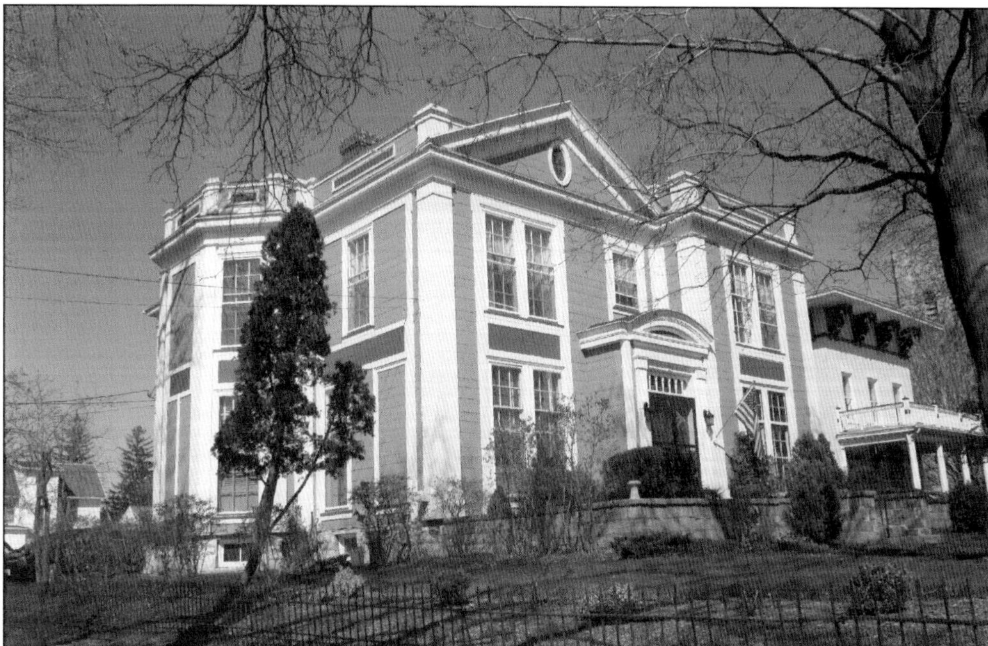

Another example of private ownership and historic preservation is this building at 401 East Main Street. Tax assessment records indicate an 1890 construction date. Once a large home, it now houses several apartments and a dentist's office. Roughly double the size of an average house, it has 4,932 square feet of floor space. (Courtesy of HCB.)

Six

Monuments and Other Public Art

Monuments and other public art in Batavia have had a mixed history. Some examples have been created by local talent, such as the murals by Vincenzo DelPlato. Other works have been the product of artists from afar, like the bust of the veiled woman that is displayed in the Genesee County History Department. Some have been well received, the Soldiers and Sailors Monument for example, but others have not, such as the sculpture that once stood outside Genesee Country Mall and that, for all practical purposes, was banished from the community. Some have had surprising longevity, like the bas-relief of a naked woman on the facade of the Mancuso Theatre that has survived the building's conversion into a church. Others have been relatively short-lived, such as DelPlato's celebrated mural at the corner of Ellicott and Liberty Streets. Not many years after its creation, it was painted over.

The fate of at least one piece of public art is an unsolved mystery. For nearly 40 years, the Woman's Christian Temperance Union fountain featuring a statue of Hebe stood at the intersection of Main and Jackson Streets. When Main Street was widened, the fountain was removed with an apparent intent of placing it elsewhere, but it disappeared. Some suspect that it went into a World War II scrap drive.

One of the most unusual monuments is the statue of William Morgan in the historic Batavia Cemetery. It's abnormal in the sense that there is no body since Morgan's remains were never found or, at least, no remains that could be positively identified as his. William Morgan had promised to reveal secrets of the Masonic orders and it was widely thought that he was murdered by Masons to protect those secrets. His murder spawned an anti-Masonic political movement that culminated with the erection of this monument more than half a century afterwards.

Perhaps the most regretful story concerns the Bessie Potter Vonnoh sculpture donated to the city in 1931. After years of neglect and vandalism, it was retrieved by the donating family and given instead to the Memorial Art Gallery in Rochester.

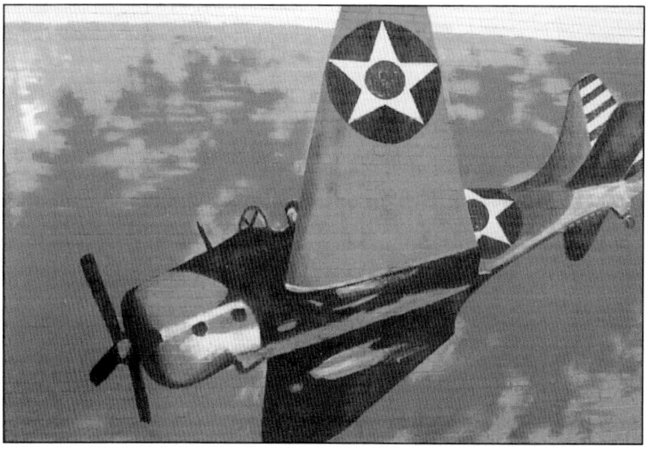

This and the following three murals are all the work of Vincenzo DelPlato. DelPlato grew up on Hutchins Street on Batavia's south side. The south side is well known for its Italian and Polish heritage, and DelPlato's work usually tapped into that history. Perhaps this mural, painted on the building at 329 Ellicott Street, was meant to remember a fighter pilot of Italian or Polish ancestry. (Courtesy of LSGC.)

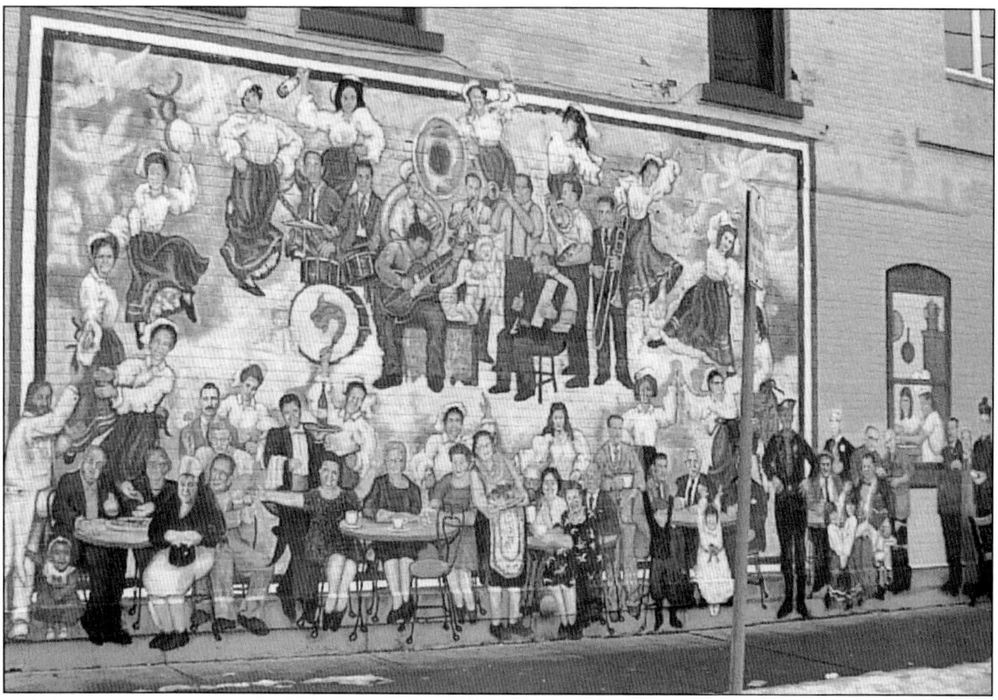

DelPlato's signature piece was this mural on the building at the southwest corner of Ellicott and Liberty Streets. Called *Heaven on Earth* by DelPlato, this mural contained the images of over 50 real people living on the south side. Unfortunately new owners of the building painted over the mural and it has been lost to posterity. (Courtesy of LSGC.)

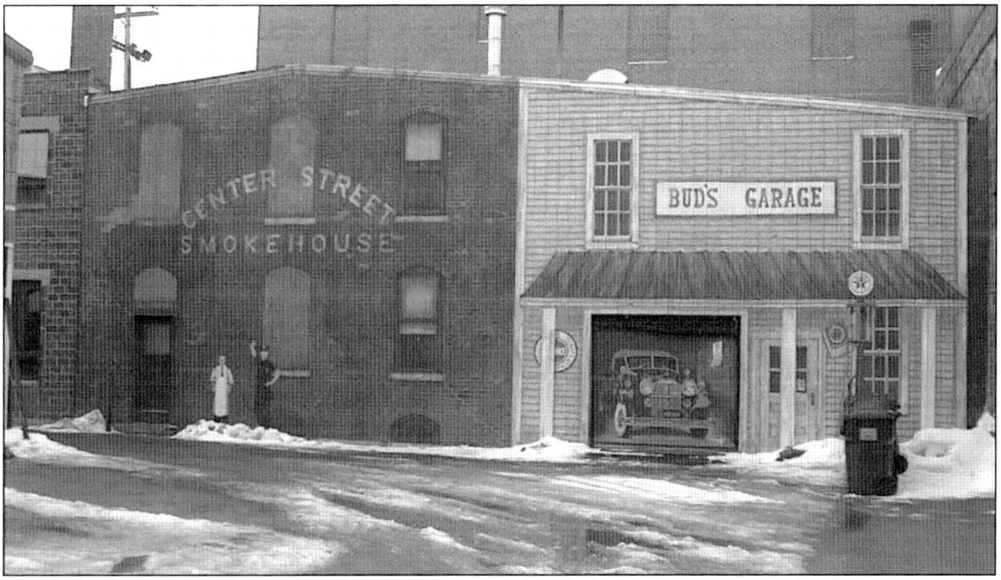

Jackson Square is a popular venue for musical entertainment during summers in Batavia. The square is centered in the only area that remains from the city's old downtown. Brick walls of older buildings stand on all four sides, perfect surfaces for the sort of murals DelPlato painted. Since this mural was painted, the Bud's Garage section has given way to a deck for the Smokehouse restaurant. (Courtesy of LSGC.)

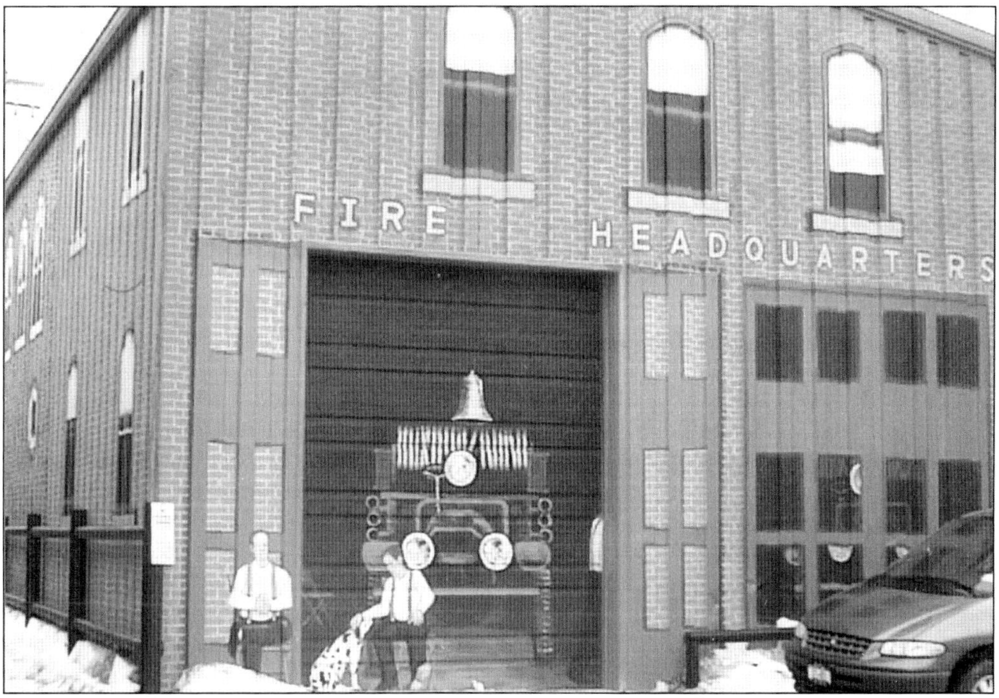

The mural seen above was painted on a building facing Center Street and backing up to Jackson Square. It appears to depict the fire headquarters that once stood on Court Street. The two figures in the mural would have been, in true DelPlato fashion, actual persons, but their identities are unknown. (Courtesy of LSGC.)

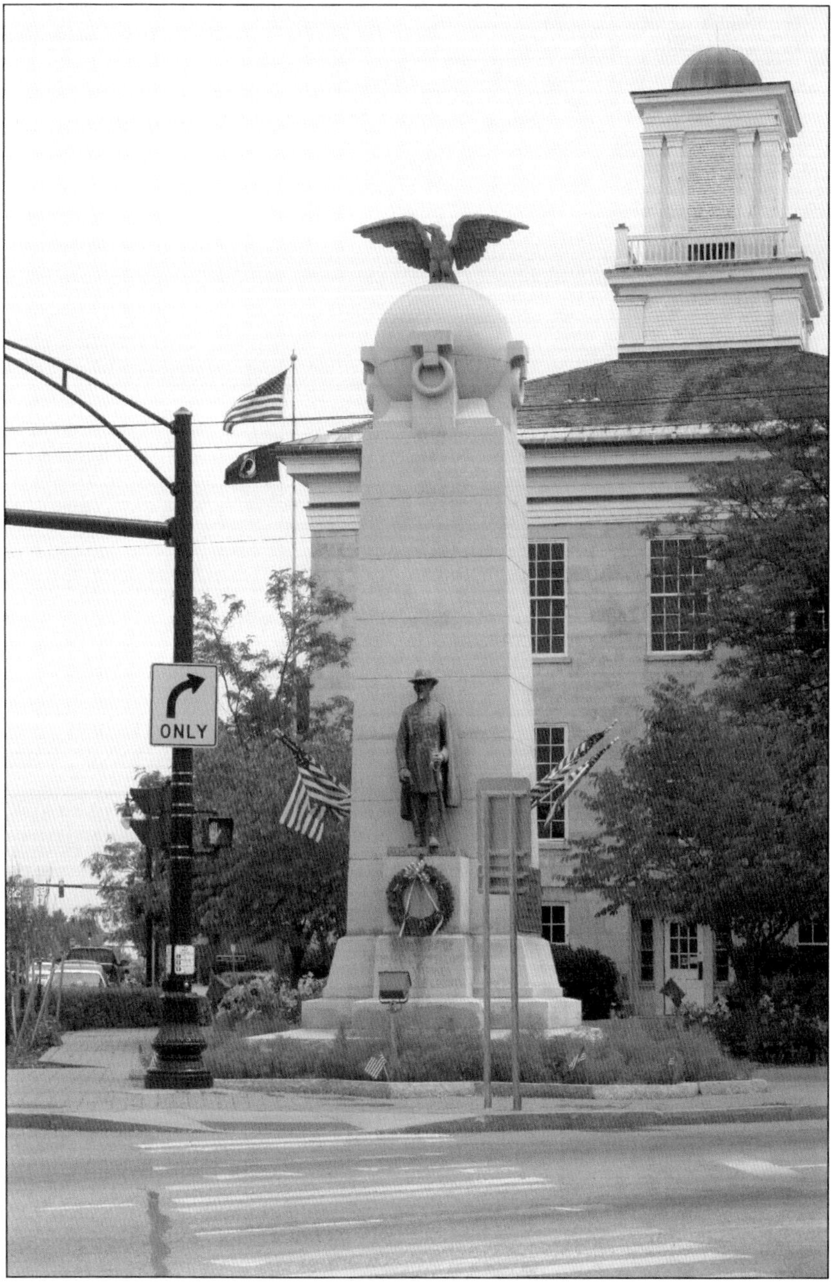

This is the Soldiers and Sailors Monument, more popularly referred to as the Upton Monument. The bronze figure on the front is that of Gen. Emory Upton, a Civil War veteran. The monument was originally intended just to honor veterans of the Civil War, but plaques for veterans of later hostilities have been added over the years. For many years, members of the Upton Post of the Grand Army of the Republic were the most active promoters of a monument. A fund-raising attempt in 1903 raised only $200, much of it from schoolchildren, and failed to meet its goal. A proposal in 1907 to provide $15,000 from tax revenue was voted down by taxpayers. Finally in 1917, voters approved a $5,000 donation in a ballot measure that provided funding for a new water filtration plant. The monument, costing $15,000, was dedicated in 1919. (Courtesy of HCB.)

Religious statues commonly have a prominent place in most communities and Batavia is no exception. This statue of St. Joseph stands at the entrance to St. Joseph's Cemetery. This cemetery, fronting both Harvester Avenue and Ellicott Street, was established about 1858 when the Rev. Francis O'Farrall purchased land for Catholic burials. (Courtesy of HCB.)

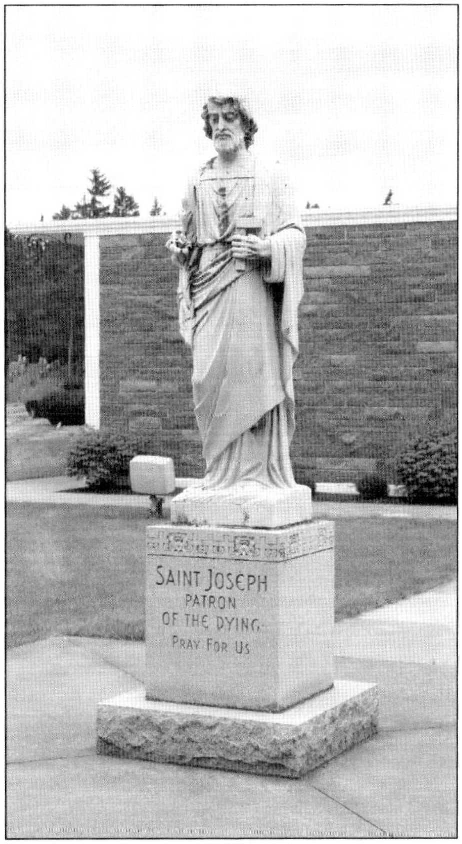

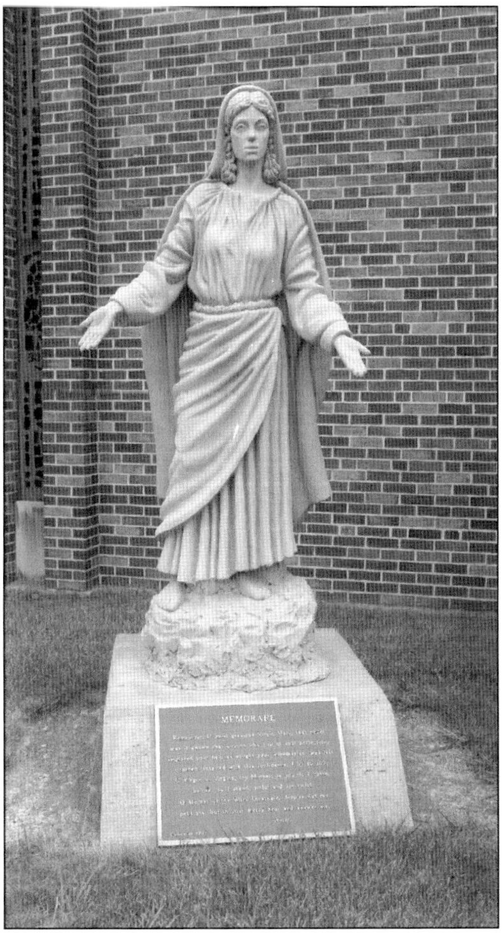

This statue of the Virgin Mary stands outside the west wall of St. Joseph's Roman Catholic Church on East Main Street. According to parish members, money bequeathed by Robert and Helen Sullivan was used to purchase the statue 15 or more years ago. The church itself was dedicated in 1970, a replacement for an earlier edifice. (Courtesy of BCH.)

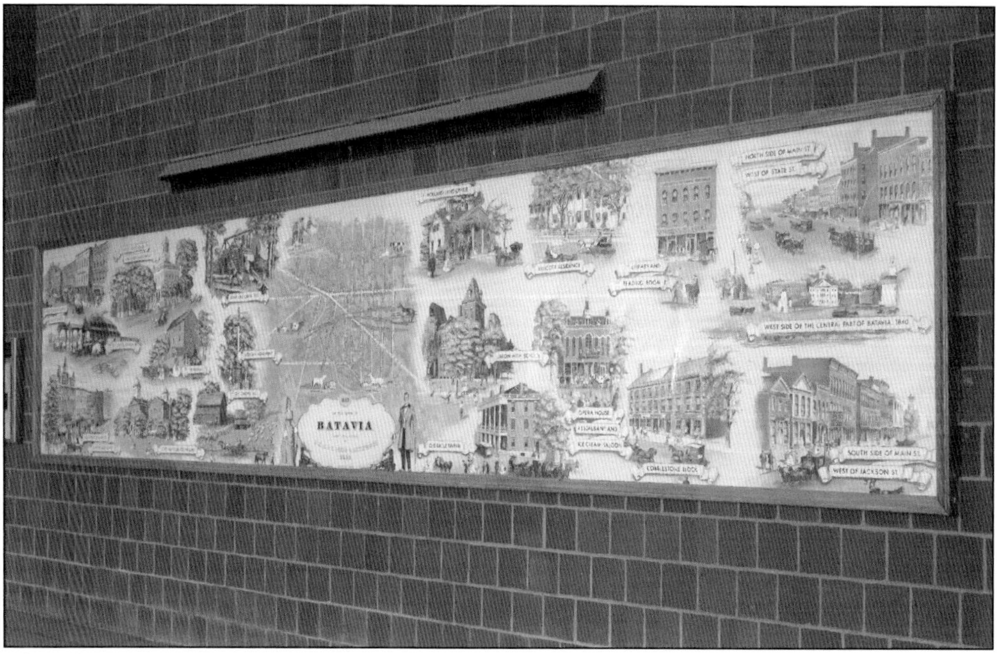

The Liberty National Bank formerly at 100–102 Main Street was expanded in 1964. Apparently at that time, this mural was attached to an interior wall. The bank building was razed in 1977 and the mural was donated to Genesee Community College. Today it is on display in the forum of the college as seen above. The picture below provides a close-up view of the center of the mural. It features a map, dated 1866, showing the village of Batavia. Unfortunately it also contributes to the confusion people experience regarding the two Batavias. The map is erroneously labeled as a "map of the town of Batavia." (Courtesy of BCH.)

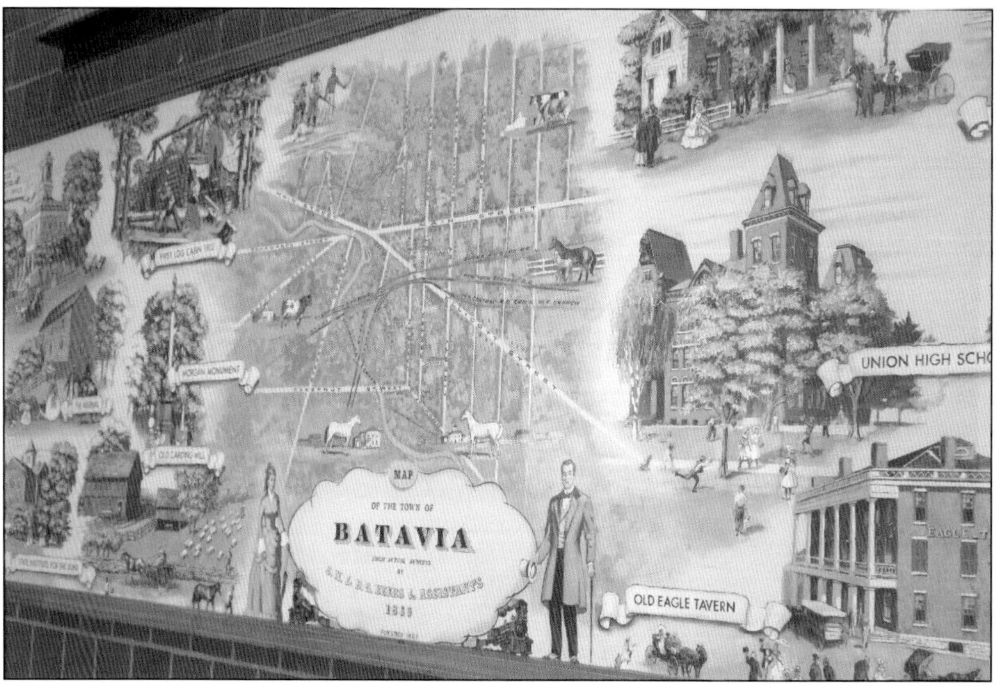

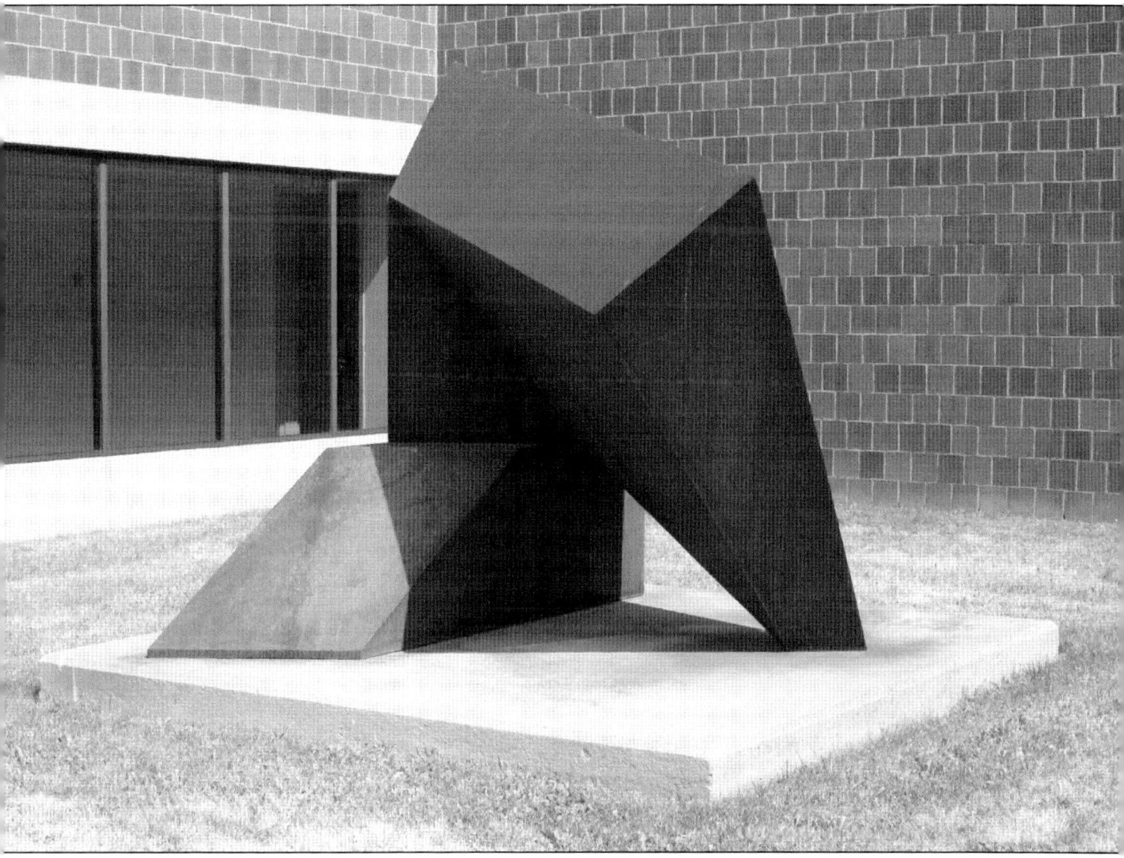

When the Genesee Country Mall was opened in 1978, this piece of sculpture graced the Main Street side along with a modest fountain. It was the creation of Henry Wilhelm. Clearly the attempt was to bring pleasure to passing pedestrians and motorists, but perhaps it was also intended to demonstrate to the world that Batavians understood and appreciated abstract art. However, the artwork was immediately the subject of critical comments. Originally a muddy brown, painting it a neutral blue didn't help matters. The college had become the recipient of other things once found on Main Street and this proved to be one more such item. The sculpture was shipped off to the college where it stands outside the Stuart Steiner Theatre. One doesn't hear much about it any longer. Since it lacks any identifying information, most students passing by probably have no idea about where the sculpture came from or why it is there. (Courtesy of BCH.)

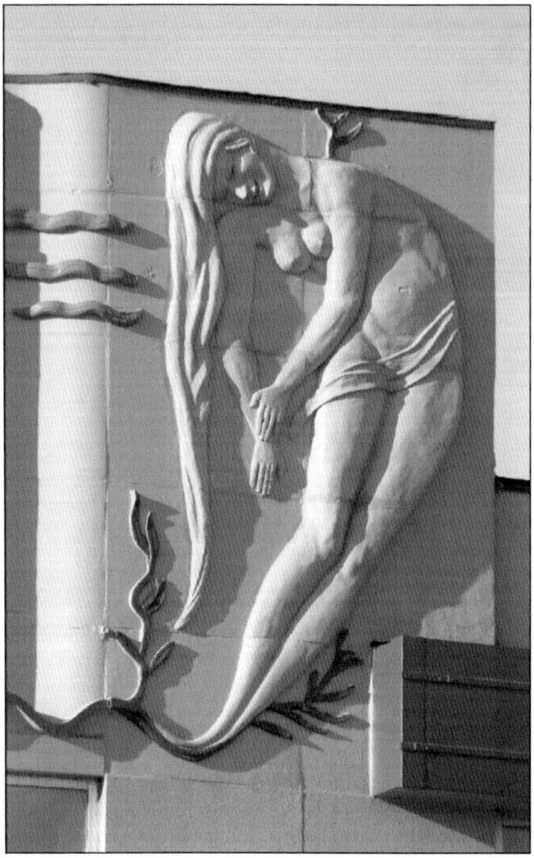

This bas-relief figure appears on the facade of the City Church building and dates back to the construction of the Mancuso Theatre in 1948. The author has never heard what the female figure was intended to represent, but a clue is provided by descriptions of the theater's interior. Along the walls were images of many different mythological beings, so one certainly might surmise that it is one more such representation. Could it be Venus? (Courtesy of BCH.)

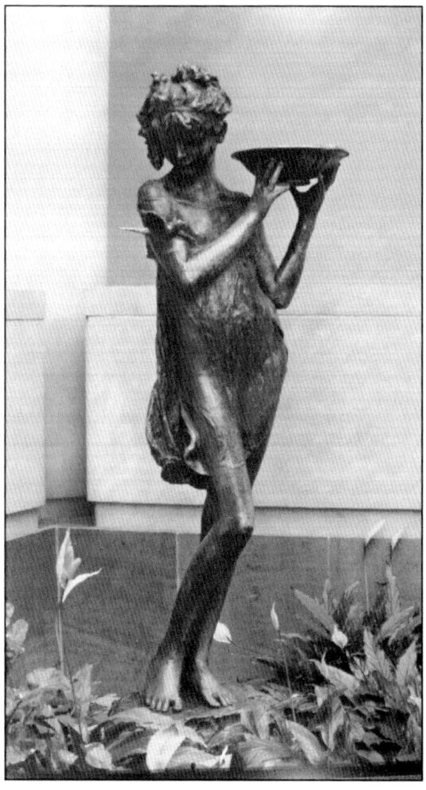

In 1931, Frances Washburn gave this bronze statue to the city for placement in Austin Park. When the city neglected its care, the figure was retrieved by family members. Today the statue stands in the Memorial Art Gallery of the University of Rochester, a gift of Edward, James, and Julian Atwater in memory of their parents and their grandparents. (Courtesy of Memorial Art Galley of the University of Rochester.)

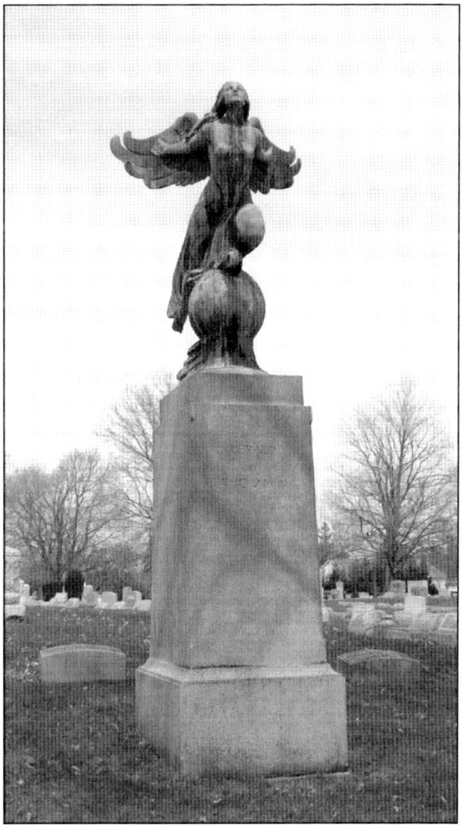

These two images provide a front view and profile of the *Herald of Dawn*, a bronze sculpture in the Grandview Cemetery. The sculpture is the work of Carl Augustus Heber of Philadelphia, Pennsylvania. It was purchased in 1925 by Kate Fisher McCool to serve as a memorial for her mother, Alice Fisher, and for her husband, Daniel McCool. The pedestal is nearly eight feet high, and the figure of a departing spirit is another six and one half feet. On the western side of the pedestal is the inscription, "O death where is thy sting? O grave where is thy victory?" (Courtesy of BCH.)

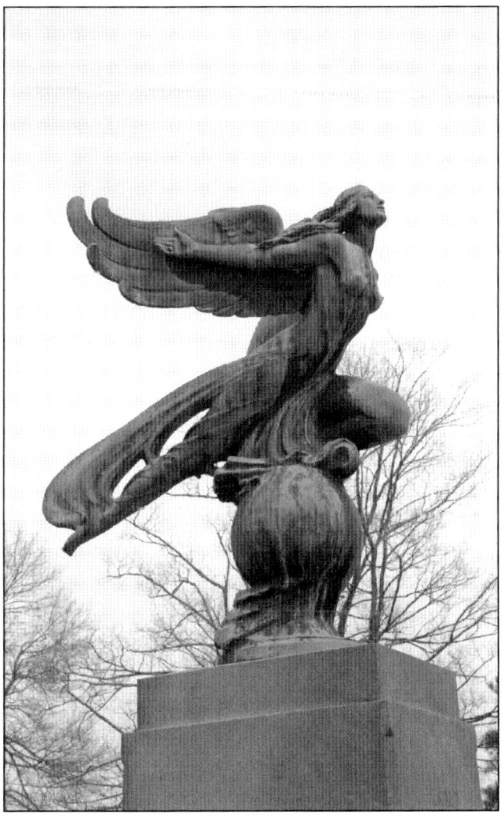

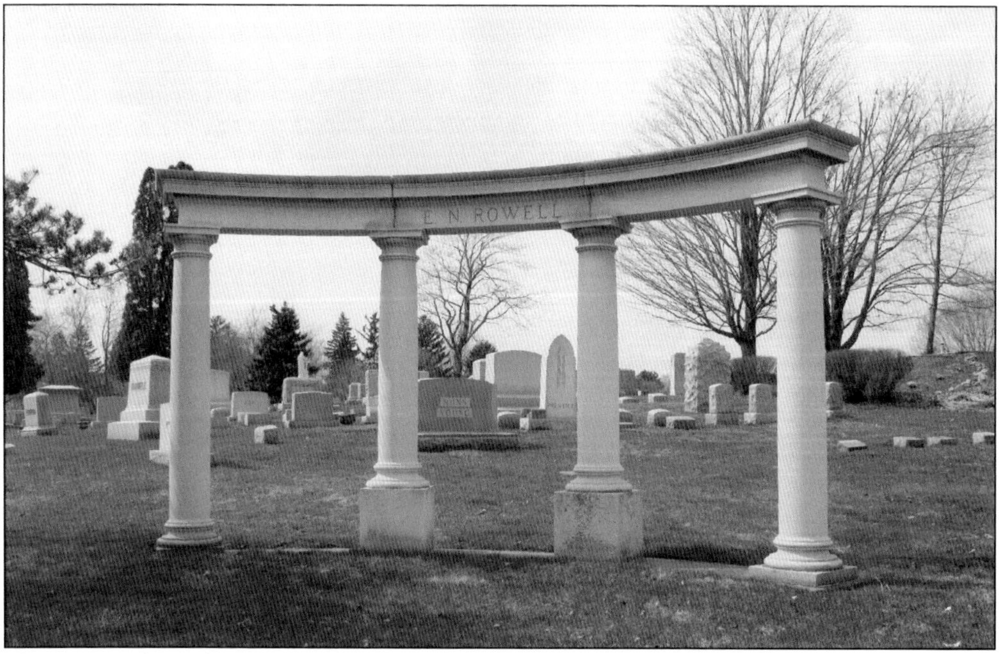

The picture above shows the E. N. Rowell memorial, also in the Grandview cemetery. It is one of the largest monuments, if not the largest, in the cemetery. There is no marker for either Edwin Newton Rowell or May Emke Rowell, his second wife. He died in 1929 and she in 1971. However, cemetery records at the Genesee County History Department indicate that both were buried where the monument stands. One interesting feature is the similarity of the monument design to that of the porch on the Rowell Mansion shown in the picture below. Both were done in a classical revival style. (Courtesy of BCH.)

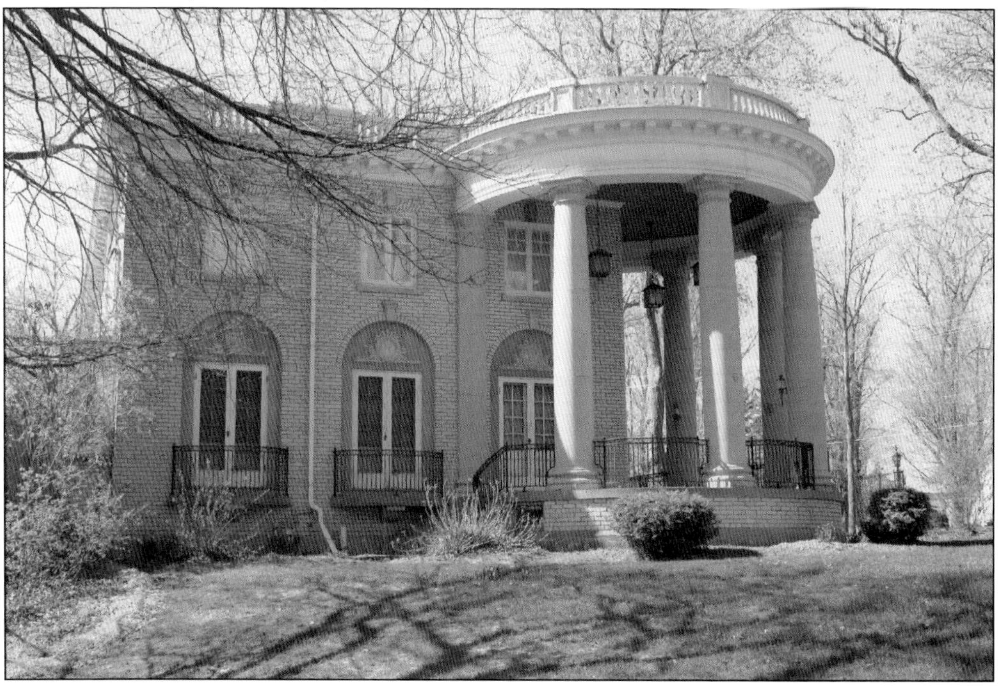

The Woman's Christian Temperance Union water fountain was at the southeast corner of Jackson and Main Streets. It was placed there in 1904 and offered refreshment to both humans and animals. The fountain had a metal base topped with a figure of Hebe, the cupbearer to the immortal gods on Olympus. The fountain disappeared in 1940 during a street widening project. (Courtesy of BCH.)

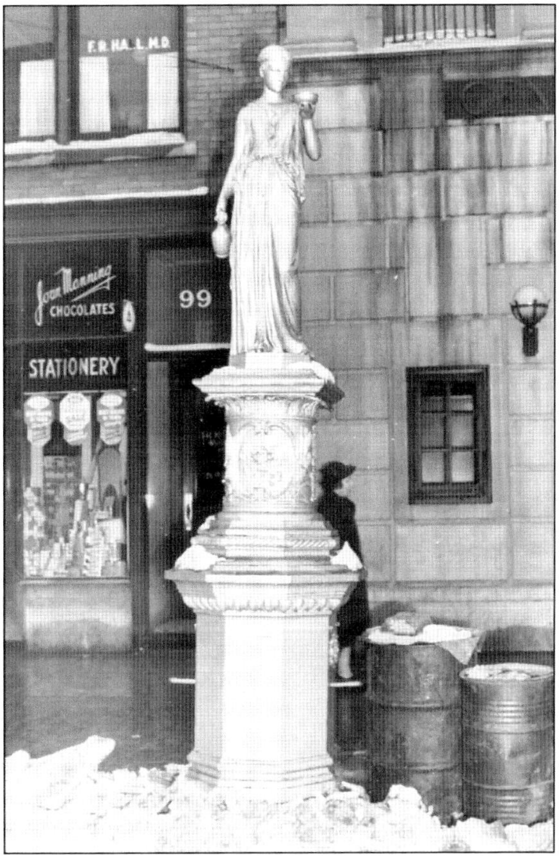

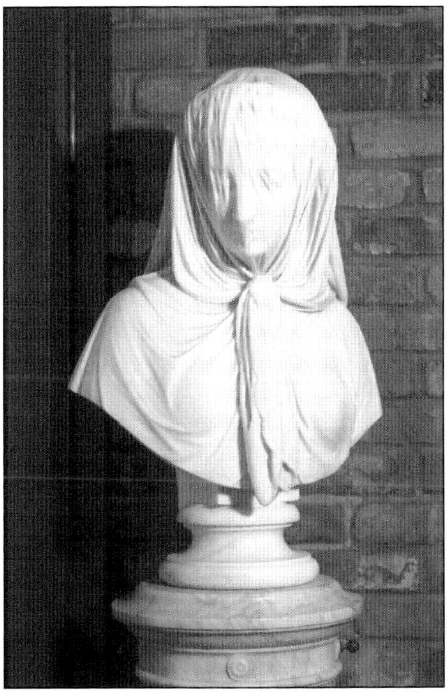

This bust of a veiled lady once stood in the Richmond Mansion. It is an 1866 creation of an Italian artist who utilized a ceramic fabric called parian. The material was unglazed porcelain almost indistinguishable from a very fine-grained marble. This bust now stands in the entrance to the building at 3 West Main Street. (Courtesy of BCH.)

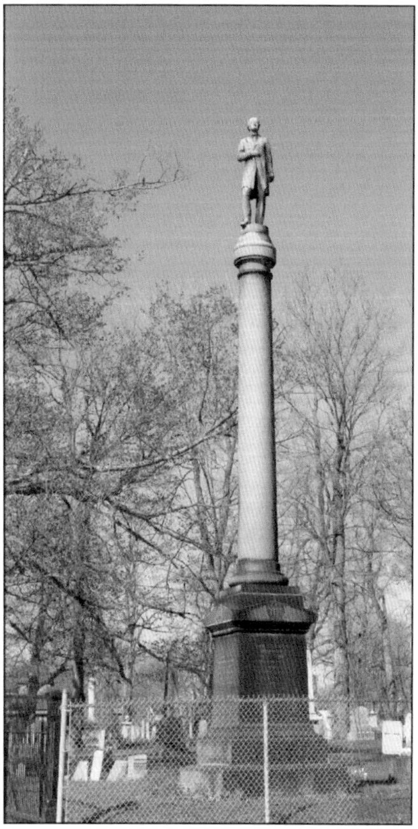

These two views display the William Morgan monument in the Batavia Cemetery on Harvester Avenue. Morgan was born in Virginia in 1774. He and his wife came to Batavia in the 1820s. Purportedly he attempted to join a Masonic Lodge in the village, but was rejected. After subsequently threatening to publish a book revealing secrets of Masonry, he was spirited away on September 11, 1826, by a group of men and was never seen again. Presumptions of his murder led to an anti-Masonic political movement. Years later in 1882, this monument was raised to Morgan by the National Christian Association, a group opposed to secret societies. (Courtesy of BCH.)

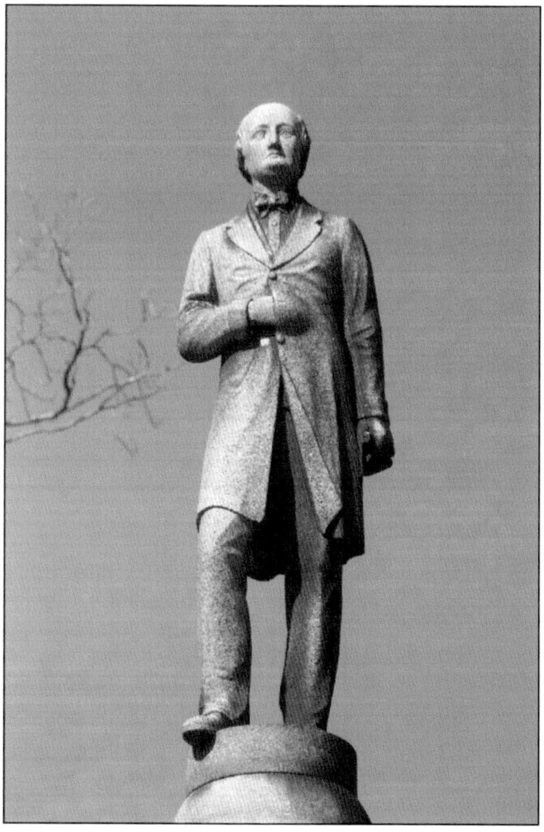

Seven

PROMINENT BATAVIANS OF THE PAST

Because Western New York was a wilderness before 1800, prominent early Batavians were almost always people who had been born somewhere else and immigrated to Batavia. That picture seems not to have changed much before the mid-1800s. The vast majority came from places on the east coast, like Philadelphia for example. Occasionally they were foreign born.

One of the foreign born was Maj. Henry Ignace Glowacki. Of noble Polish ancestry, he was on the losing side of an 1830 uprising against Russian occupiers of Poland. The U.S. Congress, sympathetic to the revolutionaries, offered them land in the Midwest. The 18-year-old Glowacki happened to stop overnight in Batavia on his way to inspect this land. It was his good fortune to meet David Evans, resident land agent of the Holland Land Company, who offered the young man a job if he wished to remain in Batavia. The job was to copy land office records by hand. Despite Glowacki being able to speak or write little English, Evans apparently thought the major was a perfect choice for the assignment. History indicates that the assessment was accurate.

Many of the early Batavians of prominent stature intermarried. A classic example is the Stevens-Brisbane-Cary family history. James Brisbane, owner of the first general store, the first postmaster, and a land speculator, had two sisters. One married James W. Stevens, chief clerk at the Holland Land Office, who held a number of other important positions including a judgeship. The other married Trumbull Cary who similarly held a number of positions in the community, was a founder of the first bank west of the Genesee River, and eventually became the bank's president. Brisbane and Cary both earned considerable wealth.

A frustration in attempting to assemble a pictorial history of these and other early Batavians is the absence of pictures, especially of the women. Perhaps the most notable lack is the absence of a picture for George Brisbane. Brisbane built the mansion that became Batavia's city hall in 1918. Neither local sources nor the Brisbane family have been able to produce a picture.

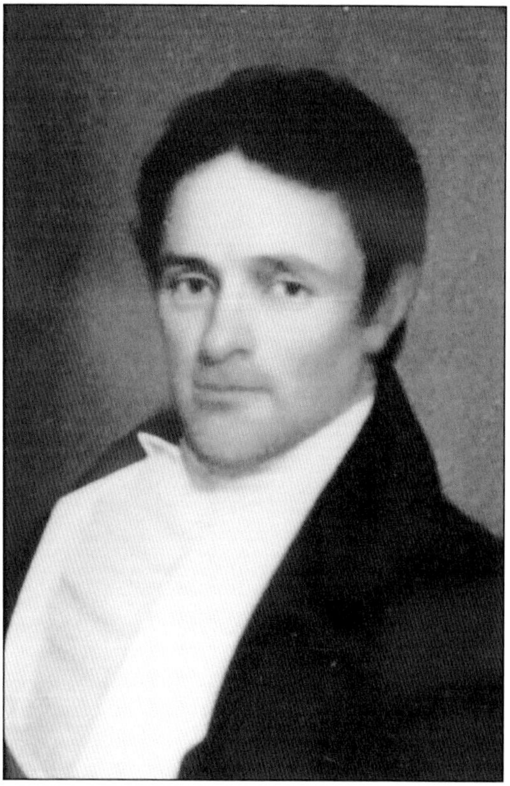

If there ever were two people chosen to be the father and mother of all Batavians, it surely would be James Brisbane, left, and Mary Stevens Brisbane, below. After working with the Holland Land Company surveyors, James Brisbane turned his attention to making money. His establishment of the first general store in 1802 was accomplished with the help of a grant from Joseph Ellicott. In 1807, he married Mary Stevens, who had come to Batavia to live with her brother, James Stevens. (As indicated previously, Stevens reciprocated by marrying Brisbane's sister, Elizabeth.) Through James's land speculation and other investments, the Brisbanes became one of the three wealthiest couples in Batavia. (Courtesy of Arthur Brisbane.)

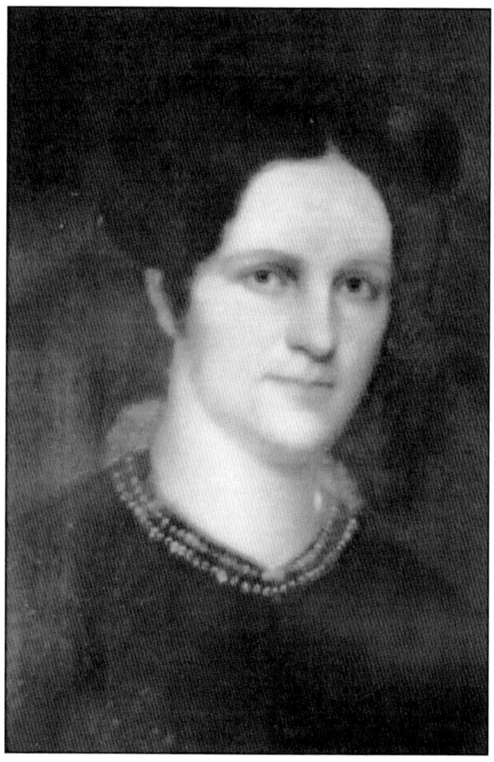

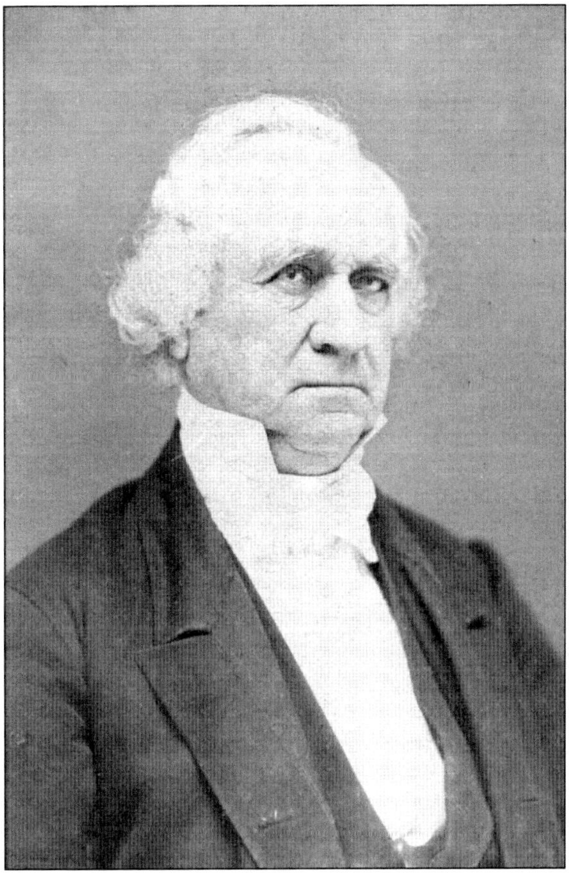

Trumbull Cary was another figure who played a prominent role from Batavia's earliest days. Among the important positions he held in addition to bank president was that of village treasurer. Margaret Brisbane was the James Brisbane sister he successfully wooed. The Cary Mansion, pictured below sometime in the 1800s, was one of Batavia's finest homes. Like the Brisbanes, Trumbull and Margaret Cary amassed significant wealth. An interesting aside is that a century later, a descendent of the Brisbanes, Arthur Brisbane, married Phoebe Cary, a Cary descendent. The intermarriage that had characterized Batavia's pioneers didn't end with the first generation. (Courtesy of GCHD.)

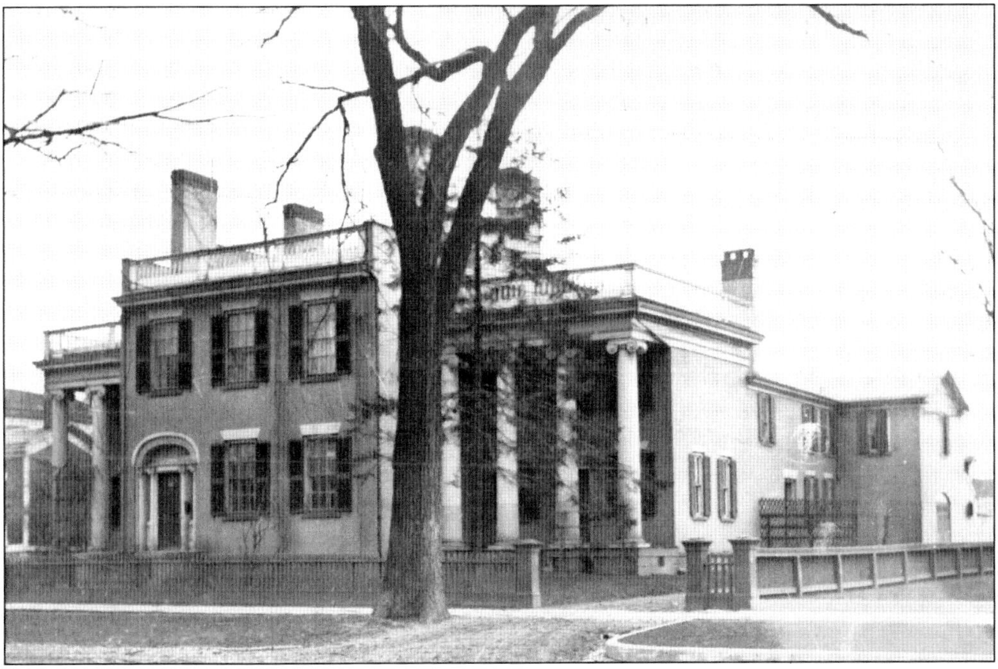

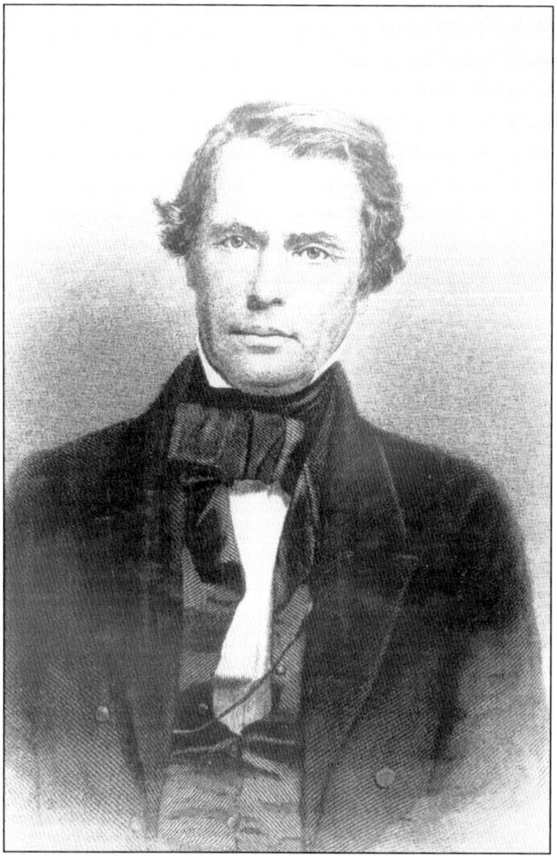

Heman J. Redfield, pictured at left as a relatively young man, was a Batavia lawyer, state senator, and district attorney of Genesee County. He also had a first name that later Batavians occasionally incorrectly record as "Herman." Redfield came to Genesee County from Connecticut in 1808, but he didn't actually settle in Batavia until 1836. Heman's wife was the former Abbie Noyes Gould. The Redfields owned a 253-acre parcel of land located at the western edge of Batavia. It stretched from the Tonawanda Creek northward across West Main Street. Redfield Parkway is on the site of the family's apple orchard. Their home is seen in the image below. (Courtesy of GCHD.)

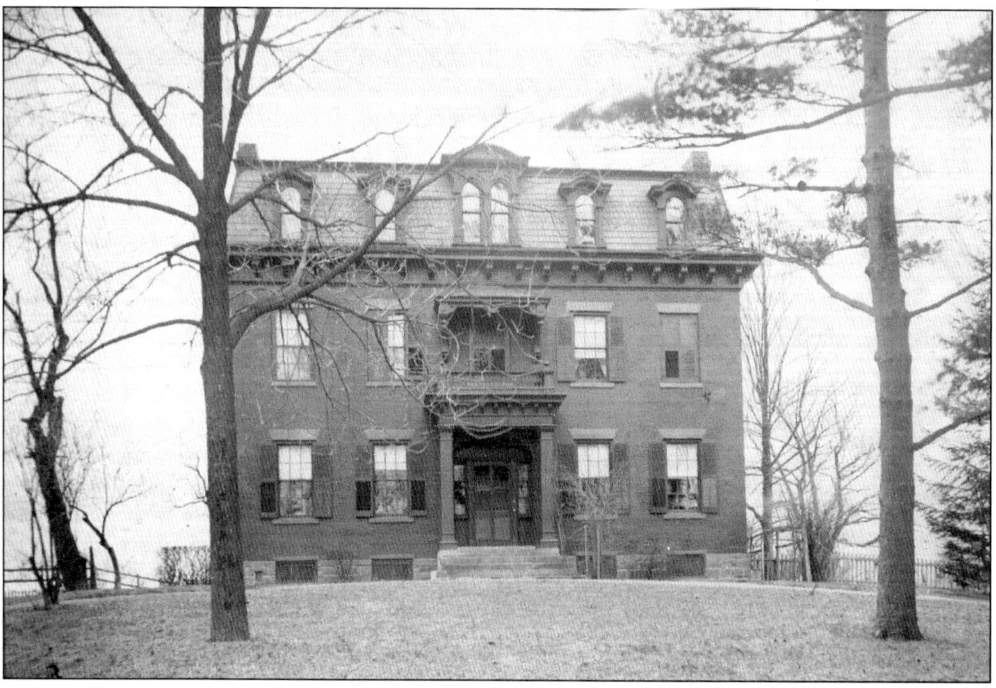

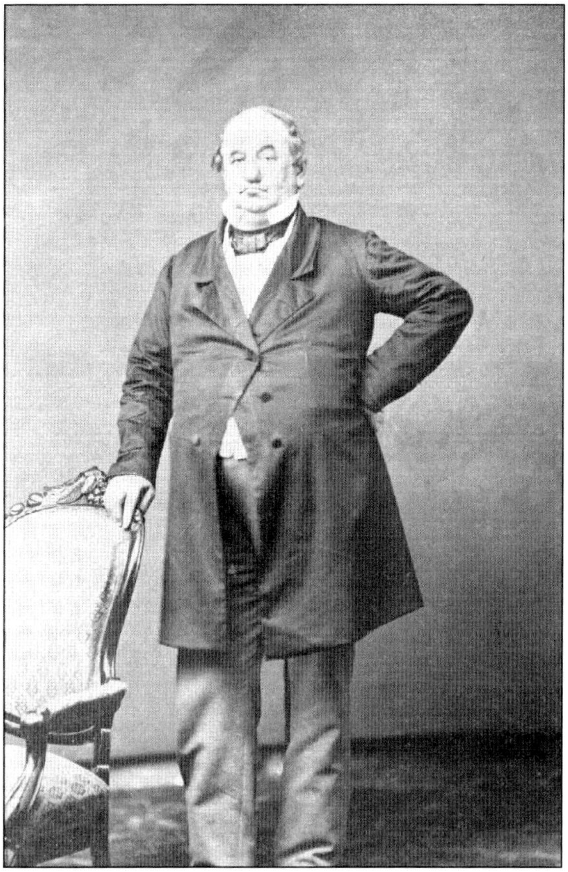

Born in Vermont in 1804, Dean Richmond became a resident of Batavia in the 1850s. Orphaned as a teenager, he had relatively little schooling and was functionally illiterate. Despite his limited education, he proved to be an astute businessman and a skilled politician. By the time he came to Batavia, he had amassed wealth from Great Lakes trade and other business investments. Richmond was a major player in the Democratic Party. Locally, he is most often remembered as the second president of the New York Central Railroad. The East Main Street mansion that he built is shown below as it looked in the very early 1900s. (Courtesy of GCHD.)

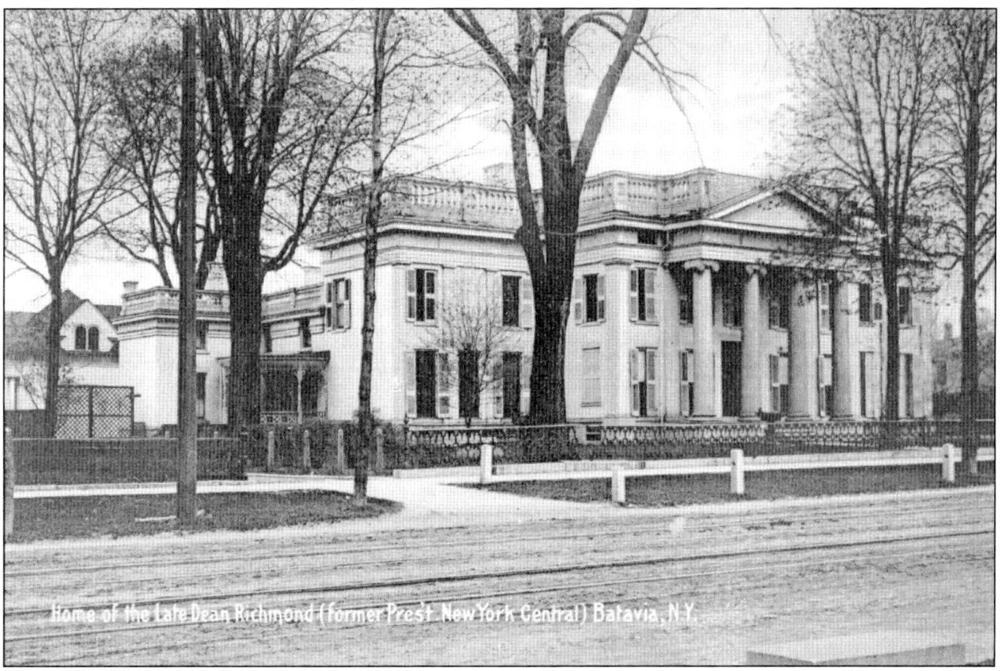

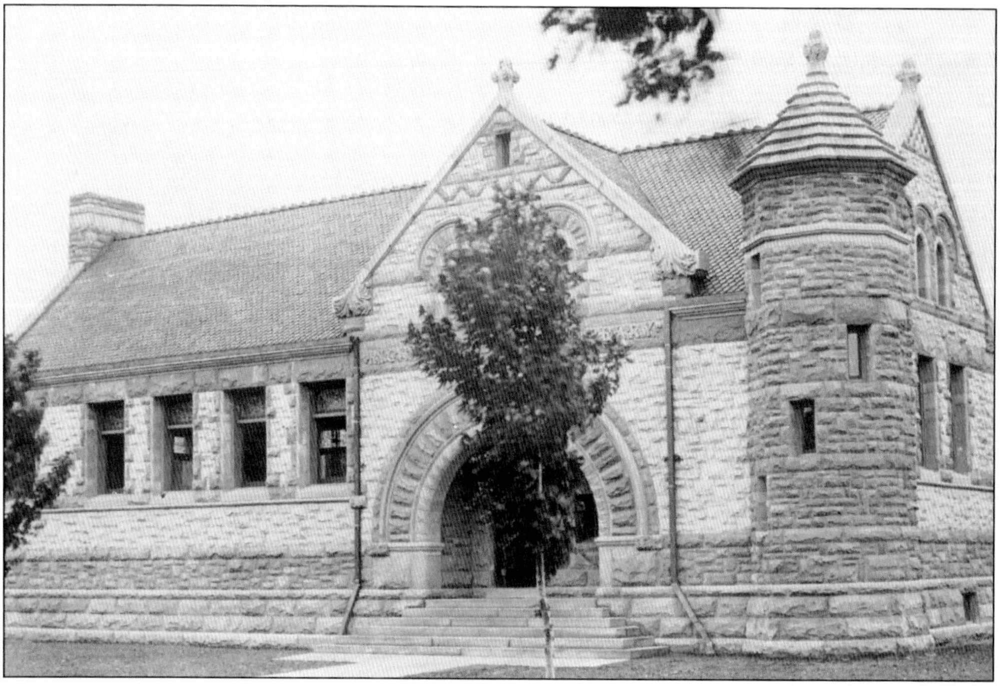

Dean Richmond died in 1866. However, his widow, Mary, lived another 30 years. During that time she managed the family's wealth so successfully that it grew beyond what her husband had accomplished. The Richmond Memorial Library building that she gave to the community in 1889 was built in a style popularized by the architect Henry Hobson Richardson. Readers may note its similarity to other buildings of the era such as the Prendergast Memorial Library in Jamestown. The photograph below is of the Richmond mausoleum in the Batavia Cemetery. It is regarded as one of the finest examples of cemetery architecture in upstate New York. (Above, courtesy of GCHD; below, courtesy of BCH.)

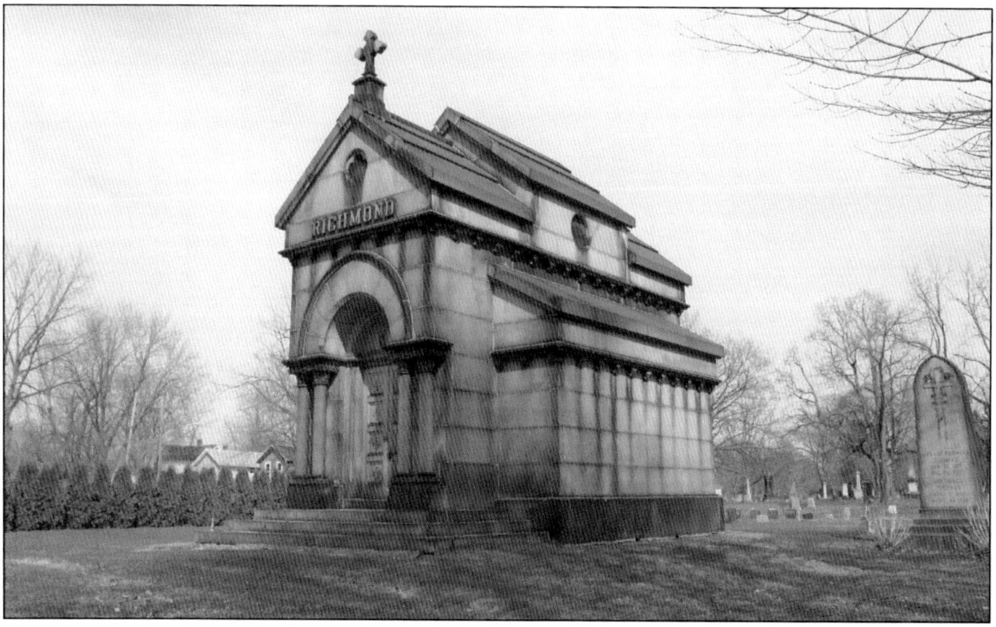

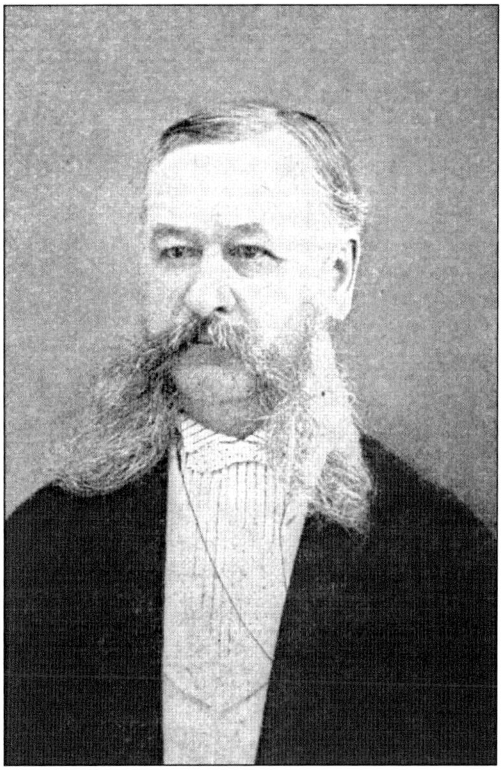

Pictured here are Maj. Henry Ignace Glowacki and his wife, Mary Redfield Glowacki. Mary was a daughter of Heman and Abbie Redfield. Henry was born in Poland in 1816. His title appears to have originated with his training at a military academy while still a teenager. Following Henry's involvement in the unsuccessful coup mentioned previously, he was sent into exile and wound up spending the rest of his life as a Batavian. Henry went on to become a lawyer, trustee of the State School for the Blind, president of the school board, and alderman. He and his wife also acquired considerable land on the north side. (Courtesy of GCHD.)

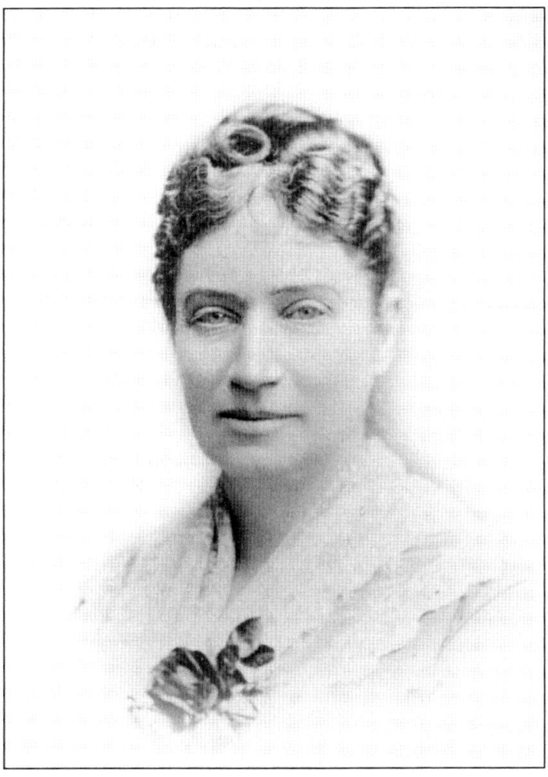

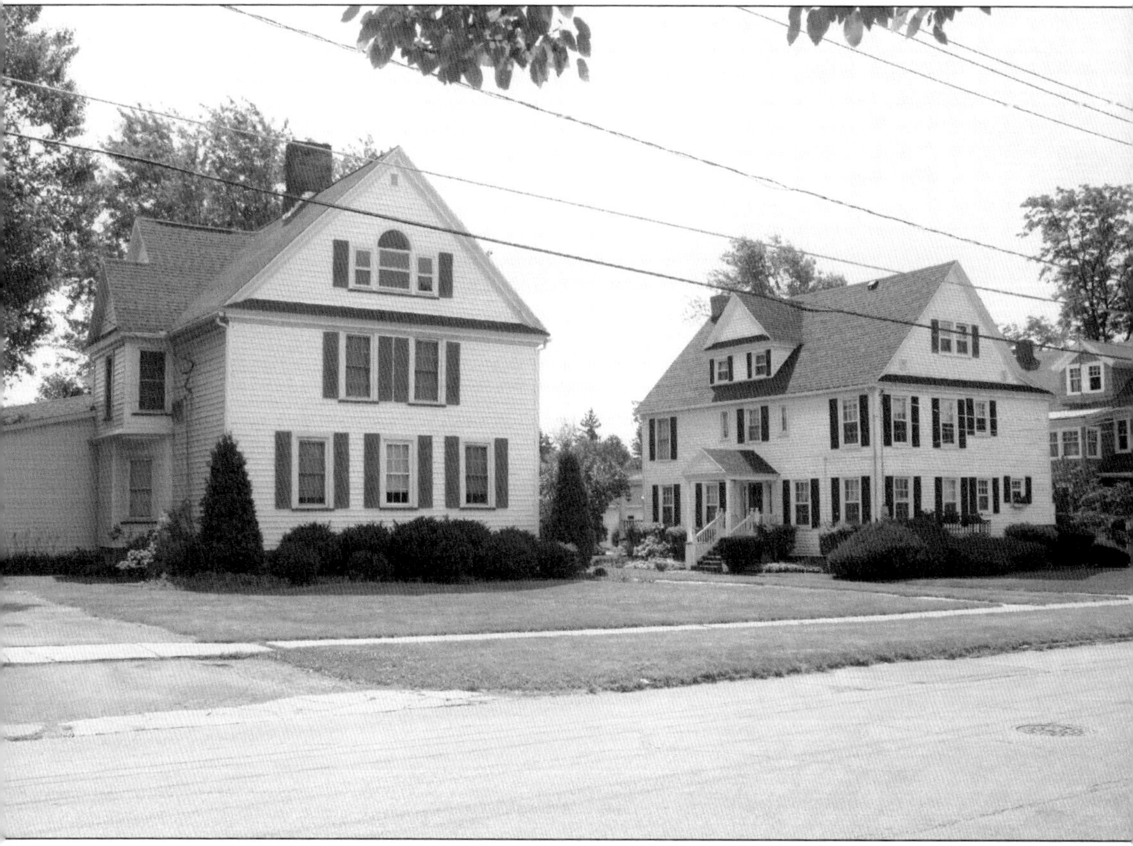

Henry and Mary Glowacki built a large home at 16 Summit Street. Evidence indicates that Mary's money funded the construction and the house remained in her name throughout her life. After the death of Henry in 1895 and Mary's death in 1908, the house became the property of their adopted daughter, Elizabeth Chandler Parker. Mary had stipulated in her will that after Elizabeth's death, the property was to pass on to Elizabeth's two sons, Glowacki and Ralph Parker. Thus, in 1917, Elizabeth's sons became its owners. Apparently neither brother wanted such a large structure, and in 1918, the house was divided into two sections as seen above. The front half remained at 16 Summit Street, while the rear half was moved to 14 Summit Street. For a time, the building at 16 Summit Street remained in the ownership of both brothers; however, the house at 14 Summit Street was soon sold to Alice Scatcherd, widow of Robert Scatcherd, who had been an officer with the Batavia and New York Wood Working Company. (Courtesy of BCH.)

This picture of Edwin Newton Rowell appeared in the 1902 publication *The past and present . . . Batavia, New York.* Rowell was married to the former Jennie Abigail Luce when the couple moved from Utica to Batavia early in the 1880s. Allegedly a motivation for the move on Edwin's part was to put distance between his wife and her boyfriend, Johnson Lynch. Time proved the move to be unsuccessful in regard to this objective, so Edwin chose an alternative plan. Pretending to have left town, he concealed himself near the New York Central train station. When Lynch appeared not long afterward, Edwin followed him to the Rowell home at 123 Bank Street. After surprising the adulterous couple in bed, Edwin fired several shots from a handgun, one of which killed Lynch. Below is a photograph of the house where the shooting took place. (Courtesy of BCH.)

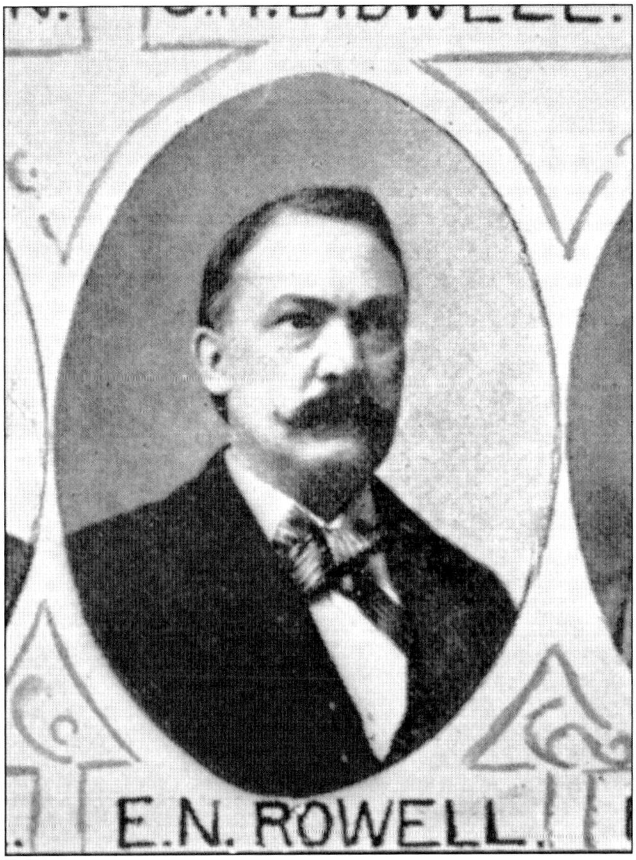

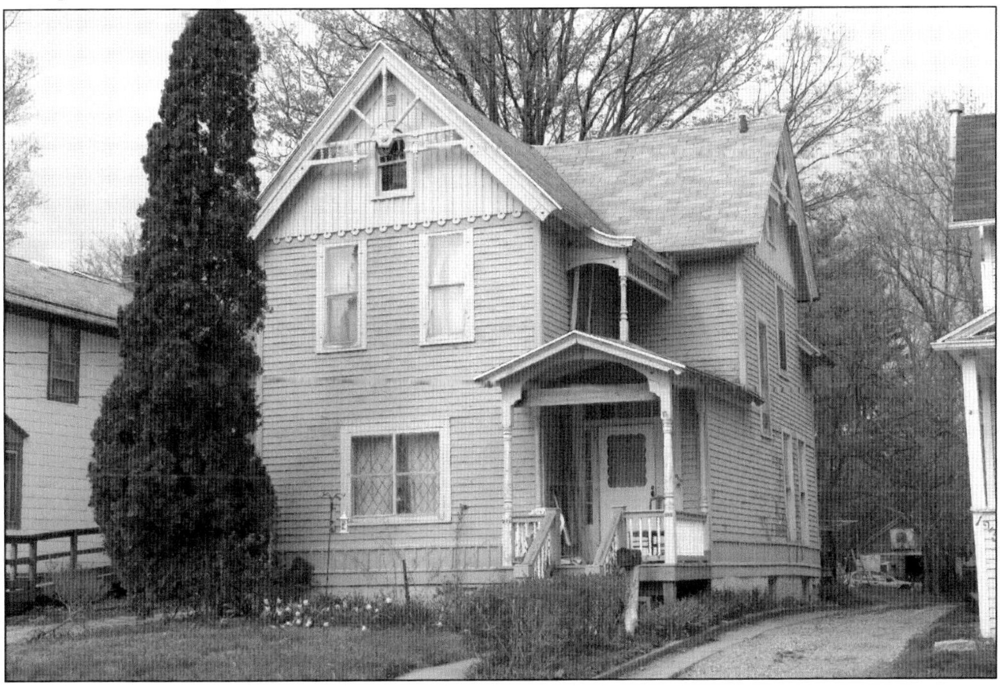

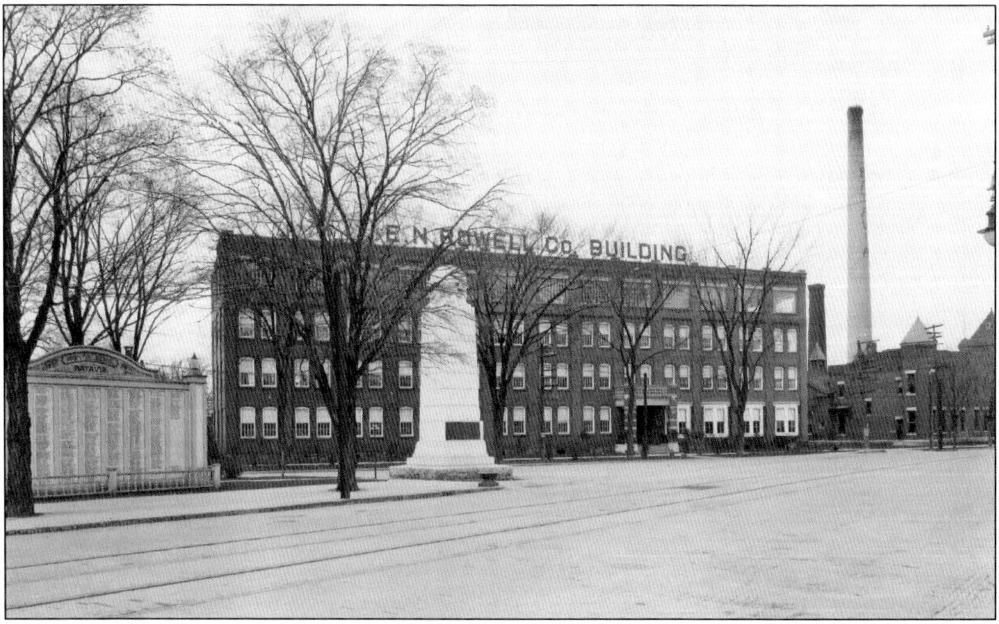

Rowell was acquitted of murder in a trial held on January 19, 1884. He later went on to be one of Batavia's most successful entrepreneurs. His company, the E. N. Rowell Company, manufactured pill and cosmetic boxes. It became the largest manufacturer of small boxes in the United States. Above is the Rowell Building on the corner of Ellicott and West Main Streets. Originally intended to be shared with the P. W. Minor shoe company, the entire space was soon needed and a fourth floor was added. The Rowell Building on Jefferson Avenue can be seen below. Formerly a factory belonging to the Mathes Shell and Novelty Company, it was acquired in 1919. (Courtesy of GCHD.)

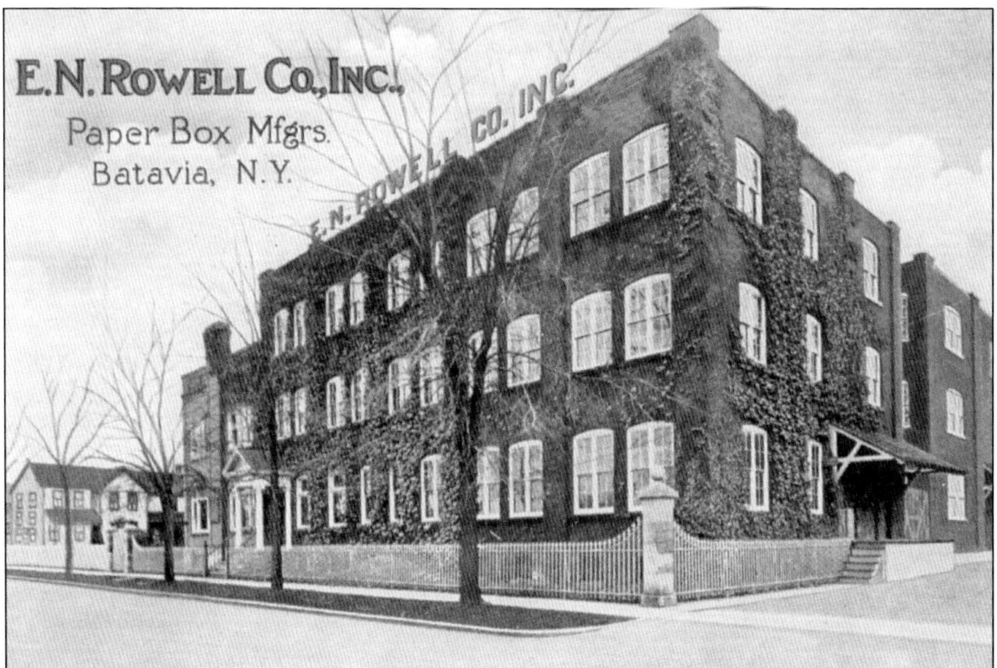

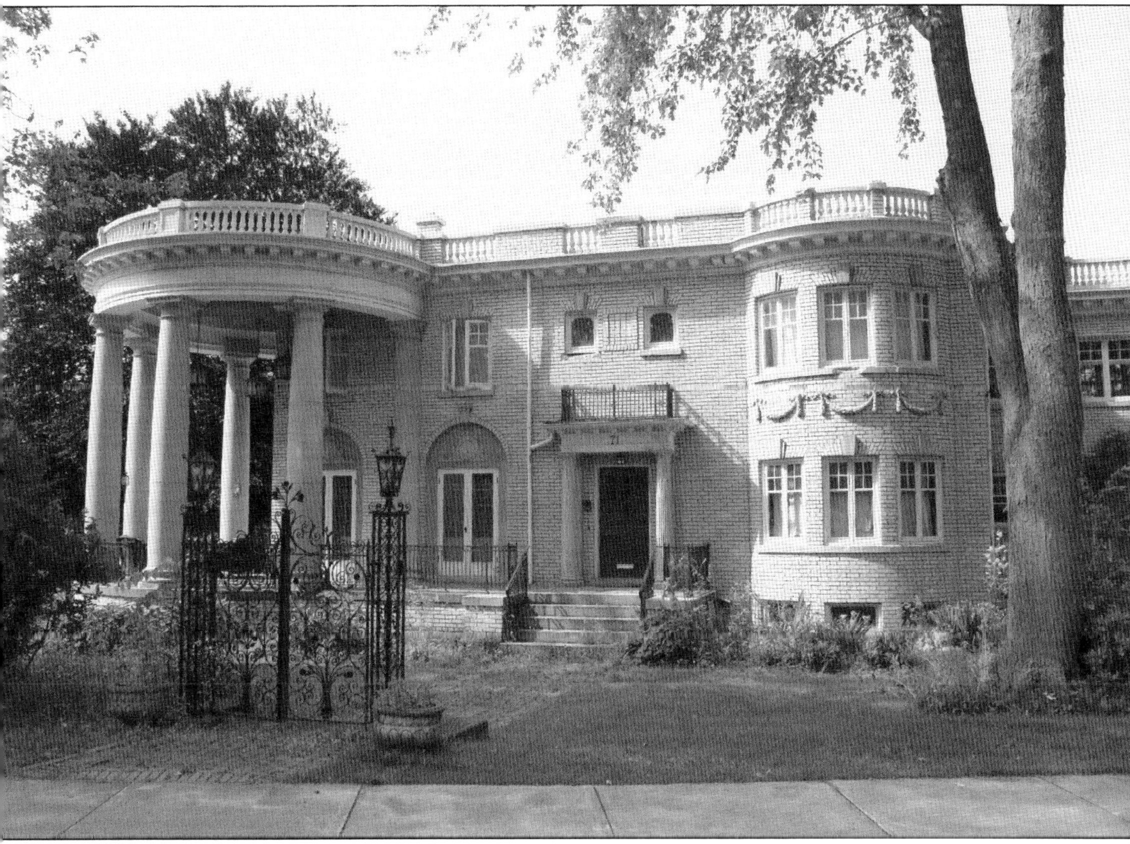

Rowell's first wife wasn't pleased by the turn of events in 1884, and she and Edwin divorced. Edwin gained custody of their two daughters. In 1915, he married May Emke, an employee of his firm. She proved to be an individual of great business ability, and she became president of the company. May retained control of the company until her death in 1971, 42 years after Edwin had died. The couple lived in this house on the corner of Ellicott and Richmond Avenues. It was built at the time of their marriage and was a gift from Edwin to his wife. The mansion was designed by the architectural firm of Otto Block in Rochester. A. Friedrick and Sons was the contractor. Since May Rowell's death, the mansion has passed through the hands of several owners, but each has endeavored to maintain its beauty. (Courtesy of BCH.)